Raiding the Gene Pool

Raiding the Gene Pool

The Social Construction of Mixed Race

Jill Olumide

Pluto Press

LONDON • STERLING, VIRGINIA

First published 2002 by Pluto Press
345 Archway Road, London N6 5AA
and 22883 Quicksilver Drive,
Sterling, VA 20166–2012, USA

www.plutobooks.com

British Library Cataloguing in Publication Data
A catalogue record for this book is available from the British Library

ISBN 0–7453–1765–0 hardback
ISBN 0–7453–1764–2 paperback

Library of Congress Cataloging in Publication Data
Olumide, Jill.
   Raiding the gene pool : the social construction of mixed race / Jill
Olumide.
     p. cm.
   ISBN 0–7453–1765–0 — ISBN 0–7453–1764–2 (pbk.)
   1. Race. 2. Race—Social aspects. 3. Racially mixed people. I.
Title.
   HT1523 .O45 2002
   305.8—dc21

                                                              2001004855

10   9   8   7   6   5   4   3   2   1

Designed and produced for Pluto Press by
Chase Publishing Services, Fortescue, Sidmouth EX10 9QG
Typeset from disk by Stanford DTP Services, Towcester
Printed in the European Union by Antony Rowe, Chippenham, England

Contents

For all our children

Racism stands apart by a practice of which it is a part and which it rationalises: a practice that combines strategies of architecture and gardening with that of medicine – in the service of the construction of an artificial order, through cutting out elements of the present reality that neither fit the perfect reality, nor can be changed so that they do. (Bauman 1989, p. 65)

Acknowledgements

I would like to thank all those who have supported the aims of the book. Those who took part in research interviews and workshops, those who provided feedback on early drafts of the book and those who were willing to discuss the various issues with me. Professor Sheila Allen provided patient and wise supervision and 'Seye Olumide shared similar qualities on the domestic front. Ishraga Lloyd, Yasmine Khan, Val Hoskins, Modupe Oduyoye, Elinor Kelly and many others offered insights and useful criticism of various versions of the text. Whatever the shortcomings of the book, it is one more step in the journey towards an understanding of mixed race experience.

Foreword

Not long after Jill Olumide began her work on the subject of this book she questioned the defining categories devised by officialdom and researchers (market or otherwise) for recording race/ethnicity. She was especially concerned with the convention of asking those of us who do not fall neatly into one category to tick a box marked 'other', rather than offering a more positive alternative such as 'many' or 'several'. The latest national censuses in the UK and the US have moved towards a slight recognition that many, perhaps most of us fall into more than one category.

Categorisation is essential, but it always simplifies the complex realities of social relations. The data it produces may serve many purposes, benign or malevolent and great care is necessary in their analysis and interpretation. The term 'mixed' now appears more frequently with reference to race/ethnicity, but usually only for those designated as minorities who are then excluded from the majority categories: 'white'; British; North American and so on. What explanations lie behind such categorisations, other than administrative convenience and computational ease, and what are the consequences which flow from them?

This book breaks new ground by exploring in some depth the meaning and provenance of what has become, popularly and professionally, termed 'mixed race' in contrast presumably to 'same race', or more pejoratively 'pure race'. Jill Olumide provides a sophisticated analysis of the theoretical and methodological dimensions of a highly contested area of social relations. Her theoretical discussion is based on a comparative and historical investigation of perceptions and perspectives of those designated 'mixed race' and their relation to racially defined institutions and structures. This enables her to put current designations of race and mixed race into context. The work thus contributes to our understanding of both the situations and views of those so designated and the professional and political discourses that have grown up around them.

Many studies of mixed race followed on from the highly politicised issues around transracial adoption concentrating mainly on the individual psychology of children. Much was made of the need for the development of an identity in keeping with racial origin and the consequences of misidentification through parental shortcomings. The contours of the debate, whatever position the protagonists espoused, remained firmly within a racialised mode and a less than rigorous methodology. Far fewer studies of adults in 'mixed' relationships or who are said to be mixed race have been undertaken, though stereotypical assumptions about the motivations of partners and pitfalls awaiting them abound in journalistic accounts. Jill Olumide's work considers the structuring of relationships where powerful others designate adults and children as problems and treat them as such. She questions the dominance of the individual psychological approach and examines the processes by which social divisions impact upon and are negotiated in everyday lives.

The ways in which she analyses the subject deserve a much wider audience than those scholars familiar with the intellectual, political and practical challenges her doctoral thesis presents. The detailed discussion of ideas and knowledge dealt with in the following chapters are germane to all those involved professionally, politically and personally in challenging accepted racialised boundaries from whatever quarter they come. Where, how and why those in 'mixed' relationships and their children are so commonly seen as problems is analysed and the voices of those currently designated 'mixed' are clearly heard. The on-going dialogue with history and the social complexities of multi-faceted identities are opened up to allow a greater appreciation of human possibilities at a time when these are being narrowed by one-dimensional ideologies.

Sheila Allen
June 2001

1 A Spell to Make Them Balance: Introduction

> And on a day we meet to walk the line
> And set the wall between us once again.
> We keep the wall between us as we go.
> To each the boulders that have fallen to each.
> We have to use a spell to make them balance.
> Robert Frost, 'Mending Wall'[1]

The poet writes of barriers, and of wilful damage to the work of boundary maintenance from animals, hunters and harsh weather. The speaker and his neighbour have met for their annual task of rebuilding the wall dividing their farms, and he questions whether the precarious balancing of stones in the wall is really necessary. But the neighbour continues to insist, 'good fences make good neighbours'.

The poem offers an allegorical introduction to the study of mixed race. The irreparable damage to sturdy social walls; the purpose of such walls and their construction; and the endless reconstruction using concepts which promote and sustain race as a means of dividing populations are all part of this enquiry. Most of all, we will need to explore the spells used to make them balance: ideologies of race and mixed race.

Dangerous Knowledge

It would be fruitless to attempt to define 'mixed race'. Its meaning alters with national boundary, position in history, class, gender, ethnicity and other factors. Each will have separate understandings of the term, and its chameleon-like ability to adapt to meanings of race. However, one distinction needs to be very clearly understood. There is a world of difference between mixed and pure race. 'The American way of life', the 'African continent', the 'British character' possess a homogeneity which rests on notions of essential difference. Mixed race implies exclusion from such constructions; in fact, it rather spoils their clean lines and makes them messy and confused. It shamelessly exposes the inadequate underwear of race and must be covered, or denied, or transformed in some way.

Mixed race is the ideological enemy of pure race as a means of social stratification. There are no universally agreed definitions of race, and we should certainly never be tempted into a belief in fixed templates for identifying *mixed* race. What I have termed *the 'mixed race condition' refers to the patterns and commonality of experience among those who obstruct whatever purpose race is being put to at a particular time.*

This cuts across the views of those who wish to see mixed race as a symbol. It has been adopted as an emblem of racial harmony, of social decay, of racial genocide, and several of the paths to peace and justice. My contention is that it is not intrinsically symbolic of anything, but simply witness to the fact that race is a wrong turning in the project of human self-classification. It is a false and shifting category upon which much has been built and in whose continuation great interest appears to be vested.

In this way, mixed race is the bearer of bad tidings for the race thinker. It carries, like the scapegoat, the sins and ill fortunes as well as the aspirations of the would-be-pure. It conceals the dangerous knowledge that race, in all its constructions, is a fiction on which complicated realities are built and lived. It is a step away from the chaos of racial disorder and the knowledge that humankind is a mongrel breed with varieties of difference and an underlying sameness.

The Importance of Studying Mixed Race

The importance of the study of mixed race lies partly in the information it can offer to an understanding of some of the effects of what Birkitt[2] refers to as 'structural inequalities, ideological misunderstandings and wasteful social controls' (p. 215) on lived experience. That some groups are identified and characterised as being, in some way, distinct from others requires attention.

I also claim importance for the subject because, in the course of human history, some of the worst excesses of exploitation have seized on race as their rationale. Where groups, or particular human differences, become racialised, any mixing of difference is, of course, tabooed. If we are, as a people, mindful of the ways in which our social organisations construct and shape our 'social selves', to progress beyond these gross inequities we must invent fairer and more just organisations for ourselves to inhabit. We can do this only when we are aware of the consequences of present arrangements and have the will to insist on social change.

Divisions

It is possible, indeed it is necessary, to make links between mixed race and other conditions that challenge social divisions. Those who are constructed as homosexual and who have responded through creative explorations of ways of being lesbian and gay are an obvious example. The struggles at the margins of gender also include serious discussion of the viability of transformations (usually) from 'male' to stereotypical 'female'. Similarly, those who contest divisions between ability and disability, or challenge age divisions, confront the power of social ascription in limiting the choices of how to live in the world.

I have concentrated here mainly on race and gender divisions as they affect relationships perceived as heterosexual, as much antipathy towards mixed race is directed towards 'breeding' between groups defined as races. This is not to suggest that there are not important bodies of experience among other subpopulations of mixed race, rather, it is to alert the reader to my particular focus.

By looking into the experiences of those who live across social divisions, we may learn not only something of the divisions themselves, but of the strategies used by, and the difficulties and the casualties amongst, those defined as trespassers. There is another part to this question of divisions which concerns political responses. In taking a particular political position, it is necessary to enquire into the kind of social organisation that is envisaged. On what criteria do questions of fairness and justice rest? Who is being excluded? What are the understandings of equality? As mixed race groups throughout the world move towards examinations of their collective positions, aims and objectives become important.

The Mixed Race Condition

This book developed from a profound dissatisfaction with existing knowledge of mixed race and an inclination to make fresh knowledge. This is an onerous task for, as we shall observe, knowledge about the subject is entrenched, particularly at the level of 'common sense'.

What I have called the 'mixed race condition' is not indicative of a rigid set of experiences which all those to whom the term 'mixed race' (or some variation) is applied experience uniformly. However, I do suggest that through the analysis of historical, empirical and documentary evidence, patterns emerge which are familiar to diverse groups perceived to be mixed or mixing race. It is not necessary, therefore, to sign up to anything, but to be aware, and ready to make comparisons.

The sources of this enquiry are various and include my PhD thesis,[3] undertaken among people in mixed race situations in the United Kingdom during the mid-1990s, historical material, professional literatures, and research findings. The thesis examined the construction of mixed race through professional welfare literature from the United Kingdom and the United States about the practice of 'transracial' adoptions. The empirical study involved interviews with people in mixed race situations, workshops on the subject of mixed race experience, correspondence and casual conversation.

Possibly unusually, I do not divide the population into 'mixed race people', 'mixed race couples' and subgroups such as 'transracial adopters'. This is because I assume that parents and children in biracial families are no more essentially different from one another than they are in 'same race' families. The separation of family members, and the insistence on immutable and irreconcilable differences are powerful themes and will be explored further in Chapter 6.

What has been lacking, certainly in my own understanding, has been a theoretical explanation of why mixed race has so consistently attracted similar sets of experiences. Further, why so little effort has been made to collect the views of those so defined *in their own terms*. Agendas for the study of mixed race have tended to be formulated in terms of pathology, or inadequacy, or insurmountable difficulty (either this, or the studies attempt to prove that these features are *not* present). Surely we must reject the idea that those of the mixed race condition are (and have been) masochists and sociopaths.

'The mixed race condition' refers, then, to common experiences over time and space of those who have been socially defined as mixed or mixing race. It is a loose term, not intended to suggest rigidity in any form. Rather than being a checklist of experiences which 'ought' to have been had, it is an acknowledgement of commonality amongst some very diverse groups. This commonality has the makings of a common history and provides the basis for group identity and political vision. Mixed race is never a community based on shared phenotypic features, common language or cultural artefacts. Rather, it is a group based on shared elements of lived social experience. It is, like the category 'woman', universal – of infinite variety but with identifiable common features.

This is not to suggest that those defined as mixed or mixing race should behave as a group with closed boundaries – far from it. It *is* to suggest that some possibilities for group solidarity lie in the ability to transcend race. Through identification with groups in the present and the past that have been similarly defined it is important to challenge the racial axes of social division. In the most profound sense, anti-racism (which has become a very moth-eaten construct) must endeavour to be anti-*race*. Nothing less will do.

However, there is a need for thinking and for strategy. There are roots to unearth, histories to formulate, analyses to be done. This business has been suppressed. The odds are long.

Group Identity

One of the salient features of the social construction of mixed race has been its characterisation as a marginal, detached and confused state in which individuals so designated are condemned to wander in search of belonging and acceptance. Sometimes mixed race is regarded as being 'in between' or, in some way 'intermediate' between racially defined groups. However, as writers such as Day,[4] Williamson[5] and many others have shown, those defined in terms of mixture have been able to construct, at certain moments, a local sense of group affinity based around their collective position.

Young,[6] in the course of an examination of the concept of the social group, takes issue with the notion of groups as aggregates of individuals. Her work is worth quoting at some length as she puts her finger on several matters of relevance to the task in hand. A first point concerns social ascription. Here Young employs Heidegger's notion of 'thrownness' to illustrate the nonelective nature of social ascription:

> For our identities are defined in relation to how others identify us, and they do so in terms of groups which are already associated with specific attributes, stereotypes and norms.
>
> From the thrownness of group affinity it does not follow that one cannot leave groups and enter new ones ... Nor does it follow

from the thrownness of group affinity that one cannot define the meaning of group identity for oneself; those who identify with a group can redefine the meaning and norms of group identity. (p. 46)

The possibility of self-definition has often been difficult for groups constructed as mixed. Current explorations of biracial or multiracial positioning in the United States, such as those explored in Zack,[7] Spickard[8] and Root[9] suggest that the North American mixed race condition is moving towards group awareness and redefinition. In a comparable way, many of the people I have spoken to in Britain expressed an affinity with those similarly defined. It is possible that there is a new interest and a growing consciousness among those defined as mixed. If this is so, it may be regarded as a positive step towards the identification of ways in which mixed race has been manipulated and exploited for the maintenance of racialised social classification.

In stressing that groups often come into being through the exclusion of certain categories of people who slowly come to recognise their commonality, Young shows a precedent for the people of the mixed race condition to recognise themselves as a group. She argues:

Even when they belong to oppressed groups, people's identifications are often important to them, and they often feel a special affinity for others in their group. I believe that group differentiation is both an inevitable and a desirable aspect of modern social processes. Social justice ... requires not the melting away of differences, but institutions that promote reproduction of and respect for group differences without oppression. (p. 47)

A further and very valuable point made by Young concerns the overlapping and crosscutting between and within social groups. Having made it clear that there are no 'essences' which all group members share and which can be cited to justify some groups being more deserving or talented than others, she goes on to suggest that groups may well form as a response to their social identification at a particular moment.

This is important in comprehending the social construction of mixed race because mixture has tended to be constructed as lacking in unity and coherence as opposed to being pure or homogeneous.

Young's point is that, because of the shifting, developing and over-lapping nature of social groups, all of us are subject to conflicting social designations through our multiple affiliations with variously constructed groupings. These groups – any of which may assume salience under particular circumstances during the course of a lifetime – are by no means part of a coherent unity. A person might be both privileged and marginalised in different situations. In this sense we are *all* mixed in our range of identity-making materials; that some are racialised as mixed *race* presents another range of intrigues, possibilities and responses.

A Theory of Lived Experience

One of the challenges in sociological research and study is to make links between experience 'on the ground' and abstract theory. To depict aspects of life without interpreting its patterns and anomalies produces only description. To theorise without recourse to the authority of lived experience, or to provide theory that cannot be applied and tested among those whose lives it addresses, is less than useful. The link is to be found amongst the questions which are asked of an aspect of social life. The people to whom the questions are put and the imagined sources of their solution are key variables in the project of sociology.

Harding[10] argues that what might be termed 'official' objectivity in research of all kinds is, in fact, the viewpoint of the powerful, who are limited in their ability to discern information about themselves and about those living different lives. The case for Harding's 'standpoint epistemology' is organised around the idea that the per-spectives of the marginal*ised* are highly critical and illuminative of the activities of marginal*isers*. It is a position quite similar to Bell's view of the need to 'study up'.[11]

Each suggests that marginalised groups are the source of signifi-cant 'problems to be explained' or research agendas. Both find that the sources of these problems are not usefully sought within the groups themselves – although these lives contain critical analyses of the sources. Hence, Bell's encitement to study the strata of people with the power to affect the lived experience of the marginalised. For example, the perennial question 'Why are the poor poor?' can-not be successfully addressed through recourse to the investigation of some essential nature shared by those who experience poverty (although this has been done). The more profitable line is to look among agents of that poverty, perhaps employers or political decision makers, rogue landlords, multinational conglomerates or those who draft policy which affects low income households.

In the same way, in studying mixed race the aim is not to remain with the descriptive account of those defined in these terms and to seek causes for 'identity problems', 'cultural confusion' and other mythical afflictions. Although, because there are so few studies which employ the perceptions of those considered to be mixed or mixing race *in their own terms*, this cannot be overlooked. It is also necessary to consider the architects and builders of mixed race experience, and to do this across time and place. What sorts of people are well placed to apply the ideologies of race mixing, and who gains from the social construction of mixed race? Certainly not those considered to *be* mixed or mixing race. How are those ideologies manufactured, and for what purpose? In what ways does the idea of mixed race benefit or threaten particular instances of social organisation?

If a theoretical account derived from grappling with these questions is to be of value, it must ring true in the lives of those whose experience it addresses. Conversely, those lives must be a part of the shaping of theory development.

Social Construction: Passing and Being Passed

Central to any new knowledge about mixed race must be the intention to free the topic from some of the ways in which it has been constructed, for instance, as a biological abnormality or a condition producing mental infirmity or identity confusion. The investigation of the subject has been marked – not to say stigmatised – by enquiries which separate populations considered to be mixed or mixing race from the social situations in which they are created. Responsibility for any deficiencies or problems tends to be placed with the group itself. The mixed race condition – that loose body of mixed race experience – becomes a kind of warning against the consequences of mixing race.

In a paper[12] I suggested that the term 'passing experiences' might cover some of the events commonly identified amongst those in mixed race situations, and three ways in which the term 'passing' might be understood. In some respects this is an attempt to link experiences of those considered to be mixed or mixing race with the wider human condition in which we may all be said to be passing for something.

What I mean by this is that each of us – men, women, children, and everyone in between – occupies a range of socially constructed positions which are sometimes paradoxical in the differential status they attract. These could most certainly be constructed in alternative ways, and sometimes changes in status and position do occur. Different positions limit, in different ways, our lives and what we are able to achieve. From within socially ascribed positions we make bids and struggle to negotiate improvements in our situations, sometimes recognising ourselves to be part of groups or movements for change. In a consideration of ways in which we are 'social selves', in the sense that personality is shaped by ideologies arising from particular forms of social, economic and political organisation, Birkitt[13] suggests:

> Social inequalities and the unnecessary controls on behaviour which keep ruling groups in power, still divide us.
>
> In these conditions, the structure of the personality is created more through external forces or internalised unnecessary restraints than through rational, self-conscious agency of the individual. The contours of the personality are marked out by the relations of power, and there are many wasteful controls and disruptive unconscious forces created through repression, which take initiatives and motives for action away from rational, conscious control. This leaves the individual feeling that they are compelled by forces and drives outside their volition. (p. 214)

It is as alienated and constricted selves that we work to mitigate the effects of social divisions in our lives; passing and being passed. Refocusing on those designated mixed or mixing race, those I have interviewed have often given very positive views of their abilities to move easily with difference.[14] Some have occupied the moral high ground and offered skills assessments of themselves as 'bridge builders' or 'peace makers' in situations of prevalent race thinking. This is at some distance from the ways in which mixed race is most usually constructed, as an inherently problematic, confused and isolated state.

This ability to 'pass amongst' is to be considered a positive aspect of the mixed race condition. This is not by any means to suggest that inter-group skills are universally acknowledged as valuable. As Birkitt has suggested, we are not yet in a position to realise our mature 'social selves' nor ready to appreciate the skills that might make for more democratic and fair social relationships. In the meantime, such skills are ignored, undervalued or attacked. They threaten to undermine the interests secured through social division – whatever these may turn out to be.

Passing As ...

'Passing as ... ' approximates to the original meaning of passing in which required social goods or contacts are exchangeable for temporarily suppressed information about the nature of individual or social relationships. As Carla Bradshaw,[15] a clinical psychologist from Seattle, suggests: 'The concept of passing uses the imagery of camouflage, of concealing true identity or group membership and gaining false access. Concealment of "true" identity is considered synonymous with compromised integrity and impostership' (p. 79). In mitigation, this can only have currency in situations of racial subordination: it is a loophole in the social construction of race. Where damaged identity is discussed as resulting from decisions to pass, it seems likely that some of the impossible and coercive situations which sometimes face those considered to be mixed or mixing race are the ground on which personal anguish is most likely to occur.

A further form of passing becomes apparent through my data from interviews, conversations and other contact with those defined as mixed or mixing race. This is usually the subject of complaint, and may be expressed as 'being passed'. This is to say that there is a distaste for having personal experience and belief denied, distorted, pigeonholed or in any way undermined. Being passed is to be considered a serious sanction, and very much a part of the mixed race condition. As we shall see later on, it is also the basis of some distinctive attempts to transform and exploit mixed race for desired social and economic outcomes.

Nakashima[16] captures something of the ways in which mixed race, in this case in the American experience, has been constructed as a group experiencing major social problems which are grounded in folk law, while having other experiences denied and hidden. In her concluding remarks she writes:

> Multiracial people and interracial families are a threat to the 'American way of life'. The US system has depended on very clear

racial categories for its political, social, economic and psychological organisation. In an attempt to keep the categories well defined, two strategies have been employed: the creation of a negative mythology about people of mixed race and their families, using biological, socio-cultural, and socio-economic arguments; and the denial of the existence of people of mixed race and their families. (p. 177)

It is possible that, in spite of differences in social and historical circumstances, this is not dissimilar to the British experience. The British welfare effort directed towards mixed race families down the years, for example, shows that they have been regarded as pitiably inadequate and requiring of state intervention, or else they have been subsumed under various minority populations and ignored.

Being passed removes autonomy from the exchange decisions of how to live in the world. It distorts and narrows the range of such options. Passing amongst social groups ideally involves autonomous decisions to employ the skills and knowledge available within the mixed race condition, and at a favourable social exchange rate.

Most frequently, mixed race has been passed as part of the least powerful and well endowed racially defined group, through devices such as the 'one drop rule',[17] apartheid and less formal social sanctions.

Structure of the Book

There are several parts to this task of creating fresh knowledge about mixed race. It is first necessary to examine some of the concepts and terms required to work with the idea of mixed race. Race and mixed race are slippery subjects to handle and there is by no means a clear set of understandings in place about their definition, nor even agreement that they *should* be defined. The suggested approach is that we consider both to be ideologies which have produced very real sets of social experience.

In dealing with mystification and ideological construction it is also necessary to understand something of the state and ways in which states employ ideology. In addition, awareness of other social divisions and ways in which these combine to structure varieties of mixed race experience is essential. These matters are discussed in Chapter 2 which examines some possible ways of conceptualising race and mixed race.

Bearing in mind the illusory and transient nature of race thinking, it will be as well to explore something of the ways in which existing knowledge has been produced. In Chapter 3 some of the scientific and other studies of race mixing are presented. As I have suggested earlier, and will suggest again and again, the study of mixed race is remarkable for its tendency to locate investigation within groups defined as mixed or mixing race. It is consistently treated as a 'thing' residing within individuals or groups, moreover, it is a 'thing' likely to cause problems of various sorts for those in whom it resides. As daft as this conceptualisation sounds, we shall observe some of the ways in which its persistence has affected the lives of ordinary people.

In Chapter 4 some historical notes on the construction of different mixed race groups are presented. Of course, the history of mixed race is not a linear narrative, but rather the history of an idea. The diverse situations considered in the chapter give some grounds for the view that mixed race experience is patterned and that perhaps it is in the analysis of these patterns that a collective understanding becomes possible.

Chapters 5 and 6 contain material concerning mixed race experience drawn from a small English research population. Chapter 5 deals with positive aspects of being in a mixed race situation and reflections on some of the issues that arise for the self and others about this situation. In Chapter 6 negative social experiences are discussed, along with strategies adopted to counter negativity. Both of these chapters pay close attention to the self-nominated topics of those interviewed.

Perhaps the most perplexing questions remain: those that begin 'why ... ?' These are addressed in Chapter 7 which combines some of the analyses offered during interviews with existing sociological thought. The theorisation of mixed race is an important task which has for too long been postponed. In Chapter 8 the main points are drawn together and some tentative conclusions are offered for consideration.

Perhaps the main point to be re-emphasised here is that mixed race is not detachable from the social world in which it is created. Whether it is pushed to the margins or embraced as a paradigm of harmony, the reasons and motives for these constructions are rightly explored in social life rather than in any essential mixed race 'nature'.

2   The Hall of Mirrors: Structures of Power

The task for sociologists is to explain not simply the multiplicity of difference but the value attached to 'different' differences. For they are not all equal in terms of affecting life chances, in affecting access to goods and services. What are the structures of power which turn difference into privilege and wealth on the one hand and denigration and poverty on the other? Which differences are selected and emphasised negatively (or positively) can not be explained with reference to difference. Difference is not fixed and immutable, nor one dimensional. Only by investigating social relations, processes and the conditions of their emergence, persistence and change can differences be explained.[1]

The Babalawo and the Sociologist

As the Yoruba proverb goes: 'bi oni ti ri, ola ki iri be, ni imu babalawo difa ororun' (Things are not likely to be the same tomorrow as they are today: this is why the Babalawo [Ifa priest] consults the Ifa Oracle every five days). Like the Babalawo, the sociologist appreciates the unstable nature of the social world and tries to keep track of some of the changes through consulting everyday items invested with significance: the news media, books, research reports. How to respond to change, how to interpret the implications of change, how to read the signs; this is important business.

Equally important are the things that stay the same. Those aspects of the social world which remain, perhaps in a different guise, after the ferment of change through which each generation believes itself to be passing. Often in social life, things that appear to have changed are simply at a different point from when we last looked. Sometimes there are tricks, illusions and strange goings-on that are difficult to detect and explain. We will need to keep our wits sharpened and not be afraid of the distorted shapes (sometimes of ourselves) that we glimpse in the hall of mirrors.

This chapter aims to reduce uncertainty about some of the concepts needed to discuss and analyse ideologies of race and mixed race. The ground is not always very level in these areas and there are major disagreements it may not be possible to resolve. It will pay to examine some of the rigid lines drawn between people and between ideas. Paradoxically, the social world is a complex place teeming with individuals and groups trying to subvert, shift or maintain positions. What counts here is that we have sufficient information to consider the salience of race and mixed race in social life and in political thinking and action. This, and to bear in mind that race is but one of the ideologies that divide us.

Ideology and State

The terms 'ideology' and 'state' require some clarification as they tend to be subject to diverse meanings and interpretations, depending on the viewpoint and circumstances of the user. We live in societies that are ordered, through the ideological construction of divisions such as race, class and gender, in such a way that people tend to develop distorted beliefs about themselves and about others. Such beliefs act to avert conflict and disorder so that social and economic life can proceed in ways which privilege some whilst dispossessing many. Those who are dispossessed may for a time be persuaded of the inevitability of their situation. This, however, is never completely successful, and has to be reinvented and re-established. Although domestic order may be created through repressive controls, in many states it is most usually (though not invariably) secured through ideological control.

This directs attention to the institutions through which ideology is produced, and where consciousness of self and others is shaped. Schools, religious groups, welfare organisations, mass media and the whole range of social institutions may be seen as contributing to the production of ideologies that maintain the status quo. Particular incentives, perhaps a financial encouragement of certain family forms, alert us to the privileging of some forms of social arrangement over others.

Here a Gramscian analysis clarifies links between ideology and state. Gramsci distinguishes civil society – essentially 'private' matters of organisation – from political society – which embodies state apparatuses such as education and legal systems as well as policing and military functions. Where one class within civil society has established hegemonic control, as the 'wealth creating' classes in Western industrialised states have been able to achieve, the class claims protection for its interests from the political society.

Police, welfare, education, the law and other institutions serve – whether knowingly or not – the interests of the dominant social group. A definition of the state by Gramsci[2] is as follows: 'The state is the entire complex of practical and theoretical activities with which the ruling class not only justifies and maintains its dominance, but manages to win the active consent over those whom it rules' (p. 244). The 'winning of active consent' is particularly important in this definition of state. Control over ideological production is a powerful means of maintaining order and dominance. And these are always capable of being reinforced with the use of force through military and policing facilities should the need arise. Mouffe[3] in a discussion of Gramsci's writing on ideology and hegemony shows the importance of a state's involvement in the welfare of those within its protection. This, as Young[4] has also suggested, becomes a question of *defining the needs* of those being provided for. It is an area to watch in the study of mixed race.

Applying the concept of ideology to the study of mixed race, it is clear that institutions such as welfare, the law and the media intervene in powerful ways to shape mixed race experience. For example, there has long been a dearth of positive representations and serious discussion of mixed race in books and newspapers. Welfare professionals have tended to be charged with the management of race mixing at various points in history. There are notable international examples of anti-miscegenation legislation over time and place. Scientific agendas have been arranged around providing information that contradicts the normality of race mixing. Each of these examples is rooted in the *ideological* rather than based on empirical evidence. Any severity of social experience among those considered to be mixed or mixing race which arises from this ideological onslaught may well have affected life chances in very real ways.

As far as the task in hand is concerned, it is also the terrain of disagreements over who may mix with whom. The suggestion here is that relations between people serve, to some extent, a dominant group. Mouffe notes:

In fact what Gramsci was trying to do was to think the role of subjectivity, but so as not to present it as the irruption of the individual consciousness into history. To achieve this he posits consciousness not as originally given but as the effects of the system of ideological relations into which the individual is inserted. Thus it is ideology which creates subjects and makes them act.

Ideology as a practice producing subjects is what appears to be the real idea implicit in Gramsci's thoughts on the operative and active nature of ideology and its identification with politics. (p. 226)

In this understanding of ideology, social position and social identity are defined (and contested) within social orders in which dominant groups have access to machinery for the production and organisation of subject realities. Thus, ideological constructs have material ramifications; they profoundly affect lived experience and the distribution of social goods and positions. The extent to which these ascriptions may be successfully disputed depends on the identification of common interests, and the knowledge and resources available to mount a resistance. Much rests on the breadth of vision for reform and change, and on the quality of intellectual work which informs this. This definition of ideology has plenty to contribute to an interrogation of the term 'identity'.

Ideology for What?

Enormous attention from various state-sponsored institutions has, over time and place, been directed towards the disruption of the 'private' aspects of race mixing. We must enquire why race springs eternal in the teeth of contrary evidence. Ideology is a key concept in this task. But ideology for what? For whom? Gilroy[5] suggests the centrality of ideology in the following terms:

'Race' has to be socially and politically constructed and elaborate ideological work is done to secure and maintain the different forms of 'racialisation' which have characterised capitalist development. Recognising this makes it all the more important to compare and evaluate the different historical situations in which 'race' has become politically pertinent. (p. 38)

This is work that will be undertaken later in this enquiry. Meanwhile, Goldberg[6] gives us cause for conjecture about the complicity of social science itself in the production of knowledge about race. This is of interest if we are to understand some of the pitfalls of anti-racist activity in state departments, in particular, where such activity apparently finds difficulty with the concept of mixed race:

> Social science is important to the modern State both *functionally* and *ideologically*. In the former sense, social science furnishes the State and its functionaries with information, and it is often employed in formulating and assessing State policies to satisfy social needs. Ideologically, the State often invokes expedient analyses and the results of social science, whether by collaboration or appropriation, to legitimise State pursuits and to rationalise established relations of power or domination. (p. 152)

It is also important to take this matter seriously in order to avoid a reification of race through the acceptance (overt or tacit) of racialised meanings in the course of investigation. Race and mixed race must be held constantly in a state of problematisation and soft options, such as the allowance of 'race' as a folk or everyday term, are best avoided. There are other ways of discussing human difference.

Race and its Provenance

There is considerable discussion of 'race' and what this term might involve. A general area of agreement within sociology seems to be that the conceptual histories of race are neither continuous nor systematic. What also seems clear is that race thinking is applied in similar ways to diverse groups of people. In the outworking of race thinking, racism often mimics itself, as it mimics ideologies of class and gender.

The provenance of the construct is also subject to varying interpretations. Goldberg[7] finds, during an erudite investigation of the development of philosophy, that liberalism 'has become the defining doctrine of self and society for modernity' (p. 4). This, in turn, is associated with the primacy of the individual over the collective as well as belief in the rational core of human affairs. 'Rationality', in Goldberg's interpretation, while denying the relevance of race, turns out to be racially determined and ethnocentric in its application.

Fryer[8] is unambiguous in his assertion about the roots of racism and its linkage with the requirements of capitalism:

> Racist ideology sprang from slavery. It arose as a justification of the enslavement of black people in the New World. At the very heart of the new capitalist system that was clawing its way to world supremacy there was a tragic anomaly. (p. 63)

The anomaly identified by Fryer was in three parts. First, while capitalism depended on free labour, slavery was, by definition, an un-free state. Second, capitalism generally made use of technological innovation, and yet slavery maintained backward methods of production. And third, as it proclaimed the cause of freedom, capitalism enslaved, indentured or otherwise oppressed its workforce. The complicity of race thinking is undeniable. However, the contributory factors are likely to be more diverse and complex.

Religion and Race

In the course of an email discussion with a friend[9] about the concept of race, my friend offered a theological perspective on the matter. His question about whether the concept of pure race coincides with a one people–one God (one religion) concept is pertinent to this enquiry. Many examples of philosophies which propose irrevocable human difference do not employ the same rationale as race thinking. They may have similar effects but are not 'racial' in origin.

Religions have been, and continue to be, either a leading or latent factor in constructions of racial or ethnic unity. The empirical study which informs later chapters shows religion as a means by which individuals are able both to affirm and to reject what they perceive as the mixing of racial differences. The question is also important as it underlines one of the areas of disagreement about the origins of race thinking.

Groups defining themselves as a 'people', a 'race', a 'nation' or a 'line of descent', whilst seeking to draw a line of demarcation between themselves and others, do not necessarily act in a hostile manner towards those perceived as the outsider.[10] However, opposition to mixing between groups is often an important aspect of the maintenance of group cohesion. An example of this may be seen in the Old Testament book of Ezra, a person who is dismayed by the wayward habits of his people as he summons them back from exile to Jerusalem. The most heinous of their sins has been to intermarry with other groups:

When all this had been done, some of the leaders approached me and said, 'The people of Israel, including priests and Levites, have not kept themselves apart from the foreign population and from the abominable practices of the Canaanites, the Hittites, the Perizzites, the Jebusites, the Ammonites, the Moabites, the Egyptians and Amorites. They have taken women of these nations as wives for themselves and their sons, so that the holy race has been mixed with foreign populations.' (Chapter 9: vv. 1–3)

This Middle Eastern melting pot has a rather modern ring to it. Similar-sounding sentiments have been echoed in recent times, often by politicians wishing to evoke a sense of national unity based on exclusion of the outsider, through constructions of 'the nation' or 'the race'. The Jews of Ezra's time were not, however, acting in the manner of ancient or modern democratic politics. Their Law and its authority were believed to come from a divine rather than political source. Disputes were conducted from religious as opposed to racial imperatives, and group boundaries, identity and genealogy were defined in religious terms.

Teaching against intermarriage (the term race may well have been inserted during translation from the original Hebrew) was, therefore, teaching against breaking divine Law – the Law that provided a blueprint for action in all areas of life. The people with whom Ezra's compatriots had intermarried did not accept the Law and were defined, therefore, as having 'abominable ways'. Certainly Judaism, like Christianity and Islam, proposed human differences and each claimed the authority of their faith and the need to keep within the faith group. Ezra's solution for redeeming the purity of his people, for example, appears now to be somewhat punitive, and he was evidently not afraid to name names:

Amongst the members of priestly families who had married foreign women were found Maaseiah, Eliezer, Jarib and Gedaliah of the family of Jeshua son of Jozadak and his brothers. They pledged themselves to dismiss their wives, and they brought a ram from the flock as a guilt-offering for their sins. (Chapter 10: vv. 18–21)

Just what provision, if any, was made for the welfare of these women and their children, we are not told. What is very clear is that this propensity for separating those who mix is by no means exclusive to the Jews of antiquity. Abandoned women with children perceived as mixed are artefacts of history. It is important to note also that it is women who are dismissed as the defilers of purity. Yet, the men folk have been free to mix and are able to resume their purity through recantation and expulsion of the impure. Religions are a means of ordering the social world. They may be made instrumental in the construction of ideas of race. They may be an effective means of separating people defined in terms of difference, but they are not the same as race.

Ethnocentricism

The existence of racial consciousness in China from antiquity to the modern era is discussed by Dikotter.[11] In what appears to be a rationale comparable to that of European colonialists, he shows the Chinese world as intellectually divided into those with 'Chinese ways' and 'barbarians'. The assumption that 'barbarians' could be redeemed by being exposed to the 'Chinese ways' displays ethnocentricism but whether this can be termed race thinking is a moot point. Dikotter shows the development of 'racial' stereotypes of different groups of non-Chinese people with perceived physical difference expressed in terms of biological immutability. An example of particular relevance to the study of mixed race deserves to be quoted here:

> Liang Qichao persistently denied any sense of equality to the coloured peoples. India did not flourish 'because of the limitations of her race. All the black, red, and brown races, by the microbes in their blood vessels and their cerebral angle, are inferior to the whites' ... For Liang, blacks and browns were simply lazy and stupid. The reformer Kang Youwei (1858–1927), perhaps the most acclaimed Chinese philosopher of the last hundred years, expounded a utopian vision of the world in a work called Datongshu, or 'One World'. Kang wanted to eliminate the darker races in order to achieve universal harmony. Darker races were inferior and should be eradicated. He proposed to whiten the darker races by dietary change, *intermarriage* and migration; those who resisted should be eliminated by sterilisation. (p. 249; my italics)

This suggestion makes an interesting comparison with the twentieth-century policy in Australia of removing mixed race children from their families to white foster families in what is sometimes called the 'Whitening of Australia'. The pseudo-scientific reasoning for 'racial' difference is also noteworthy and comparable with the scientific racism attempted in Europe.

It is possible to present an endless array of eclectic examples of what, by present-day understandings, *appear to be* examples of race thinking. That the idea of race is evident in ancient Greek and Roman writing, for instance, is disputed by Hannaford.[12] This is a painstaking evaluation of the legacy of Greek and Roman political thinkers and the development (and ultimate decline) of the political ideal. In this view, the citation of philosophical texts – such as Plato's *Republic* – as evidence of early division of the world into races was a failure of political imagination on the part of nineteenth-century thinkers. The idea of race was attributed retrospectively as being grounded in antiquity. As Hannaford suggests: 'Race is about the Hellenism consciously revived at the beginning of the nineteenth century by reading out the political idea from Greek texts' (p. 60). For Hannaford, this represents a failure of – or departure from – political ideas concerning governance, citizenship and involvement in public life. It is a deliberate rejection of the political ideal and a lack of similarly profound replacement. It may be argued that the development of capitalism required changes in the way government was enacted. From being a means of public participation, political activity and collective action became a liability.

It is this question of provenance that most divides those dealing with the subject of race. The reader will, in this area, no doubt be influenced by the intellectual tradition that appears to offer the best explanatory framework. Perhaps of some help in this area is part of Momoh's critique of borderland theories relating to partitioning in West Africa.[13] The passage is long, but very relevant to the question of the development of race thinking as it suggests the complexity and similarity of capacities between peoples of the world:

> I hold the view in African philosophy and, logically, that view has to be extended to the thesis of this paper – that there is nothing unique in Africa and about Africans. *A fortiori*, there is nothing unique in Europe and about Europeans. If history has taught us anything, it is that there are patterns and paradigms of behaviour, actions, experience, and through which man, irrespective of race, colour, religion or ideology has displayed, again and again, over time and space ... Europeans colonised the Africans. Europeans

partitioned the Africans. They (the Europeans) did those same things on a larger and even more inhumane scale to themselves ... In contemporary memory, the white man partitioned Poland, Germany, Vietnam, China and Korea. Even now they are partitioning Great Britain and Canada. (p. 56)

The author goes on to suggest that although Europe had no business slicing up Africa, Africans too had been prone to similar actions:

I am not aware that the Fulani Jihadist refused to conquer peoples and annex lands whose language and ethnicity were different from theirs. The same thing applied to the Benin Empire, the Oyo Empire and the Ibadan Empire ... Africans were and still are capable of conquering and partitioning people although they probably would have done it more humanely than the Europeans. (p. 57)

The importance of these points lies in the fact that while race and the propensity to annex and partition people is generally held to be a European invention, Europe really cannot take credit for an original idea. It is responsible merely for a specific development of the idea under particular political and economic circumstances. There have been attempts to theorise human difference from non-European sources. Further, these have led to all manner of conquest, cruelty and domination among human groups. This is not to excuse or diminish what became a specific ideology of race. Nor should we minimise the damaging inequalities constructed on the back of race. It does, however, draw attention to the view that differences between the peoples of the world may not be as great as expected when it comes to theorising difference itself. This may be of great importance in understanding mixed race experience, which often is not structured solely by a belief in race, but through a complexity of beliefs about the mixing of different differences.

European Roots of Race Thinking

Smedley,[14] an American anthropologist, traces the European origins of race and finds evidence of a peculiarly English 'racial world view'. This was widely disseminated through colonial encounters and most particularly in the trading in African slaves established in the United States and Caribbean islands. This, she suggests, precedes encounters with the New World and Africa. With the long transition from feudalism to a capitalist system of organisation, land and labour were commodified and separated. Common land was, from the fifteenth century, increasingly enclosed and exploited by the putative 'landowners' as private property. The emergent English culture of individualism and unrestrained profiteering was, Smedley suggests, different from that of the rest of Europe (although, given the vast inequities, it can hardly have been a homogeneous affair). England was particularly notable for its hierarchical social order and for the displacement of large numbers of people from the land. The gap between rich and poor was considerable (and, of course, is still remarkable).

The origins, and much of the substance, of later ideological con-structions of race and races are, Smedley argues, to be found in English responses to the Irish. In this matter, Gaelic culture is associated with an attachment to animal herding as opposed to the English preference for settled farming. These pastoralists were provocative to English entrepreneurs wishing to commodify Irish land and exploit its use in a systematic manner and in order to maximise profit. The same English perplexity over Aboriginal Australian views of land 'ownership' is most apparent, even among descendants to the present day. Struggles over land ownership suggest an economic motive in the constructions of difference here. The dec-laration that Australia was an 'empty territory' gives an indication of the views of the first settlers about the indigenous population.

Given the subsequent intertwining of histories of the United Kingdom, United States, Africa, the Indian subcontinent and Australia, each of which has been embroiled in claims which rest on notions of racialised difference, this suggestion has merit. Smedley's account dates back to the twelfth century, and embraces plans by King Henry VII to colonise Ireland. As Momoh, quoted in the last section, suggests, Europe was well accustomed to partitioning her own territories and peoples. The Irish were regularly portrayed as a wild and brutish people, unclean and ungodly. She notes of sixteenth-century writing about the Irish:

> Some Englishmen argued what was to become a familiar strain in European attitudes towards Indians and Africans in the New World during the coming centuries: that the Irish were better off as slaves of the English than they were retaining the brutish customs of their traditional culture. (p. 57)

It seems that the Irish were constructed in the same vein as (and before) those who made up the 'Aboriginal problem', the 'Indian problem' and a whole succession of 'native problems' identified by British colonial and imperialist thinkers. The underlying issue in these putative 'problems' seems to have been that the problematised group was often the sitting tenant of a commodity – often land, sometimes their labour – required by certain groups of entrepreneurs.

Remaining with the Irish for a moment, accounts of the random murder of Irish people are deeply resonant with, for example, Rowley's account[15] of the 'picking off' of Australian Aborigines as 'vermin'. It seems to be in the ability to detach racially designated groups from their full status as human beings that constructions of race are particularly significant. (The same may also be argued of the highly exploitative labour relations during the early and subsequent stages of the capitalist mode of production.)

Spain

As well as the 'Irish problem', Spain, a model of multi-faith cooperation when compared to England, began during the fifteenth century to separate along ethnic-religious lines. Whereas Moors, Jews and Christians had long coexisted, the question of conversion to Catholicism began to be more pressing. Those who had converted voluntarily, in particular former Jews, began to be denounced for 'secretly' practising the Jewish faith. This suggests that individuals of Hebrew descent were believed to possess an 'innate' Jewish character which could not be changed. Poliakov[16] explains the situation in this way:

> During the Renaissance, the Spanish statutes relating to 'purity of blood' brought about a type of segregation similar to that of the racial laws promulgated in the twentieth century by the Nazis and Fascists. This case is highly instructive since it shows how, given appropriate circumstances, religious bigotry, under cover of a perverted theology, was able to bring about discrimination against Christians said to belong to a biologically inferior stock. Even so, though the 'inferior race' of the conversos (i.e. Christians of Jewish or Moorish descent) was persecuted by the Inquisition and, in the case of the Moors, expelled from Spain, it was not exterminated. No doubt the anthropology of the Church acted as a brake in the last resort, thus saving Christian honour. (p. 259)

The suspicion of the covert Jew is one that arises again in the context of Nazi Germany (especially in situations where it became difficult to distinguish by dress and physical appearance between Jew and Gentile). This signifies a situation whereby racialised 'taint' is constructed as immutable and anxiety provoking, particularly if undetectable. The interesting intertwining of religion and race as hereditary factors provides a clear example of the fallacy of race thinking and its capacity to rationalise cruelty.

This area of anxiety around the covert racial infiltration is also to be found within constructions of passing by mixed race people in America. While this is often now couched in terms of the personal damage done through denial of 'true' identity, it is also clear that the outrage is over the avoidance of incorporation of 'coloured blood' into 'white' veins. In a similar way the social work discourses around the 'transracial' adoption of children emphasise a perceived need to avoid concealment or suppression of the 'true' and inherited cultural heritage of the child.

At worst, such sentiments of immutable and racialised difference (through whatever discursive rationale) have facilitated a range of responses – from genocide to enslavement – and have underwritten belief in the need to 'control' racialised groups 'for their own good'. Depictions of poor people, women and racially designated groups are remarkably similar in their construction in terms of lawlessness, fecklessness and a general inability to manage their lives successfully. Such discourses have often been managed through the construction of scientific discourses, which have tended to re-emphasise the immutable nature of such traits.

Classification and Race

Ideas about difference, whether those used to defend the keeping of slaves in ancient Greece and Rome or to justify the cruelty of Catholic Spain, stem from particular intellectual traditions. Each tradition has a discernible development and set of discourses and philosophies about the human condition. Difference defines the enemy, the subordinate, the potential marriage partner and the 'other'. It often favours the interests of the powerful and circum-scribes the lives of the powerless.

The race thinking of modernity is no different in these general respects, but highly specific in the context of emergence. Goldberg[17] finds that the 'elements' of what he terms 'the racist project' 'include classification, order, value, and hierarchy'. These elements, he finds, are embedded within 'modernity's sociodiscursive structures and scientific vision' (p. 49). It is the 'naturalisation' of these within social and scientific thinking that makes race such a tenacious concept. As Goldberg explains:

> *Classification* is basically the scientific extension of the epistemological drive to place phenomena under categories. The impulse to classify data goes back at least to Aristotle. However, it is only with the *'esprits simplistes'* of the seventeenth century and the Enlightenment that classification is established as a fundament of scientific methodology. With its catalogues, indices, and inventories, classification establishes an ordering of data; it thereby systemizes observation. *But it also claims to reflect the natural order of things* [my italics]. This ordering of representations accordingly always supposes value: Nature ought to be as it is; it cannot be otherwise. So the seemingly naked body of pure facts is veiled in value. (p. 49)

It is upon these principles that scientific racism rests. The authority of a system of classification, whether that of anthropologists or biologists, derives from the belief that human difference (including the arbitrary differentiating criteria for races) is natural. Further, that the 'facts' imputed from those differences (some races are superior to others; people in different racial groups are essentially dissimilar) are part of a natural order. Earlier attempts at human classification were based on perceived physical 'types'. Later, factors such as psychological make-up were imputed. In fact, there was always considerable debate and disagreement about the ordering criteria and the differences that would be noted (or ignored).

This is of critical importance in comprehending *mixed* race experience in the modern era. Notions of 'own-kind', so frequently used as a term of exclusion of those perceived as mixed or mixing race, appear to stem from a profound belief in immutable (and natural) differences between peoples. The 'unnaturalness' of mixing whatever constitutes perceived racial differences is a foregone conclusion for the race thinker. It is unnatural. Whilst race excludes and differentiates, mixed race blurs the criteria for exclusion and is itself excluded in the process because of the dissonance it causes.

Not all exclusions of mixed by own-kind are justified in racial terms – we have the ever-present fluff of 'cultural' difference to consider too. How a group responds to diversity and to strangers will say much about the group itself, and mixed race has more enemies than the overt race thinker. The carriers of group responses, moreover, are often alarmingly close to home: family, religious group, neighbours and so on.

The Ground of Racialisation in the Capitalist Era

The development of race thinking and the hierarchical ordering of humankind into greater and lesser races was fertile ground for capitalist development requiring labour, land and markets. Also important is the style of thinking that is able to reduce thinking, feeling humans to the status of factors of production. This kind of 'rationality', which spawned rudimentary responsibility for the 'welfare' of its casualties, still finds perversity in notions of human equality. The point is missed where profit maximisation is the aim of applied rational thinking.

If race ideology in the capitalist era can be convincingly linked (in part, at least) to the desire for control over factors of production, it is also important to emphasise the diversity of the racialisation project. While in some quarters, race equates mainly to perceived skin colour, the omnivorous ontology of race has also incorporated religious, cultural, linguistic and other differentiating factors. An important understanding of racism here is that it is the *operationalisation of race thinking*. That is to say that any thought or action proceeding from the view that race is a meaningful division of humankind is to be counted racist.

As Anderson[18] famously suggests: 'racism dreams of eternal contaminations transmitted from the origins of time through an endless sequence of loathsome copulations: outside history' (p. 150). This suggests the essential and eternal nature which race is constructed to convey. It is irretrievably located 'inside' the person, as a property of the group to which the person is thought to belong. This becomes evident in the Inquisition's search for the covert heretic, in the stereotypical portrayals of the African (both in Africa and as slaves) and the Nazi proposition of a racial hierarchy. We can also begin to see something of the finality of mixing race – it cannot, in this view, be unmixed (although 'sinful' women and their 'mixed' children may be banished, to repair the breached boundary). Indeed, it is unsafe to consider mixing it at all with such understandings in place.

Anderson and others (for example Sivanandan)[19] link race ideology to that of class. The British colonial experience enabled bourgeois and petit bourgeois to ape the lifestyles of their 'betters' when away from the domestic setting. This is also most certainly true of those who managed the slave plantations of America and the Caribbean. We can glimpse this through sources such as the diaries of white women in the slave communities, collected by Fox-Genovese[20] and through slave narratives and accounts of life on the plantations.[21] Elaborating on what he terms 'the codes of breeding' in England, Cohen[22] locates race as:

> part of an ideology of inheritance through which the aristocracy asserts its hereditary entitlement to govern, either against the claims of a rising bourgeoisie (as in the European countries) or as a means of transforming itself from a feudal rentier class into 'gentlemen capitalists' as occurred, uniquely in Britain. (p. 64)

We shall be meeting Cohen's 'freeborn Englishmen' and 'gentlemen capitalists' again, as they stalk the world and appear in all sorts of transnational dramas.[23] It says much for the versatility of racial ideology that the very different racial orders of, for example, the United States, Australia and the United Kingdom have each been able to adapt the concept of racial difference to fit their own unique styles of social development.

Race has also been constructed to embrace the lower social classes of a nation. The elaborate class codes devised to establish rank amongst those involved in the colonial enterprise emphasised hierarchy of social class. However, the 'nation' capable of such acts of imperial and colonial strength could shelter all within a national polity, each with an understood position in the social order. Anderson[24] links colonial racism to an imperial concept which

> attempted to wield dynastic legitimacy and national community. It did so by generalising a principle of innate, inherited superiority on which its own domestic position was (however shakily) based, to the vastness of overseas possessions, covertly (or not so covertly) conveying the idea that if, say, English lords were naturally superior to other Englishmen, no matter: these other Englishmen were no less superior to the subjected natives. (p. 150)

Opportunities for claims on the basis of this form of hierarchical ordering vary, and social class and race ideologies have developed in markedly different ways in different countries.[25]

As Zack[26] points out, American white family identity depends on successful claims to the complete exclusion of blackness from family ancestry. She also links ideologies of race to those of class and heredity both in Europe and the United States. In explaining the persistence of the concept of race, Zack finds that its European origins are associated with a line of descent, which would have indicated a person's family in the sense of kinship as opposed to biological family. The modern American meaning, on the other hand, employs family as a medium for assigning an individual to an abstract racial category. Underlying each instance is the assumption of race as biological inheritance. This also highlights the convergence which has occurred between the notions of social and biological family. The increasing assumption that the two are the same may well have heightened the need to control the fertility of women in order to ensure that social fatherhood coincides with biological fatherhood.

Biddiss,[27] in discussing the importance of Gobineau's ideas to right-wing political philosophy, finds that the social background of nineteenth-century France contributed to Gobineau's ideas about the inequality of races. Born into the bourgeoisie, he became disillusioned by the outcome of the 1848 revolutions and by what he perceived to be a general degeneracy within political circles. Biddiss makes an interesting comparison between the thinking of Marx and Gobineau:

> Again we see connections between Race and Class, here associated in their identical function as secular symbols of group loyalty in an age when political theory had lost almost completely its earlier role as a servant of the city state or of the Church or of a dynasty. The major works of Marx and Gobineau, directing loyalty to Class on the one hand and Race on the other, are in essence responses to the same crisis – that of alienation from the social, economic and cultural state of contemporary Europe. (p. 21)

But, of course, the solutions were diametrically opposed. Whereas Marx theorised a move towards social equality, Gobineau's proposals were founded on a 'natural' inequality existing between groups defined as races. Marx made no claims of a 'natural' order, social class being defined in relation to ownership of the means of production. It may be argued that Gobineau's was also a class position, since the elite or highest group in the racial hierarchy was the very one in which Gobineau's economic and social interests lay. What seems to emerge from the comparison of the two is that each was writing at a time when political theory and earlier styles of governance were failing to address questions of social order. The crisis, to which class and race were alternative forms of intellectual and organisational response, seems to have been political and economic. Race, in this understanding, is a political response to the question of order and the maintenance of social hierarchy.

A Missing Link: Whiteness as a Racial Category

A missing link in much of the social scientific work on race has tended to be the inattention to whiteness as a *racial* category. Yet in the earlier stages of human classification, mainly attempted by white men, whiteness was argued to be a positive and superior racial state. By equating whiteness with superiority, panic was often engendered about the quality, morals and health of lower-class whites. This goes a long way towards an understanding of the anxious need to control or keep in check the behaviour of the lower orders both at home and in the colonies. This has been almost forgotten with the hegemonic naturalisation of whiteness in many Western democracies. Whiteness is 'normal' and non-whiteness has come to be described by series of ethnic or racially defined populations.

The business of claiming whiteness requires some consideration. White has been used to indicate deserved privilege or superiority, and white people constructed as the perpetrators of racism. Leaving aside for the moment the likelihood that much of the world's population is likely to be mixed, whiteness is by no means a homogenous category. White, the world over, is a category riven with divisions and situations of white-on-white exploitation. Gender, class, age, sexuality and disability are some of the social constructs that secure inequity and exclusion amongst those defined as white. White is also a highly conditional privilege, particularly when the question of mixing it arises, and most particularly for white women who mix race.

Frankenberg[28] investigates ways in which whiteness is constructed as a racial category in the United States. Through interviews with 30 white American women, some of whom are in interracial relation-ships or who have mixed race children, she contextualises the views expressed within common American discourses of race and race mixing. Race mixing, Frankenberg suggests, threatens 'a power structure in which race, class and gender are linked' (p. 75). The social construction of whiteness is an ideological device, and one from whose privileges many white people are actually excluded.

This point is driven home on United Kingdom ethnic monitoring forms which tend to offer the opportunity, for white British people faced with selecting their ethnic group, to select only 'white'. This notion of whiteness as an ethnic affiliation is most perplexing and hides the deep divisions and more realistic notions of affiliation which might more accurately depict a variety of situations. Perhaps this observation misses the point of ethnic monitoring altogether.

At the point of its perceived mixture, whiteness becomes overtly racialised and gendered. Its exclusiveness is threatened. It seems reasonable to pay attention to the career of whiteness as it moves between its 'pure' (and often undifferentiated) state into the areas of its mixture where it becomes a compromised privilege. As one woman reported during the course of a workshop on mixed race issues:[29]

> As a white woman out on my own, I can go anywhere. As a white woman with my black kids I am called names. As a white woman out with black kids and a black man, I am a 'white bitch' and my kids are 'black bastards'.

The degree of compromise is structured by gender and social class position, as well as by more local features of individual situations. In this respect, whiteness behaves like other racial criteria. Its advantages are claimed through the control of ideological production which has normalised and universalised a fragment of 'white culture'. However, whiteness is not the only basis for claims to exclusiveness and purity.

Ethnicity

Ethnicity, a concept which some sociologists have tended to eschew,[30] has some explanatory potential in the study of human affairs.[31] Cohen[32] whilst regarding race as an ideological construct which 'signifies a set of properties of inheritance which fix and legitimate real positions of domination or subordination in terms of genealogies of generic difference' (p. 23) separates out ethnicity and links it (as he does race) to class. Like Bauman,[33] Cohen places ethnicity as part of human individuation activity. It is seen as a means whereby a collectivity identifies itself through language and cultural practice and transmits the practices through the generations, sometimes with a territorial aspect to ethnic claims.

The processual nature of ethnicity, in this version, anticipates change and adaptation through time and circumstances; it is usefully seen as a dialectical process between the group and the social world. Both are changed in the process. Ethnicity is a way of explaining the world, and of organising within particular contexts. It is independent of race unless linkage is attempted. The view that ethnicities are part of the necessary substance on which race works renders ethnicity problematic since racialisation, requiring concrete bases for the manifestation of racist ideology, appropriates, but distorts and fixes, processes of negotiation and adaptation.

Cohen also finds that the hegemonic domination of one class may well also result in an ethnic hegemony. This certainly contributes to an understanding of the 'normalised', non-ethnic constructions of whiteness and highlights links which we need to keep in mind between race and class. In this understanding, both race and class subordination are equated with the 'naturalisation' of a particular ethnicity. A transclass appeal to race or ethnic solidarity, emphasising common elements of ethnicity, is made possible at times of war and economic boom, requiring additional sacrifice on the part of the working classes. Racial pride, social solidarity, unity of purpose supplant the underside of unemployment, exploitation, poorer social facilities for the majority. An emphasis on 'racial fitness' masks anxiety over the poor state of those required to perform protective or productive tasks for the nation.

This source of solidarity also rings true in situations where there are distinct and well circumscribed ethnic groups, often rewarded through local systems of funding and space at negotiating tables. Failure to keep within the allotted 'ethnic spaces' brings forth recrimination, since order is in jeopardy. Devices such as family control and reliance on the sound moral reputations of womenfolk work towards the closure and defence of ethnic group boundaries.

It is not difficult to understand that mixed race is something of a loose cannon in these settlements over ethnic spaces. Apparently a failure in socialisation into the finer points of the racial order, it becomes the source of anxiety over social change and disorder. It represents the failure of 'family' and a whole range of institutions to manage racially ordered behaviour. This was true in Africa and India during colonial rule and remains true in Western nations which persist in racial and ethnic classification. American civil rights funding allocation, for example, relies on the identification and quantification of distinct ethnic groups. Mixed race is certain to reduce numbers in a headcount needed for funding, or may imply a double counting that could bring the system into disrepute.

The blurring of the distinction between race and ethnicity is apparent in the 'racial' census categories in the United States and elsewhere. It has been apparent in the conflict over the divided Yugoslavia with religious and ethnic affiliation signifying apparently intractable and immutable difference. In a similar way ethnicity in Nigeria, and other African states, appears to be 'hardening' through the re-emphasis of religious, cultural and linguistic differences.

Ethnicity in the Nigerian context appears to be providing a way of responding to the circumstances of post-colonial experience. The population has, in recent years, been assaulted by a series of corrupt military regimes (often supported by Western alliances and trading agreements) and the corrosive manipulation of multinational conglomerates. Older certainties, forms of wealth and social positioning are fragmented. Appeals to origins and common ancestry, as well as recourse to religious fervour are the channels of resistance available at present. The concept of ethnicity was emphasised in this area, as in the southern states of Africa, through missionary and colonial activity and the writing of histories of ethnic groups in terms of profound difference. How these divisions will progress is not yet clear, although, in the case of Nigeria, some of the northern states are attempting to introduce Sharia Law while the Yorubas and other groups further south emphasise their Christian allegiances.

Vail[34] examines the ideological construction of ethnic consciousness in South Africa from the early twentieth century. He finds three factors that were essential for its creation: a group of intellectuals or 'cultural brokers', African intermediaries required to administer subordinate peoples ('indirect rule'), and the willingness of people to accept a rendition of 'traditional values' at a point of great social upheaval. Local African intellectuals, missionaries and anthropologists were part of the construction process and missionary groups (throughout Africa) had great influence on the organisation of spoken languages into written forms with formal divisions identified between different languages. Missionaries also – and this was particularly influential because of their monopoly on schooling – prepared historical accounts of tribes which attributed customs and cultural practice to newly identified groups. In turn, this information was used by pupils to define aspects of local politics based on the notion of ethnic grouping. As Furedi[35] discusses, fear of the 'detribalised native' was a preoccupation in the West during the inter-war years, and appeal to traditional values of the tribe was a means of avoiding this situation. Indirect Rule, a product of Lugard's thinking on the management of Africa, used the indigenous systems of organisation to administer the populace, thus underlining 'tradition' and continuity for the masses.[36]

On the position of women in this relatively new ethnic settlement in South Africa, Vail is specific. It was the male migrant worker that had the vested interest in the newly formed 'traditional' arrangement which secured the surveillance of land and family during times of absence – with maintenance work carried out by womenfolk. Further, those not tied to migrant labour (including Cape Coloureds) were less enthusiastic about ethnicity. Vail also shows something of the interplay between class and ethnic interests in southern Africa:

In those situations in which labour migrancy was not a pressing reality (the Africaaners, the 'Cape Coloureds', the Luso-Africans of Mozambique and to a lesser extent, contemporary Swaziland and Ciskei ...) or in areas from which men did not migrate in large numbers, such as Southern Zambia and Central Malawi, the ethnic message has clearly had less popular appeal, reaching no further than the petty bourgeoisie in most cases. In the case of the Africaaners effective class alliances between the bourgeois elements of society and the 'poor whites' were brought into being only in the 1940s and afterwards. In the case of the 'Cape Coloureds' and the Mozambican Luso-Africans – and possibly Swaziland and the Ciskei – the gaps between well-off and poor were too great to be easily overcome by appeals to ethnicity ... In these situations, class identity – or at least class-tension – has tended to overshadow ethnicity. (p. 235)

This tension between group affinity and administrative convenience makes ethnicity an awkward concept. Although the term may be used to describe loose collectivities of people with some similarities such as shared language, it also classifies such groups in fairly rigid terms and enables inequalities to be sustained within the group boundaries. Vail's point about the control of women and property through the mechanisms of the group is not confined to the South African situation. Ethnic group leadership is by no means a democratic affair and is open to manipulation by national and local governments. Liaisons between ethnic groups are often bound by protocols and mixing and partnering across groups is policed through this medium. What may begin as a local realisation of commonality between people may become a rigidly defined set of differences and obligations.

Women and the Racial Order

If ordering on the basis of race, ethnicity and class relies on the transmission of inheritance, culture and capabilities through breeding, constructions of women require very careful control since they are integral to the processes of reproduction and child rearing. Women have also been the source of considerable reserves of free or low-paid labour. Links between the structuring of class and race positioning and the subordination of those defined as women within and across these categories are complex and ever shifting. Gender, like race, is heavily defended at its boundaries, with struggles over dissent from binary gender definition mimicking, at certain points, mixed race experience.

Anthias and Yuval Davis[37] take issue with the failure of feminism to account for racialised women and those subordinated through class positioning. Responsibility must also be extended to those theorists of race and class who persistently fail to account for gendered forms of subordination within race and class positioning. Ideologies of race, class and gender are frequently a means by which social orders attain the stratification of the workforce in order to maximise the appropriation of labour for profit.

It is most unfortunate if social divisions are intellectually separated in this way and analytical links are not made. As Ware[38] suggests, there is much to be gained from studying such connections. She gives examples of women who have made links between situations such as the exploitation of slave labour in the United States, the conditions of factory workers in Britain and the structural position of women of all classes and origins.

bell hooks[39] takes a somewhat wry view of this type of linkage, particularly in the context of white American women's claims to suffrage, which was extended first to black American males. It is worth quoting hooks at some length here as there are one or two points which are of interest to the present discussion. She notes:

No 19th century white woman could grow to maturity without an awareness of institutionalised sexism. White women did learn via their efforts to free the slave that white men were willing to advocate rights for blacks while denouncing rights for women ... It did not enhance the cause of oppressed black slaves for white women to make synonymous their plight and the plight of the slave. Despite Abby Kelly's dramatic statement, there was very little if any similarity between the day-to-day life experiences of white women and the day-to-day experiences of the black slave. Theoretically, the white woman's legal status under patriarchy may have been that of 'property', but she was in no way subjected to the de-humanisation and brutal oppression that was the lot of the slave. (p. 126)

This latter point may have been true for bourgeois women with sufficient leisure to consider their lack of voting rights. However, as social theorists (such as Engels)[40] have shown, the conditions of the working poor, particularly women, were far from ideal. There is also the question of the ideological construction of women as inferior in all respects, and the extent to which women were persuaded to accede to this.

The second point which needs to be made concerns the distinction between awareness of something (here it is 'institutionalised sexism') and the ability to articulate that position, and ultimately to dispute it. This process takes time and considerable resources. Women's access to education is a huge issue here. hook's suggestion that the plight of white women and black people were in no way comparable is understandable; however, it is also possible to argue that the subordinate status of each benefited a similar group. It is in the comparison of the different forms of exploitation managed within a particular economic order that these kinds of comparisons become valuable.

Ida B. Wells, in the context of writing against lynching in the South,[41] makes a similar point about women of goodwill joining in the fight against oppression. Of the work shared by white women she notes:

They became social outlaws in the South. The peculiar sensitiveness of the southern white men for women never shed its protecting influence about them. No friendly word from their own race cheered them in their work; no hospitable doors gave them companionship like that from which they had come. No chivalrous white man doffed his hat in honour or respect. They were 'nigger teachers' – unpardonable offenders in the social ethics of the South, and were insulted, persecuted and ostracised, not by Negroes, but by the white manhood which boasts of chivalry towards women. (p. 14)

Adrienne Rich[42] considers something of the differential constructions of womankind in the United States:

But the polarisation of black and white women in American life is clearly reflected in a historical method which, if it does not dismiss all of us altogether, or subsume us vaguely under 'mankind', has kept us in separate volumes, or separate essays in the same volume. (p. 291)

Brah,[43] in addressing the experiences of women of Indian and Pakistani origin living in Britain, finds links between ideological constructions of race, class and gender originating in the relationship of capitalism to colonialism and imperialism:

Ideologies of 'race' have featured centrally in historical constitution and contemporary elaboration and reorganisation of the internal division of labour, and they have been pivotal in the reproduction of a racially divided British working class ... The British claimed they were a liberalising force in the colonies, especially for women, yet as Liddle and Joshi show, colonial policy on issues concerning the position of women was shot through with contradictions. While they liberalised the law on some issues, on others their policies had the effect of either reinforcing existing gender inequality or creating a new form which was as oppressive to women, if not more so. (p. 68)

This is very much in tune with Vail's point that ethnicity, as it was constructed in South Africa under Indirect Rule, did not benefit men and women in equal ways. Brah goes on to suggest a continuity in the discourses about 'Asian women' between their construction under colonial rule and as inhabitants of Britain. The term 'Asian women', in the British context, is a catch-all which encompasses religious, ethnic and class diversity. However, racialisation processes have tended to fix constructions of gendered ethnicities and to allocate stereotypical positionings in relation to work and to social resources. The fixing of varieties of women suggests that ethnicity has been appropriated as a means of 'breeding in' social differences through socialisation within discrete and, most importantly, distinctive ethnic groups.

Women, then, are constructed not only as being essentially different from men and from children, they are also constructed as an internally divided category. There are different sorts of women, and these different sorts are assigned racial and class positions. They pass and are passed, and adopt positions based on assessments of what might be socially possible. At best, they make links between their own positions, the position of other women in the world and between other, related, forms of ideological oppression.

Gender, in simple terms, may be seen as sets of ideologies that organise differences in sex and reproductive capacity between people. From physical differences, many other differences have been constructed, such as historical assumptions that those defined as women have been physically and mentally inferior to those defined as men. Such disputes need not detain us long, except that we need to note the structural inequalities that have arisen from these constructions. Struggles over the rights of those defined as women to participate in democratic processes, to own land, to hold money in their own right, or to work outside the home are the stuff of very modern world history. Female self-determination is a struggle which has by no means been universally won. Neither have the socially constructed differences between women been sufficiently analysed and removed. This is nowhere more evident than in the study of race and, in particular, mixed race.

Endpiece

This is a highly eclectic, partial and necessarily incomplete look at some facets of ideologies that divide us. When gender, class, race and ethnicity are discussed, it is often with the confidence that all parties have a corresponding understanding of what the concepts refer to and a shared belief in their reliability. If this chapter achieves nothing else, it shows the wide range of meanings attached to common terms. If race is a can of worms, mixed race is a pit of snakes in its diversity of meanings.

What we can also begin to see is that privileges claimed on the basis of class, race, ethnicity or gender are not distributed equally.

These divisions do not arise from a desire to name interesting features of difference on the human landscape; they are each loaded with inequity and differential rights and capacities. Race ideology may be shown to have developed from multiple influences and sources and has been of particular value in the capitalist project. Whether race thinking was present in ancient Greece, or whether it emerged exclusively in nineteenth-century Europe, racialised difference has been used to justify exclusion and privilege.

Mixed race experience is never the product of a single ideology but of the intertwining of ideological constructions accruing to different differences. It is complex not only because of its differential construction between groups and societies. An individual is assigned social position not only on the basis of race but of other social criteria of difference. Little wonder then that we see ourselves, and others, as distorted shapes as we pass through the hall of mirrors. But this confusion has never prevented groups and individuals from finding common ground and contesting their position.

3 Parallel Fictions: Writing About Mixed Race

In a parallel set of texts, those of the 'human sciences', a parallel creation of fictions is undertaken. Like those fictions of 'high art' the fictions of psychology, biology, anthropology, sociology, genetics and medicine relate, directly or tangentially, to perceived realities. Their point of departure is not the assumption of a closed world of fiction but the nature of humanity. But the very act of perception is, of course, coloured by our mental representations of the world. Science creates fictions to explain facts, and an important criterion for endorsing these fictions is their ideological acceptability. Science, in spite of its privileged status in the West as an arbiter of reality, is in this respect a blood relation of art.[1]

We come now to some documentary evidence about the ideological construction of mixed race. In this chapter we glance briefly at some of the areas of writing which have contributed to and fuelled the discourses that constitute common knowledge about the subject. There is a severe limit to the amount of documentary material that can be considered here. In fact, an analysis of the various genres of writing about mixed race would usefully run to several volumes. The selection of examples of writing only scratches the surface of some of the ways in which mixed race ideology has been produced over the last century or so.

'Natural' Science and the Social Construction of Mixed Race

Useful starting points for the consideration of 'natural' scientific writing about mixed race (for the non-expert in this field) are two reviews of biological research by Provine[2] and Graves Jr.[3] During the 20 years that separate these two papers there has been a renewed interest in genetic explanations for various human differences. This has been given considerable impetus by the human genome project, and, from this source, conjecture about the genetic origins of, for example, criminality, sexuality[4] and 'racial' attributes has become available.[5] In popular usage 'it's in the genes' replaces 'in the blood' as a folk expression for deep-rooted and allegedly inherited tendencies. Steinberg[6] examines some of the metaphors employed in the embedding of the language of social division within genetic narratives. She suggests:

> Common to all of these utopian narratives are investments in elite (classed, gendered and racialised) knowledges and discursive practices that have been historically implicated in both the (re)production and normalisation of social divisions. Indeed, all invest the agency of both social stability and social change in scientific 'readers' and 'writers' – in both the experimentational and representational senses of the term. (p. 166)

The double helix model may have left many struggling for comprehension. Newer gene narratives (which have the advantage of being simplified and relayed through newsprint and other mass media), appear to be capable of rivalling those of blood as dramatic discursive devices through which essential human features are passed on. The character of the 'scientist', who alone can interpret and reassign genetic features, remains a powerful force in the definition of the borderlands of biology and the social domain.

Provine, in his review, suggests that European colonial expansion and the freeing of slaves in North America prompted greatly increased and altered interest in the subject of race mixing. Perhaps inevitably, in the transition from a tightly racially ordered society to a situation in which control became diffused, anxiety over order and the ordering criteria became marked. It was certainly a desire to address the perceived problems of social order that originally inspired Gobineau in his writings outlining a hierarchy of races, an idea which has proved highly influential down the years.[7]

By the early twentieth century an interest in Mendelian theories of plant genetics was revived. There was a tendency to apply new botanical insights to human beings, without rigorous investigation of the species barriers crossed in the process. Much of this work displays an anxiety over race crossing that implicitly or explicitly relies on the earlier writing of Gobineau:

> The observations of naturalists seem to prove that, in the animal or vegetable world, hybrids can be produced only from allied species, and that, even so, they are condemned to barrenness. It

has also been observed that between related species intercourse, although possibly fertile, is repugnant, and usually has to be effected by trickery or force. This would tend to show that in the free state the number of hybrids is even more limited than when controlled by man. We may conclude that the power of producing fertile offspring is among the marks of a distinct species. And nothing leads us to believe that the human race is outside this argument.[8]

A logical conclusion to draw from this would have been that since humans of all sorts successfully interbreed they must, therefore, be of a single species. However, distaste evidently clouded judgement in the area.

Davenport, a leading geneticist of the time, wrote of the considerable problems he felt might confront 'racial hybrids'. Basing his ideas on observations of interbreeding between hens, Davenport[9] advocated restrictive breeding among humans to carefully combine desirable human characteristics. Those who followed him were more specific about 'racial' inferiority and heredity, and more ready to condemn race mixing – by law, if need be. A number of leading geneticists worked with plants and lower animals and generalised their findings to human 'inter-breeding'. For many there was the expressed concern over physical disfigurement, which might occur through race crossing. This focus on the physical tended to give way to an even more abstract (and data-free) worrying over mental disharmony as the century progressed.

The classificatory systems and terminology of experimental breeding, devised for plant and animal life, are not necessarily appropriate to humans (and may not even always be relevant to plants and animals). This is an important point for those who look on factors such as ethnicity, phenotype, religious persuasion, or other socially constructed variations, as evidence of irreconcilable and racialised difference. As Zack[10] notes of anomalies in the classification of humans which cannot accommodate what she terms 'the slippery slope of mixed race': 'if the existence of certain human beings causes problems for certain concepts or systems of categorisation, then it is the concepts or systems of categorisation and not the human existents which need to be criticised and changed' (p. 17). However, it is evident that, by classifying some groups of people as similar to one another and inferior to other groups, a ruling elite will be spared the necessity of looking into possible social causes of differential achievement between groups. It is these sorts of areas that work such as Graves Jr's review addresses.

Politics of Biology

The review paper by Graves Jr explores the political and social motivations informing this attention to race mixing. Graves Jr considers issues such as the social origins of biological research questions and squares up to essentialist notions of race by painstakingly dismantling biological theories that purport to demonstrate features of essential human difference. He does this, as does Steven Rose, from the perspective and training of a biologist, offering a critique of both Eurocentric and Afrocentric claims to superiority. Such claims, he suggests, are rightly disputed in the social rather than biological domain.

Among the problems to be addressed in the field of biological research, Graves Jr identifies matters such as differential access to scientific careers and the promotion of certain lines of questioning over others. This is particularly important in any examination of the research agendas drawn up to investigate race mixing. Both Provine and Graves Jr acknowledge the view that science serves the dominant social order. Each questions the longevity and persistence of the idea of human races well beyond the point where racial theory has been discredited. On this subject Zack enquires:

> The ordinary concept of race in the United States has no scientific foundation. Yet rational people still retain this concept. The question is, why? What purpose does the ordinary concept of race serve? What prevents otherwise rational people from abandoning this concept as a means of designating individuals? (p. 18)

These are not easy questions, but they are important ones. Cartographers abandoned the notion that 'here be dragons' once the oceans were more fully understood and more sophisticated maps were possible. It is reasonable to expect that race as a classificatory device would also have withered away were it not for its exploitative potential. Race does not describe human differences in neutral terms; it ranks perceived differences and enables the uneven distribution of privilege. It is in this territory that we must look to comprehend the longevity of race as a means of explaining human difference and the fear of blurring 'racial criteria' which is so important to the study of mixed race.

What Graves Jr aims to show (and what is now largely accepted within social science) is that there are greater biological differences within groups defined as races than there are between such groups. This is to say that the narrow range of phenotypic traits, which tend to be used as part of the stuff of racialisation (such as shade of skin, hair type and so on) are accounted for by a tiny range of genes. He looks in close and challenging biological detail at research purporting to identify differences and provides an impressive array of counter-evidence and counter-argument for the existence of race and the salience of superficial differences.

The social nature of race is summed up by Provine:

> The danger is not that biology changes with society, but that the public expects biology to provide the objective truth apart from social influences. Geneticists and the public should realise that the science of genetics is often closely intertwined with social attitudes and political considerations. (p. 796)

Eugenics

Eugenics, first proposed by Galton,[11] was a popular pseudo-scientific way of thinking about national human resources and 'breeding in' human qualities perceived to be superior, while eliminating those considered to produce inferior people. Galton, a relative of Darwin, was specific about 'racial' differences, arriving at the notion that 'Negro' intelligence was, on average, two grades below that of the 'Englishman'.[12] Without enquiring too closely into what constituted a 'grade' (or even what, for Galton, constituted 'intelligence'), the problem of intellectual degradation of white populations would, he felt, not be helped by race mixing.

We need to be clear that the 'two grades advantage' that Galton had in mind for the Englishman was not evenly distributed amongst all Englishmen (a not insignificant number of whom were not particularly white and at least half of whom were not men). As well as there being a racial disadvantage, there was also a social class differential. Furthermore, overpopulation among the working classes was a constant preoccupation for those who followed Galton's ideas.[13] There seems also to have been some failure to tackle the estimation of intelligence of English*women*. As writers such as Cohen and

Biddiss suggest, the projects of race and class were closely inter-twined, and each ideology was responsive to anxieties, within ruling elites, over social order.

Eugenics was a set of ideas[14] that became interwoven with concerns across Europe about the general standards of health and the fitness of 'national stock'. Populations, depleted during the nineteenth century through wars and some very unhealthy social conditions in towns and cities, carried general anxiety about the quality of their citizens (and, presumably, their capacity to defend and produce for the nation). There were various approaches to tackling the problems of improving 'national stock'. Although some of these appeared benevolent, all relied on the notion of race.

A tension between hereditary and environmental explanations for differential human capacity and achievement exercised social science in the early twentieth century. Sociology, as well as the more thoroughly implicated discipline of anthropology, was considerably involved with eugenic concerns, and it was thinkers such as Hobhouse who urged closer attention to social conditions rather than an overemphasis on heredity.[15]

The logic of Galton's argument suggests that people with the capacity to transmit positive intellectual abilities should be encouraged to do so whereas those with lower abilities should be dis-couraged from reproducing. Certainly the mixing of higher with lower abilities (as broadly defined by race and class ideologies) was anathema. Anti-miscegenation legislation[16] (for example the South African Immorality legislation and the numerous American anti-miscegenation statutes)[17] reflects governmental attempts to establish these (or similar) principles. Although deeply concerned with racial exclusion, eugenics was by no means confined to the control of race mixing. Other groups targeted by the eugenics movement were 'mental defectives' who were considered to be in need of isolation from the general population. Underpinning these concerns was not a wealth of empirical evidence. Rather, it seems to have been a fear of chaos and desire to maintain the status quo.

UNESCO and Race

The culmination of nineteenth-century European anti-Semitism was its institution, in the 1930s, as a centrepiece of Nazi race ideology. This advocated an extreme and applied form of eugenics for the maintenance of Aryan racial purity and elimination of potential 'contaminants'. It was not a set of views that could be entirely disowned by any of the European or transatlantic countries. All had toyed with race thinking, considered the possibilities of segregation and believed in 'contamination' in one form or another.

In the National Socialist construction of race, citizenship and race became twin concepts. Citizenship was awarded on the basis of race – only those of the German race could be German citizens. Those not considered to be racially German were, therefore, not within the citizenry and were without the protection of the state. Beginning first with concern for lesser people within its own ranks, Germany initiated a programme of sterilisation of citizens with physical, social or psychological problems along sound eugenic lines. Needless to mention, in this campaign to tidy up the race, intermarriage with Jews, as well as with disabled fellow Germans, was forbidden. The Nazi position on race mixing contained few ambiguities: it was a sin. Hannaford[18] identifies some key ideas:

> Hitler's state was bonded by a culture of purity of blood and posited on the deepest longing of the triumph of the German spirit. The words he used to describe the dying cultures were medical, evoking public health concerns: sclerosis, putrefaction, virus, bacillus, parasite, syphilis, sanitation and cleansing. The causes of the collapse of cultures are 'profanation of blood': 'Blood, sin and desecration of the race are the original sins in this world and the end of humanity which is surrendered to it'; 'All who are not of good race in this world are chaff.' (p. 363)

It was politically expedient for the international community to move swiftly to a more neutral position on race and race mixing and to distance itself from the Holocaust. The newly formed United Nations Economic and Social Council (UNESCO) attempted to attack the notion of race. Ideologies of race were running scared. A first attempt to issue a Statement on Race, from a meeting in Paris of internationally renowned social scientists in 1949, failed.

UNESCO's first attempt did not find acceptance with the international community and with the academic world. A main criticism was that the conceptualisations of race had erred on the side of sociology and had failed to deal with the 'facts' of race still held to be current in the field of biology. However, in 1951 a further statement was issued after consultation between members of an expanded group of academics. It was accompanied by qualifiers from main disciplinary areas (anthropology and genetics were both interested and implicated in the idea of race). Furedi[19] makes the following comment about this:

> The co-operation of the international intellectual community against racism under the aegis of UNESCO stood in sharp contrast to its inaction in the period during the Second World War. Both the League of Nations and the International Institute of Intellectual Co-operation had failed to take a stand on this issue. (p. 13)

This new approach to race appears to have cut across some of the former arguments about race mixing, although these too did not receive universal acceptance. One inclusion of major importance here was the view that no evidence exists either to suggest that race mixing might produce inferior 'results' or that any innate difference in capacities between peoples are evident. This *volte-face* was effected without, as Provine points out, an increase in the already scarce evidence about race and race mixing. He also suggests: 'Thus the 1951 Unesco statement marks a clear point at which the public attitude of geneticists on the issue of race crossing had reached the current dominant view: that race crossing is at worst harmless' (p. 796). It was part of an enormous shift towards establishing the principle of race equality and heralded an apparent retreat in overt race thinking. Racism needed to diversify.

Stonequist and the Psychologising Tendency

Race mixing, as I have suggested already (and will continue to emphasise), is an area almost exclusively researched and written about in its own terms. This is a remarkable phenomenon. It suggests that questions which purport to address the problems and pathologies of race mixing are framed in such a way as to indicate that these problems are somehow intrinsic to the group rather than dependent on social processes. Psychological investigations of mixed race have tended to assume and to investigate this problematic nature.

Stonequist, in his highly influential study,[20] constructs his account of marginality from international sources and from biographical writings. The people identified as 'Marginal Men' in the study are those in various migrant situations as well as those whom Stonequist considers to be of 'mixed blood'. Forms and purposes of structural inequality appear to be neglected by Stonequist in favour of the problematisation of group responses as a form of personality dilemma. The experiences of North American 'mulattos' – those of 'mixed blood' – affected by social sanctions applied on the basis of 'blood' or ancestry, are portrayed in the following manner:

> From the white point of view, a drop of negro blood makes a person Negro, no matter how 'white' he may appear. The very fact that the mulatto is closer to the white man in cultural attainments and physical traits renders it all the more difficult for him to accept this extreme colour line. It has meant bitter frustration and mental conflict. The mulatto has found himself unable to enter the white world and unwilling to belong to the black group. (pp. 111–12)

It is not difficult to bring charges of ethnocentrism against Stonequist for his interpretations of the aspirations of a particular social group in relation to a white, privileged norm. Yet it needs to be said in mitigation that Stonequist and Parks were, within the context of Chicago in the 1920s and 1930s, attempting to counteract some of the extremes of mainstream racist thinking of the era. What each appears to have failed to bring to bear fully on the matter is a critique of the concept of race and race thinking.

It is clear, from any reading of social history, that the term 'white man' cannot be used to reliably represent a homogeneous group whose aspirations have been fully and equally met. Acknowledgement, for example, of the part played by the economic institution of slavery, under whose auspices many 'mulatto' children were conceived through acts of rape and coercion, is virtually absent from the analysis of 'marginal man'. That these children were arbitrarily privileged or reviled, attests to the capacity of some social groups to manipulate the life experiences of others at a given time. Ambivalence towards the ancestry of many of Stonequist's 'mixed bloods' was encoded at the act of conception, yet, it is conceptualised as a *dilemma for the group* rather than for the society which differentiates according to 'blood'.

It is inattention to social forces which is particularly limiting in the work of Stonequist and other Chicago sociologists of the time. While they provided often brilliant ethnographic accounts of city life and particular groups within the rapidly expanding city, their accounts are not fully contextualised nor analysed with reference to economic and social structures which affect those experiences.

People of mixed race are, therefore, conceptualised as victims of unmet aspirations or, as Everett Hughes[21] has described it, faced with a 'status dilemma'.[22]

Marginal Man Goes East

'Marginal Man' as a conceptualisation of mixed race experience became popular on both sides of the Atlantic. It might be argued that the characterisation was the forerunner of the investigation into 'identity problems'. 'Marginal Men', bereft of cultural attachment and social acceptance, were discovered and studied in dockland areas of England and Wales.[23] These studies tended to neglect the coercive forces at work in the construction of a much documented but little analysed situation. Marginality was a concept available to account for any apparent tendencies towards underachievement, criminality or other social pathology detected among groups perceived to be mixed or mixing race. In an earlier set of accounts it was biological degeneracy which served this purpose. Mixed race as a social and psychological disfigurement inevitably tended to be met with pseudo kindness and concern. In the 'best interests' of all concerned, race mixing was best prevented.

It appears that mixed race is particularly prone to this nominal research location, divorced from the social structures that create it. The persistent selection of individual or group experience as a topic for investigation over the study of factors shaping that experience is problematic.

This highlights a further issue: mixed race is often presented as dependent on the goodwill and acceptance of the cultures of its constituent parts. The presumption being that ambiguity arises from being torn between the two (or more) such groups. Much depends on who 'owns' and 'performs' the ambiguity. Perhaps more importantly, the social space in which to be mixed has so frequently been absent that reliance on ancestral cultures has been assumed to be a defining necessity for mixed race rather than an interesting range of possibilities.

Stonequist acknowledges the influence of Lord Lugard's thinking on the conceptualisation of *Marginal Man*. A preoccupation with African intellectuals who had supposedly stepped away from 'traditional' ways of life but found no place within the Western traditions masked a concern over social change (a final loss of Empire). The notion of the deracinated individual, those torn between two cultures, the breaking of traditional and conservative ties were of particular concern in the West. Looking forward to the 1950s and 1960s and the launching of independence movements in former colonial territories by leaders such as Nkrumah, it is evident that these fears over change were not without foundation. Furedi writes:

> The interest that academics displayed towards Marginal Man, the detribalised native, the mulatto or half-caste was the product of their interest in the problem of change ... Maladjustment did not merely imply the difficulty of adapting to new circumstances. It also underlined a problematic mental state. Being uprooted and not being accepted in the dominant culture were seen to expose intense insecurities. The tendency to psychologise dissent by labelling it as oppression psychosis or an inferiority complex dominated the literature. (pp. 137–8)

This touchy oversensitivity detected in *Marginal Man* was, it seems, an unburdening of fears that social orders were changing and old boundaries and certainties were shifting. That these fears were capable of being transformed into mental problems for mixed race groups (and other dangerous groups) is an indication of the ideological forces opposing change.

Mixed Race and the Question of Identity

The concern of the natural sciences with physical feebleness among those considered to be racial hybrids often contained allusions to mental as well as physical deficiency. Race was, after all, an almost spiritual quality in some of its incarnations. With the subduing of biological theories of race mixture in the wake of the Second World War, the minds of the mixed race increasingly became a focus of study and knowledge production. This industry has tended, as in Stonequist's work, to be couched in benevolent, for-your-own-good terms. The inclination to psychologise is now central to the way in which mixed race is investigated and managed.

'Racial identity' is the peg upon which much writing about mixed race, within the genre of psychological writing about mixed race, is currently hung. Few authors (Zack is among the few) call into question the notion of promoting or embracing an identity based upon an untenable biological categorisation of the species. Because of the lack of social identities which depart from bipolar models of race, mixed race has tended to be depicted as problematic. Again, it is within the group that putative problems of identity tend to be located rather than in the wider social world where restrictive and inaccurate racialised identities are allocated. Much writing retains greater or lesser degrees of loyalty to the psychological possibilities of adapting current racialised systems to the viewing of a mixed race self.

One example of this line of enquiry is the study by Ann Wilson[24] of 51 children in the United Kingdom considered to be mixed race. Wilson employs a variation of the Clarks' 'doll test'[25] in order to determine the children's self-perceptions of their racial ascription. Early on a point is made about the 'need' of the children to accept both black and mixed race identities. This is, reasons Wilson, because black is disparaged in British society and, therefore, the mixed race child must come to terms with the fact that she will be defined, by society, as black.

Accommodation, it is claimed, is best achieved where the child is aware of, and accepts, her ascribed or 'realistic' identity as defined by skin colour. Emphasis is placed, in the study, on parental ability to convey these salient details about the racial hierarchy to the child and to socialise an awareness of racism – countered by black pride – into the family ethos. Omissions of variables (other than perceived race) seriously undermine the importance of factors such as economic position and parental occupational status in shaping children's experience of the world in the study. Such variables are likely to contribute to the material and experiential worlds of children. Poverty or opportunities for expensive education and foreign travel (for example) seem likely to shape childhood perceptions of social structures well beyond the confines of an individual researcher's frames of reference.

Yasmine Khan, addressing an audience of clinical psychologists,[26] considers the complicity of psychology in pathologising the identity of the mixed race child. She writes:

Rather like the permanently infantilised learning-disabled, the multi-racial become firmly fixed to the sides of their parents in this discourse, the role of biology firmly underlined, and symbolised, by the new label of 'mixed parentage'. The concerns, the intelligence and agency of the multiracial person become invalidated and subsumed under those of the parents and parental authorities, such as teachers, social workers and therapists.

This is an important point, since the identities of the mixed race seem to be particular targets for intervention and for the issuing of 'ought' statements. Who, it is useful to wonder, has greater expertise in living the social designation 'mixed' than the mixed person or those in a mixed family? Who knows better than they the limitations and lack of space allocated to those departing from the bipolar models of identity?

A study of adolescents in mixed race families[27] shows a somewhat broader picture of 'racial identity'. The authors suggest that:

> According to much theorising, both past and present, only those young people who defined themselves as black should have felt positive about their racial identity. The rest could be expected to yearn to be white, or to feel confused about whether they were white or black, and in general to feel unhappy about, and ashamed of their mixed ancestry. In fact we found that, using fairly stringent criteria, including definite pride in their colour, 60 percent of the sample had a positive racial identity. But of this 60 percent, nearly three-quarters thought of themselves as 'mixed' rather than black. They were proud of their mixed parentage, and saw many more advantages than disadvantages in it, particularly in their ability to feel comfortable with black and white people and to see their point of view. (p. 161)

There seems to be a great deal of difference in writing about mixed race between that which is based on presuppositions and that which enables the self-definitions of those concerned to emerge. In Root's most recent anthology of writing on the theme of mixed race it is evident that there is a determination towards unravelling the complex position of mixed race in American life. Further, in Song and Parker[28] there is evidence that similar tasks are being shouldered for a multidisciplinary exploration of the subject based in the United Kingdom. These two books are examples of writing by those involved in living mixed race, and show some of the ways in which mixed race is being negotiated and redefined.

Fostering Mixed Race

Opposition to transracial adoption is of interest as a genre of writing about mixed race. It is a discourse that was taken up by social workers in the United States[29] and which has been carried through professional welfare discourses. The main plank in this argument has been that children in need of placement for adoption or fostering should be allocated to families of the same race as themselves. Subtexts to the discourse have included the problematic nature of race mixing and the contest over defining racialised identities of children and families perceived as mixed. Historical circumstances between peoples defined as races have been incorporated into the discourse and much has been conveniently left out – not least the ways in which people defined in oppositional terms have always been able to make lives together.

Bartholet[30] provides a comprehensive account and discussion of the origins and implications of same race rhetoric in the American childcare system. A major difference between America and Britain in this area is that same race comes within the legal definition of race discrimination in the former but not the latter. Bartholet's exposition is complemented by three reviews of the impact of writing about transracial adoption in Britain.[31] Each raises concerns about the nature of professional discourses concerning children considered to be black.

Macey views the attack on transracial adoption as an unintended consequence of a particular form of anti-racism and perceives wider implications in the separation of races. Does this represent a move towards segregation in Britain which might encompass other forms of relationship?

The paper by Allen makes a case for the development of social policy, as it currently embodies racial ascriptions, to be informed by sociological knowledge. Allen expresses dissatisfaction with the transracial discourse because of the narrowness of its terms of reference. As she points out: 'No binary divisions are adequate to encompass the social diversity of everyday life and attempts to erect them are symptomatic of struggles over the power to define others and to privilege particular difference as an absolute' (p. 3).

Peter Hayes regards the opposition to transracial adoption as ideological and as originating in separatist movements in the United States. A particularly important summary in the Hayes paper analyses the organisation of knowledge in opposition to transracial adoption. It parallels ways in which research has historically constructed mixed race out of very little empirical data. Hayes finds:

> In the face of the evidence that refutes them, opponents of TRA have defined their position in a forceful, persuasive, seemingly

scientific and apparently convincing manner. This has been done in three ways: (1) By distorting and fitting empirical evidence to support the claim that TRA is harmful, rather than using evidence to test this claim. (2) By adopting absolutist positions that admit to no exceptions and justifying these claims through logical deductions without reference to empirical evidence. (3) By discounting current evidence in favour of predictions concerning the future. (p. 5)

In discussing same race matching policies in relation to American race relations law, Bartholet finds:

Current racial matching policies are in conflict with the basic law of the land on race discrimination. They are anomalous. In no other area do state and state-licensed decision makers use race so systematically as the basis for action. In no other area do they promote the use of race so openly. Indeed in most areas of our community life, race is an absolutely impermissable basis for classification. (p. 169)

The British Associations for Adoption and Fostering (BAAF) displays no such reticence. This highly influential organisation advocated a complete ban on transracial adoption. Their proscriptions and those in writing such as that of Stephen Small, who suggested that transracial adoption entails a process of 'pathological bonding', cast serious doubt on the capacity of non-adoptive mixed race families to 'bond'. They are new tunes on an old fiddle, interestingly extended to adoptive families which represent one of the few areas in which race mixing may actually still be prevented. BAAF practice notes for social workers, for example, contain the following advice presented as questions and answers:[32]

1a *Are children of mixed parentage really black?*
Children of mixed parentage who have a white and a black parent are no different from other black children. Almost invariably they will be identified as black by society. They too need to feel proud of their black heritage and it is this that is hard to achieve in Britain today.
   Such children with parents from different *races* [my italics] should feel good about having one white and one black parent. Society will make them feel good about being white. It follows

that the children are best placed in homes which will redress this balance and make sure they are proud of being black too.

The paper then moves into the realms of hypodescent:

1c *But the child may look white*
If this is the case, and it is rarely so, it does not change the fact that the child should be proud of both parents and of their *different races and cultures* [my italics]. If the child denies the black parent and attempts to 'pass for' white, this can cause psychological problems in the child's future. The child is a black child and should be treated as such.

Part of the interest here lies in the opportunities that this discourse has provided for the reinvention and reaffirmation of opposition to race mixing over the past two decades in America, Britain and elsewhere. The subject has provided a platform for professional social work to define the racial 'needs' of poor children.[33] It has become a focus for various forms of anti-racist activity within professional groups. It has also been a channel for the news media to recycle perennial public discourses of race mixing. The importance and functions of exclusive knowledge-claims to professional groups is well documented.[34]

There are several points of curiosity in the literature on race mixing through adoption. The most striking of these is the extent to which it is conducted without reference to the progress of families which are mixed race via means other than adoption. Usually step-families, mixed race families and the many permutations of people living together in family groups are, as noted previously, outside the immediate scrutiny of the state. They mix wantonly, in spite of any objections. Whether the racialised vocabulary of the transracial adoption discourse accurately reflects the reality of their family life is not widely tested.

The brief history of state-sponsored adoptions both in the United Kingdom and the United States shows the rapid shifting of views on childhood and the capacity to separate out issues of race and class. Cohen[35] finds that discourses around transracial adoption are not specific to racial oppression but arose as a means of legitimating the transfer of children from the poor to the families of the better-off. As he suggests: 'Transclass placements, which continue to be the norm, have always been articulated to discourses of "race" and nation. It is only recently that black people in Britain have become their main focus'(p. 48). Transclass is rarely mentioned in adoption literature.

Proving That Mixed Race Works

In assessing the outcomes of so-called transracial adoptions, research imagination is characteristically directed to detection of pathology within mixed families and individuals. A much quoted study by Bebbington and Miles[36] shows the 'risk factor' of mixed race in the United Kingdom from a study of 2500 children taken into care in 1987. In the case of ethnic origin, the authors find:

> Single race children from ethnic minorities are not over repre-sented amongst the children entering care ... On the other hand, a child of mixed race is two and a half times more likely to enter care than a white child, all else being equal. (p. 356)

This is an outstandingly interesting finding, and one almost entirely ignored. Why should this be the case? What factors can be found to explain this disproportionate representation of mixed race among families held to be in need of state intervention? Bebbington and Miles already show that poor economic circumstances are one of the other risk factors but even so, those of mixed race are in a par-ticularly risky situation. Barn[37] is now seriously investigating this matter.[38]

Much of the research that investigates transracial adoption suggests positive outcomes.[39] While this supports the possibility of 'survival' among such families, methodological and conceptual assumptions do not always do credit to the subject. Bartholet[40] finds that 'the nature of the studies that exist reflects a bias on the part of those responsible for funding, sponsoring and conducting research' (p. 162). This is very much the case, and the anticipation of putative 'problems' through the research designs echoes earlier writing about the problems of race mixing.

Bagley and Young,[41] for example, rely particularly heavily on psy-chological testing in their studies of transracial adoption. Bagley has worked extensively with adoptive families in the United States, Canada and the United Kingdom and is sympathetic to his subject. As with most investigation in this area, research questions are concerned with events following the adoption of mixed race children into white families rather than being focused on events leading to the adoption. By implication, the research diminishes the achievements of the families of origin and questions their ability to function adequately. Of the adoptive families we learn: 'The majority of these parents were middle class, and all were comfortably off, with adequate accommodation. Overwhelmingly they were a warm, loving, caring group, indistinguishable (and this is reflected in their children's adjustment) from the general run of parents' (p. 209). By contrast the families of origin are disorganised, with poor economic prospects and the children mainly 'illegitimate'. (If their 'legitimacy' is already in doubt, what other recognised civil rights are in question?) They are poor and they are not the kinds of people who could be expected to coach their children to perform well in IQ and other psychological tests. Here, psychological testing is the gold standard of proof that all is well with the newly mixed families.

The ideal of a harmonious society against which the research is set also begins to alert us to some possible biases in the research. Further, it begs the question of whether adoption (and mixing race) is to be seen as instrumental in the creation of a new utopian order or whether it is to provide children with alternative carers in situations of perceived need:

> The general model which we are putting forward is one of *multi-racialism*. This can, ideally, be achieved at the community level, reflected in multi racial education, multi racial friendships, multi racial marriages and multi racial families. Within integrated communities, white families who adopt black or mixed race children should have frequent and equal status interactions with black families. (p. 202)

We learn little of the arrangements for attaining this integrated society. Nor why the black families with whom the white adopters are to have status interactions were not, themselves, adopting children, nor indeed why such a world is not already in place. Whether it will come through revolution, unfettered market forces or the sheer goodwill and common sense of the population we are left to wonder.

The authors administered a range of psychological tests to groups of adopted and non-adopted mixed race children as well as to adopted and non-adopted white children. These were to assess 'adjustment', 'self esteem', IQ and other regions of the psyche. Throughout, the non-adopted mixed race children fared badly on test scores. (This seems a far more interesting and obvious topic for research than the progress of prosperous families.) Possibly their families too, given decent incomes, work and adequate housing, might have been able to facilitate enhanced test scores.

Psychological testing, and its obsession with quantification and the establishment of statistical 'norms', is considered in Nikolas Rose's study[42] of the development of the psychology of the individual. Rose shows ways in which this form of psychology has become part of mechanisms of social control. The setting-up of statistical norms has edged psychology away from the study of the variety of normal mental functioning and towards the pathologisation of those who are considered deviant to institutional norms which are measured and established by forms of psychometric testing. It is a circular situation.

Rather than present further evidence of psychologising in this area, I would like to query methods of testing 'adjustment', or any other identified region of the psyche, particularly where these rely on acceptance of racialised divisions while neglecting factors such as class and gender. They do not begin from reasonable premises and aim to tell only a fraction of a story. After all the testing is over, we know little of why the mixed race families of origin were perceived to have failed and why the mixed race children made such excellent progress when placed in middle-class, white homes. These are structural questions, far more difficult to tackle, either in research or in policy.

The Mothers of Mixed Race Children

The transracial adoption debate promoted, through the uncritical use of concepts such as 'racial identity', 'heritage' and 'needs', a partial view of mixed race experience that contributed little to its analysis. White women with mixed race children were located in a very awkward social space since the rhetoric made clear that their capacity to fulfil these racial duties was virtually absent. Their vulnerability as mothers may well have contributed to the disproportionate numbers of their children under state care and this may still be the case. The possibility must certainly be included in designs for research in this area.

Banks,[43] in an enquiry into the placement needs of what he calls 'children of Black mixed parentage' in Britain, makes use of a piece of unpublished research which looked at particular outcomes for mixed parentage children arising from being designated 'black children in care'. Banks writes about the implications of the United Kingdom's Children Act of 1989 for mixed race families. In particular, he comments on the situation for a single white parent of mixed race children wishing to adopt:

> One may ask what the resistance is to such a placement? One of the agency respondents in the study by Gascoyn provides us with a clue to the social perceptions of one of the interviewees who said 'while placing a mixed parentage child with an inter racial family may be seen as the ideal for that child, difficulties are raised for the organisation in terms of assessment, in that mixed relation-ships are inherently complex and have tremendous amounts of pressure upon them.' As Gascoyn notes, such stereotypical images of inter racial families bear a stark similarity to the pathological images historically (and some may argue currently) attributed to all black families. (p. 22)

Banks comes tantalisingly close to questioning the racialisation of relationships in the adoption assessment process; however, he pulls back from a thorough assessment of the notion of racially defined 'need'.[44] The definition of this need, for those considered to be associated with mixed race, challenges existing assessment orthodoxy and Banks finds:

> The issue that is likely to affect the assessment of a single white woman or 'mixed race' couple is one of 'entitlement'. Are mixed race relationships to be sanctioned as socially legitimate and are the children who are the offspring of such relationships to be celebrated in their difference?
>
>   At the psychological level, part of the agency and individual resistance to the idea of single white women with historical Black relationships resulting in mixed parentage children often allows white practitioners to openly indulge their racism without fear of challenge from those Black colleagues who are also critical of such relationships.
>
>   Therefore, both Black and white workers may collude in racist practice whether intentional or not. (pp. 22–3)

Are white mothers not 'entitled' to their children? This denigration of white women in mixed race relationships has historical precedence which will be discussed in the next chapter. Attacks on reputation are mounted on the basis of such associations. However, through the adoption and fostering process, it seems that this inadequacy extends to their parenting skills.

Banks also turns up some distinctions between 'race' (as a biological and political construct) and cultural factors needing to be taken into account in child placement. Thus, we are introduced to another weasel word which runs riot through the transracial adoption literature: 'culture'. What, we must enquire, exactly are cultural differences? Of what is culture constituted? How is culture transmitted, and does everyone from the same cultural group act in unison? Monolithic views of culture and language do tend to preclude human ability to adapt to the unfamiliar and, in the case of some mixed race families at least, to celebrate such difference.

Mixed race is a contested site. In recent years specification of the 'needs' of mixed race children has constituted part of a package of professional knowledge. Single issue arguments, notably those which underpin the transracial adoption discourse, make eclectic use of the concept of mixed race. They are, in this sense, exploitative, even as they promise to create a fairer world. The discourse has provided one of the main means of reiterating opposition to race mixing over the past two decades in the United Kingdom and the United States. Further, much of this opposition has been carried through the professional literature of state employees.

Referring back to Provine's review of genetic research, there is a similarity between features of this discourse and Hayes' claim above. Opposition to race mixing has tended to be characterised by a lack of empirical evidence, being powered by political expediency. The ideological attack that Hayes identifies is part of a wider set of ideological material on race mixing. The questions receiving priority assume the view that it is 'better to stick to one's own kind' – common sense that is so often undergirded by severe legal, political and social sanctions to ensure that 'common sense prevails'. We learn little about the mechanisms of race and mixed race nor do we find any effort to dismantle action based on race thinking in this adoption literature.

Counting Mixed Race

A popular target, among the people I interviewed, for locating anecdotes about being pigeonholed and for demonstrating the fallacies of racial classification, was the ethnic monitoring form, and particularly the 'other' category. This is a highly specialised form of writing about mixed race. Ethnic classification is an inexact science as far as those defined as mixed race are concerned, a point made evident in attempts to collect statistics about 'ethnic minority populations'. In *Population Trends* (Spring 1988) an attempt to estimate 'mixed marriages' and to report on the classification of children from such relationships in the United Kingdom is made by Shaw.[45] Apart from ambiguities around who is included in the 'white' category, it is evident that rampant confusion occurs where parents, captured in the 'mixed marriages' category, are required to select an ethnic classification for their children. Evidently, this is the sort of confusion which arises when the people of the mixed race condition are trusted to self-identify. They confuse the system. This has now shifted somewhat with the changes in United Kingdom and United States census categories towards a more flexible form of self-identification. It is likely that ethnic classification statistics, as they deal with mixed race, are in the nature of a leakage assessment.

Aspinall,[46] reviewing large survey sources of numerical information on mixed race from the United Kingdom, reaffirms this classificatory confusion.[47] Pointing to evidence of the apparent disadvantage of mixed race groups in Britain (Bebbington and Miles;[48] Rowe, Hundleby and Garnett;[49] Charles, Rashid and Thorburn),[50] Aspinall calls for the better collection of information as a basis for an improved provision of policy and services, including health and social services.

Against this argument must be set the views of those who see an additional 'racial' category in more negative terms and who resist any racialised self-identification. Rather than allocating and tailoring social resources on the basis of 'race', might it not be possible to aspire towards societies where *all* were adequately provided for, irrespective of perceived differences?

In the United States, the picture is somewhat different, with a 'multiracial movement' in favour of the opportunity to express more than one ethnic affiliation (the terms ethnic and racial being somewhat interchangeable). The historical background to the classification of mixed race people in America is well set out by Fernandez.[51] The Office of Management and Budget (OMB) in the infamous Directive 15, required that racial or ethnic information be expressed in a monoracial form which, as Fernandez points out, enshrines the notion of hypodescent in classification. Everyone, until the 1990 census, was subject to classification in one of five categories (white, black, Asian/Pacific Islander, American Indian/Alaskan Native or Hispanic). Those of mixed ethnic origins had long been classified according to the non-white parent's grouping in the case of mixes involving whites. This is an interesting contrast with the United Kingdom, where ethnic classification and notions of hypodescent have been less explicitly handled and are mediated in different ways by social class.

By 1997 the OMB had arrived at the solution of allowing mixed race people to tick more than one box on the census form to indicate diverse ethnic origins. Again, it will be interesting to observe the outworking of the OMB's plans in this area and the way forward for mixed race. What the census discussions in different parts of the world have achieved is the establishment of a focal point for the discussion of mixed issues. The calls to remove the 'race question' altogether from the United States' census are detectable through web sites and other texts. The United Kingdom's call is less clearly heard, although there are occasional newspaper references to the folly of racial classification.

A correspondent from Fiji, now lecturing in Sydney, Australia[52] where she works mainly with Aboriginal Australians, explained the contrasting forms of racial classification in Australia and Fiji in the following way:

> these days the Aboriginal category allows for self definition and re-classification owing to the impact of dispossession and genocide on Aboriginal Australians ... American Indians, Canadian Indians and the New Zealand Maori have similar situations, although their classificatory system is not as flexible as Indigenous Australians. We have a similar situation in Fiji-registered natives and non-registered Fijians (Kailomas).

The Kailoma are the mixed race community in Fiji and have, since the colonial era, only been able to claim Fijian registered status if registered by a Fijian relative at birth. Otherwise, they have been consigned to a highly ambiguous social position outside the classification system.

Struggles over ethnic or racial classification are emblematic of struggles over the right to a social identity and over the matter of self-definition. It is not always clear why ethnic or racial statistics are collected. Certainly, a more even distribution of social advantages does not always follow an increase in statistical knowledge. However, it is very clear that the slowness to address the challenge posed by perceptions of mixed race in classificatory systems seems to be an international issue, and one of the ways in which the exclusion of mixed race may be effected.

Multiracial People

Two edited volumes (each edited by Root)[53] show something of the development of a mixed race or multiracial consciousness in the United States. In the later volume, Root outlines a programme of resistance to the American racial status quo, enshrined as a 'Bill of Rights for Racially Mixed People'. Given the rigidity of racial categorisation, it is perhaps inevitable that the emphasis on the individual's right to self-define is prominent. Certainly, the lack of space and vocabulary for those outside the existing systems of racialised classification requires the establishment of a more flexible vocabulary. However, the extent to which the individual psychology of the multiracial person is prioritised is of interest. The outcomes of this individualism are yet to be assessed.

For example, Root suggests the following, in the middle group of rights:

I have the right
    to identify myself differently than strangers expect me to
    identify
    to identify myself differently than how my parents identify me
    to identify myself differently than my brothers and sisters
    to identify myself differently in different situations. (p. 7)

The first and last of these, including the practice of 'situational ethnicity', seem reasonable. However, the detachment from family is less obviously progressive. One of the motifs of mixed race experience, which spans time and space, is the separation of families perceived as mixed. The Australian 'stolen generation', the disproportionate numbers of mixed race children placed for adoption or fostering and many examples of street abuse show that people in mixed families are not generally perceived as belonging together. They are either internally divided by race, or divided from other 'whole' or 'pure' populations by their mixture. From a different perspective, research such as that of Folharon and McCartt Hess[54] also shows that wider family pressure, withdrawal of support and rejection are vulnerable areas for mixed race families – and potentially factors that precipitate family break-up.

Amongst people I interviewed, children were often made to feel shame because of their parents' perceived differences. Individual parents were criticised for their choice of partners and identified, through the appearances of their children, with race mixing. Ifekwunigwe[55] writes of the commodification of mixed race children in the adoption process. Boushel writes of the particular vulnerabilities of poor mixed race families. Root explains the right to 'identify myself differently than my parents identify me' and begins:

> Parents are not usually aware of the identity tasks their multiracial children face unless they, too, are multiracial. Parents often will racially identify a child in a way that they feel will make for the most welcome reception of their child socially – this means not challenging convention but usually acquiescing to our country's rules around race which enforce singular racial identities. (p. 10)

Small[56] considers the 'mixed race movement', including the proposed 'Bill of Rights', and finds it to be an essentially middle-class discourse concerned heavily with psychological issues such as identity formation. There are many web sites and local groups that support the movement's aims, but the tendency to psychologise rather than to detect broad patterns and advance coherent strategies (beyond the census alterations) is evident. Ifekwunigwe too notes a class bias in Canadian and United States writing about mixed race and the relative paucity of such writing in the United Kingdom. This she puts down to additional limitations of the British class system in publishing work on mixed race.

A slightly different perspective on parental responsibility for mixed race children is found in Frankenberg.[57] Looking at hostile responses to interracial relationships in America within her data, she finds:

> All these stories, rather than holding society to blame for the problems of 'mixed' children, blame the parents ... In contrast ... women actually in interracial families frequently drew attention to the impact of racism on their relationships, on their partners, and on their children. (p. 98)

The process of constructing one's own stories about the world is evidently influenced by one's position *in* the world. It would be foolish to deny that each generation must be free to move on from the ideas of its parents and form its own views of its environment. It is equally damaging to suggest that partners considered to be mixing race will produce children that are 'racially' different from themselves – more different than the children of any other racially defined group.

That said, if race is allowed to divide mixed race families on the inter-generational level, there is little hope for continuity and stability and even less for the deconstruction of race.

Biographical and Autobiographical Writings

There is no shortage of biographical writing about people in mixed race situations. It is, however, frequently subsumed within other group accounts. What we lack is a coherent account both of the history and the personalities involved in what has been perceived, down the years, as race mixing. One collection of biographies by Asher and Martin Hoyles[58] does begin to address this deficit.

Equiano,[59] a former slave who married a Welsh woman, writing in the eighteenth century, makes impassioned arguments for reason to prevail in the division of humankind into 'races'. Sayers,[60] in a biography of the composer and musician Samuel Coleridge Taylor, gives evidence of the importance of social attitudes in the shaping of mixed race experience and scope for achievement. Mary Seacole, child of a Scottish father and Jamaican mother, was not prepared to allow racism to prevent her from assisting the wounded in the Crimean war. These are among the heroes and heroines of mixed race, whose lives are not characterised by physical nor psychological degeneracy and confusion, but by determination to challenge or to sidestep the racialised positions allocated to them in the social domain. There is also now a growing autobiographical literature which deals with more modern experience of mixed race.

A contemporary British writer who has explored the influence of a mixed race designation in his life is Hanif Kureishi. In the introduction to the plays *My Beautiful Launderette* and *The Rainbow Sign*,[61] Kureishi provides some reflections on his early life. Again, the focus is not on his innate, hybrid shortcomings but on the social world which cannot accommodate perceptions of mixture. He describes a shame over being identified as of part English and part Pakistani ancestry, wishing instead to be 'like everyone else' and describes a fascination with writing down political speeches:

> In 1967, Duncan Sandys said: 'The breeding of millions of half caste children would merely produce a generation of misfits and create national tensions'.
>
> I wasn't a misfit; I could join the elements of myself together. It was the others, *they wanted you to embody within yourself their ambivalence.* (p. 11; my italics)

Kureishi gives an important account of the development of his thinking about the United Kingdom's politics of race during the 1960s and beyond. He considers tensions between African American political positions, expressing disappointment with separatist positions and an admiration for the complexities of James Baldwin's work. He also, after a lengthy stay with relatives in Pakistan, makes some observations about the links between racism and class, finding that whilst British racism did not differentiate between classes of Pakistani migrants:

> The Pakistani middle class shared the disdain of the British for the *émigré* working class and peasantry of Pakistan.
>
> It was interesting to see that the British working class (and not only the working class, of course) used the same vocabulary of contempt about Pakistanis – the charges of ignorance, laziness, fecklessness, uncleanliness – that their own, British middle class used about them ... Racism goes hand in hand with class inequality. Among other things, racism is a kind of snobbery, a desire to see oneself as superior culturally and economically, and a desire to actively experience that superiority by hostility or violence. (p. 29)

Of particular interest to the study of the mixed race condition in this introductory essay, are Kureishi's thoughts on the right-wing political thinker Roger Scruton's ideas about 'natural prejudice and the company of one's kind':

> The crucial Conservative idea here is Scruton's notion of 'the company of one's kind'. What is the company of one's kind? Who exactly is of one's kind and what kind of people are they? Are they only those of the same 'nation', of the same colour, race or

background? I suspect that this is what Scruton intends. But what a feeble, bloodless, narrow conception of human relationships and the possibilities of love and communication that he can only see 'one's kind' in this exclusive and complacent way!

One does seek the company of one's kind, of those in the same street, in the same club, in the same office. But the idea that these are the only people one can get along with or identify with, that one's humanity is such a held back thing that it can't extend beyond this, leads to the denigration of those unlike oneself. It leads to the idea that others have less humanity than oneself or one's own group or 'kind'; and to the idea of the Enemy, of the alien, of the Other. As Baldwin says: 'this inevitably leads to murder', and of course it has often done so in England recently. (p. 31)

Another autobiographical piece of writing about mixed race worth mentioning is journalist Sue Arnold's account of her Anglo-Burmese family and their migration to England from Rangoon when Arnold was three years old.[62] There is a passage at the beginning of the story in which Arnold conveys some of the awkwardness over her Burmese ancestry:

During my years as a student in the United States I slotted comfortably into whatever ethnic minority happened to be around – Puerto Rican in New York, Navajo in Nicaragua, Mexican in Texas, Chinese in San Francisco. Someone in Vancouver thought I was Eskimo. But no, I am half Burmese and the fact that until relatively recently I have neither known, nor wanted to know anything about my origins (that word again) stems principally from the fact that I was ashamed of them. It wasn't my fault. It was my mother's. And to be fair it wasn't her fault either. It was society's – isn't it always – and it was conditioning. (p. 3)

The early shame and denial parallel Kureishi's account of wishing to 'blend in' rather than to be distinguished and racially bullied. However, like Kureishi, the author did eventually take the opportunity to visit and maintain contact with her Burmese family. This feature of mixed race experience, whereby people reach a point of wishing to investigate and reclaim a part of their ancestry that has either been denied or denigrated, is worth considering more fully. Often those who are critical of race mixing speak in terms of an inevitable 'identity crisis'. It is likely that struggles, such as those described by Arnold, Kureishi and others, to claim and integrate and explore fuller versions of their personal life histories can explain this infamous diagnosis. Certainly, where an aspect of family background is either held in social disesteem or is denied, a more mature perspective or more congenial circumstances seem to be required in order for individuals to feel sufficiently secure to investigate their situation.

A final piece of autobiographical writing here is the work of Australian writer Sally Morgan[63] about the recovery of her Australian Aboriginal family history. The author grew up as part of a three-generation family with her mother, grandmother and siblings. It is some time before she comes to realise that the maternal side of the family has Aboriginal relatives. This information is guarded by the mother and, most heavily, the grandmother (Nan). Morgan's efforts to find out more about her family are frustrated because of Nan's reluctance to relive very painful early experiences.

The unfolding family story is carefully pieced together from family sources and reveals something of the life experiences of Australians with dual ancestry over the twentieth century. Nan's story (and that of her brother), is coaxed out by Morgan, and stands as very powerful evidence of the disrupted lives of Australians living across racialised divisions. The vulnerability of the mother–child relationship is evident throughout and at one point in Nan's story the Australian mixed race dilemma is expressed clearly:

> In those days, it was considered a privilege for a white man to want you, but if you had children, you weren't allowed to keep them. You was only allowed to keep the black ones. They took the white ones off you 'cause you weren't considered fit to raise a child with white blood.
>
> I tell you, it made a wedge between the people. Some of the black men felt real low, and some of the native girls with a bit of white in them wouldn't look at a black man. There I was, stuck in the middle. Too black for the whites, and too white for the blacks. (p. 336)

And Finally

This chapter has touched upon some areas of writing about mixed race. The subject has been maintained in the public consciousness and has entered 'common sense' knowledge through all manner of writing and other mediums. It has been resited and reinvented but the message has remained essentially intact – stick to your own kind.

There is, of course, much, much more. One area of writing well worth exploring is local documentation of campaigns to 'rescue' or control perceived outbreaks of race mixing in cities across the world.[64] Another rich area for investigation is the portrayal of mixed race in local and national newspapers. The fiction and essays of Alice Walker contain some intricate and important insights for those who live across racialised divisions and these deserve further analysis. It is all work that needs to be done, along with archive searches of official documents and records concerning the lives of ordinary mixed race families and individuals.

Perhaps most exciting at present is the openness with which mixed race matters are now being discussed. Websites, magazines and educational courses devoted to mixed race issues are blossoming throughout the world. It looks as though mixed race is able, at last, to tell its own stories. As Morgan, quoted above, writes in her dedication: 'How deprived we would have been if we had been willing to let things stay as they were. We would have survived, but not as a whole people. We would never have known our place.'

4 Changing Illusions: Some Excerpts From the History of Mixed Race

> In all our diversity, we have been one people – just as the peoples of the world are one people – even when the most vicious laws of separation have forced us to believe we are not.[1]

The signs are now becoming familiar, human differences become organised into polarised explanations of the world. This is order of a sort. Disorder, and therefore anxiety, are generated when the differentiating criteria become less reliable; when populations constructed in terms of absolute difference begin to mix. Mixed race is usually afforded no legitimate social space, being outside these polarities. It becomes an object, investigated in its own curious terms, away from the cut and thrust of social life. That, or it becomes institutionalised as a 'third race'.

Patterns in the Career of Mixed Race

The variety and apparent randomness in the career of the concept of mixed race requires some investigation. This may lead to the view that the experiences of those defined in terms of mixed-ness, for mixed race is a relatively modern and highly contested term, describe a finite range of possibilities. The shifting purposes and processes of racial definition and the incorporation of, for example, religion, language, ethnicity and perceived physical differences into those processes render mixed race an elusive topic. The concept frequently labours in whatever capacity race (and its derivatives) are being made to act at a particular moment. Most often this is in the ideological construction of forms of social inequality and here there is a multiplicity of racisms.

Sometimes mixed race is in the way of clear racial definition and sometimes it is instrumental in the social construction of race. Where, for instance, race defines community, mixed race may be constructed to demonstrate lack of community. Where race

70

classifies, mixed race is used to advertise the imagined perils of defying 'natural' classification. There appear to be five features which often accompany constructions of mixed race: it is defined as an ambiguous social location; it is a contested site; there is a measure of dependency involved; it is a conditional state and it serves as a point of articulation in the creation, ordering and underlining of race, gender and class divisions. These are not always equally emphasised. They do, however, permit mixed race to be maintained as a particularly malleable social construct. The consequences of this unstable social location for lived experience are the focus of this chapter.

There have been circumstances in the history of the mixed race condition which may have appeared relatively benevolent in the initial encouragement of race mixing, for example, the early Anglo-Indian experience. At extremes of prohibition, such as those integral to the development and eventual abolition of slavery in North America, ideological material concerning race mixing becomes available to be transformed for various symbolic or material purposes. The structuring of mixed race has always been crucial in the processes of racial ordering and reordering of societies. Above all, there have been times of indifference; times where people, later to be incorporated into definitions of national, racial or ethnic group, mix, marry and become part of racially undifferentiated populations, as happened, to some extent, in England during the eighteenth and nineteenth centuries, New Orleans prior to the collapse of Reconstruction and in Germany prior to the Second World War. The mixed race condition has often been the lived experiences of people picking their way through the minefields of changing racial ideologies.

Heredity

While race has long been discredited as a biological fact, as a social fact it retains vitality in the structuring of social relationships and distributive inequalities. It is the parent of ideological children who promiscuously mate with other ideologies of inequity. Constructs such as gender, age, class, race and ethnicity have all made appeal to biology in order to legitimate ideological claims. In the end, their retention as social constructs conveniences dominant social, political and economic interests in the distribution of social resources and exclusion from access to forms of privilege and power. Their construction rests securely in the social domain (which, of course, continues to borrow, where necessary, from 'scientific knowledge', which has *always* borrowed its agendas from its social milieu). The struggle over ideological production is to be regarded as a key area for groups seeking to renegotiate, contest or to subvert their defined status.

The retention of a *hereditary* component in group definition and self-definition, as well as in claims to group superiority, is highly problematic for those identified as mixed or mixing race. It enables 'mixed' (in itself a nebulous concept) to be defined as dilute, or disloyal, or in some way lacking by interested parties. Response through constructions of duality or multiplicity of 'heritage' is sometimes employed in defence against the predictions of fragmented identity and loss of group belonging rumoured to afflict mixed race populations.

The essence of this putative inheritance is difficult to determine; it is possibly not an area on which those of the mixed race condition are wise to concentrate their imaginative resources. Certainly, where real or imagined ancestry is appropriated to explain present reality, the mixed race condition tends towards an underdeveloped *collective* mythology of origins or culture. This sometimes works to its disadvantage – as in current streams of race politics. Mixed race mocks and confuses any emergence of superiority claimed on the principle of heredity and this has the potential to be turned to good advantage. Against this, the 'dreams of eternal contaminations' postulated by Anderson[2] inform some serious social sanctions which tend to be experienced as a negative aspect of mixed race experience.

In the business of heredity, certain strategies regarding women have always been required in order to ensure their cooperation in the process of passing on the imagined inheritance and preventing its dilution or contamination. The position of women and what womankind is constructed to represent are of critical importance in the structuring of mixed race experience. It is essential, in any analysis of mixed race, not to allow this reproductive requirement to wander far from centre stage, since the experiences of populations considered to be mixed or mixing are circumscribed, to some extent, by struggles for control of female expressions of sexuality and of children born of such expression. This seems to be as true amongst my research population in England as it has been in other racialised societies at other points in history, albeit the means of struggle have taken different forms and sanctions have been applied with differing degrees of severity.

Division and Exploitation of Race and Gender: Slavocracy Style

In social constructions of mixed race the position of accomplice has often been filled by aspiring social groups, amply assisted by powerful forms of institutional support. It is tempting to suggest the primacy of economic motives, but there are instances where the exercise of power is apparent beyond perceptions of economic necessity. Ideological contributions from legal, scientific, religious, artistic and family sources have often accomplished a complex juggling of gender and class with race to produce a polished ordering of mixed race experience. Repertoires of experience vary, but they are, as I have already suggested, finite and patterned.

Erlene Stetson,[3] in an account of her search to assemble material through which to teach about the lives of black women in the slave communities, provides evidence of a quintessential moment in the construction of mixed race experience in the Deep South. The gradual institution of slavery from indentured servitude (and other exploitative employment practices) as a response to the perceived need for abundant and reliable supplies of labour, seems to have superseded all other moral and human considerations. It was the legislative process, in this instance, which articulated 'race', linked this with class and gender interests, and established both the desirability and the condemnation of race mixing through a complexity of ranked social standards and degrees of privilege. As we may deduce, it was a legislature which favoured the interests of the 'inherently superior' Englishman in the creation of a self-reproducing slave community which provided both economic and sexual benefits. There are many, perhaps most notably Angela Davis, who argue that rape, in these circumstances, was never about sexual expression but rather was an extreme example of the oppressive use of power and control. Stetson writes of the legal process:

> The first of these statutes declared that if any white indentured servant ran away with any Negro, the white servant must not only serve more time as a punishment, but must serve the life term of the Black person, too.
>
> By 1662, the Virginia colony had passed nine laws determining the status of newborn children. That is, all children born within the colony of Virginia would follow the condition of the mother. This law was significant in two ways. It was a change from English common law, which declared that a child's status was determined

by the father's condition. It implicitly condoned sexual intercourse between white men and Black slave women, in effect
allowing white men more legal, social and psychological freedom
by not holding them responsible for any offspring resulting from
sexual relations with female slaves. (p. 72)

In this way, ambivalence was encoded for the mixed race child who
had the legal status of slave and could, therefore, be sold away from
her mother, or who might find favour with a father prepared to take
a sentimental view of his child conceived under circumstances of
extreme exploitation. These were the antecedents of Stonequist's
Marginal Man, although works such as those by Williamson[4] and
C.L.R. James,[5] show some of the complexities and alliances made by
various mixed race (and unmixed) groups under the diverse circumstances of slavery. The construction of mixed race as a mental
health problem has proved popular and informs research to the
present day. Much of this work locates ambivalence as arising within
the group itself – an extreme irony of history.

The early use of the law, in the Southern colonies, also made
possible the greater control of white women who had, for a short
time, claimed a degree of autonomy. With children now following
their mothers' status, it became essential to secure inheritance rights
of property through legitimate children. The importance of marriage
and the absolute control of wives' property by their husbands was,
therefore, an integral part of the establishment and maintenance of
the plantocracy. It became essential for preserving the integrity of
the estate not to officially mix race, and was completely out of the
question for white women.

It was in 1967 that a final challenge to Virginia's laws on intermarriage was successfully granted. These had, with the withering of
slavery, become even more convoluted on the subject of 'miscegenation'. In the *Loving* v. *Virginia* case (1967), heard in the Supreme
Court in April and decided in June 1967, it was found that Virginian
statutes preventing marriage on the basis of racial classification were
in violation of the Equal Protection and Due Processes clauses of the
Fourteenth Amendment.

White Women and Black Women

Fox-Genovese,[6] through an examination of some of the diaries of
bourgeois women during slavery, and Frankenberg's engagement

with whiteness as a racial construct,[7] each offer insights into ways in which ideologies of gender, race and class have been manipulated to structure aspects of white experience in relation to black (race has to be a relational concept). The analysis of the racial nature of whiteness is necessary work in the unravelling of mixed race and of the social locations of black and of white women in relation to one another. Other approaches to these female relationships include an examination of ways in which white women have written about race in Roberts.[8] Much less seems to be written about the poorer white population in America during and after slavery – the extent to which they mixed and merged, or, conversely the extent to which they found it important to hold the colour line in order to claim slight social advantage.

The accounts from white women are sometimes testimony to the privilege available to claimants of brands of ideological superiority structured by race and class. Most make explicit this relative privilege as mediated by subordinating experiences of gender. This is particularly so where the forms of exploitation of black and of white women during slavery are contrasted. Where there is the suggestion of race *mixing*, white women instantly exchange any privilege which whiteness was constructed to confer, and become outcasts. Whiteness is to be seen as a conditional privilege – at least where women are concerned – which race mixing seriously jeopardises.

In a historical study of black women in America[9] Gerda Lerner draws extensively on slave narratives. Of the position of women she writes:

Under slavery, black women were savagely exploited as unpaid workers, as were black men; black women bred children to the master's profit and were sexually available to any white man who cared to use them. Mulattos or especially beautiful black girls were sold at fancy prices as concubines.

The sexual exploitation of black women by white men was so widespread as to be general ... The privileged house servants and artisans were usually selected from among the mulattos, thus giving rise to a caste system within the slave group which served to divide and weaken the oppressed group. On the other hand, many of the leaders of the slave rebellions were mulattos who had benefitted from their relatively more privileged position to become effective leaders. (pp. 45–6)

It was this manipulation of race and gender which informed strategies of social control of black and white women and black men both during and after the economic institution of slavery. A centrepiece of this was premised upon the need to protect an idealised confection of white femininity.[10] As far as race mixing between black women and white men was concerned, the power differential was such that this mixed race condition can only be described as the ruthless use of power claimed on the basis of perceived 'ownership', although James and many others others suggest that strategies of resistance were always in evidence. Michele Wallace[11] also considers some features of race mixing on plantations in the Southern States as part of her examination of ways in which relations between black men and women and white women continue to be racially manipulated.[12]

The dependency of the entire female population was secured within the racially divided community of the plantation. Female labour was appropriated for minimal outlay as women served either as wives or slaves. Reproductive work was required to provide the master with legitimate children or to replenish the slave stock and children were positioned according to skin colour. The extent to which unequal power differentials continue to enable social ordering on the basis of race and gender in Britain and the United Stares is pertinent to the analysis of mixed race.

Davis[13] writes of this cynical manipulation of race and gender. Her analysis of the functions of rape includes an engagement with other women theorists (such as Brownmiller[14] and Firestone[15]) and involves the following observations:

> Racism has always drawn strength from its ability to encourage sexual coercion. While Black women and their sisters of colour have been the main targets of these racist inspired attacks, white women have suffered as well. For once white men were persuaded that they could commit sexual assaults against Black women with impunity, their conduct towards women of their own race could not have remained unmarred. Racism has always served as a provocation to rape, and white women have necessarily suffered the ricochet fire of these attacks. This is one of the ways that racism nourishes sexism, causing women to be indirectly victimised by the special oppression aimed at their sisters of colour. (p. 177)

Also notable is the misogyny of some male writings which were published in the United States during the 1960s. Eldridge Cleaver,[16] for example, openly advocated rape of white women as a means of attacking the white man's 'property'. This seriously missed the point as far as many feminists (of all shades) were concerned. However, tensions between racial and gender oppression have taken some time to unravel. Ida B. Wells, [17] writing during a much earlier era, put her finger on an essential point here. During the post-reconstruction period at a time when lynching was rife, she wrote:

> True chivalry respects all womanhood, and no one who reads the record, as it is written in the faces of the million mulattos in the South, will for a minute conceive that the southern white man had a very chivalrous regard for the honour due to the women of his race or respect for the womanhood which circumstances placed in his power. Virtue knows no colour line, and the chivalry which depends on complexion of skin and texture of hair can command no honest respect. (p. 12)

Losing Caste

The question of losing caste is important for the women of the mixed race condition, and sometimes for the men. It is apparent that membership of some social groups is highly conditional and frequently expires when individuals are perceived to enter mixed relationships. A more literal loss of caste is evident through the establishment and eventual social exclusion of mixed populations formed through Portuguese and Indian, and later English and Indian, marriages in the India of the sixteenth and seventeenth centuries. These early arrangements were of expedience in the formation of trading relations and were explicitly encouraged by both the Portuguese government and the British East India Company. The Roman Catholic Church (under the Portuguese) and Protestant denominations (under the British) legitimated the marriages that were, by definition, out of sympathy with indigenous Hindu beliefs. (Although, quite what the unofficial view was is not entirely clear.) Indian women converting to Christianity and entering Christian marriages were effectively outcastes in Hindu society and much of their story is yet to be recovered.

Such marriages were, therefore, heavily dependent on the goodwill of the European entrepreneurs and appear to have been encouraged across all strata of the expanding English expatriate community. Henriques[18] gives details of grants and land offered to support newly formed Anglo-Indian families. Successive generations of Anglo-Indians married freely into white settler and Anglo-Indian populations, although not into Indian populations in which they were not even eligible for employment. They were able to travel to England for education and work prospects and, for a time, occupied jobs at all levels of expatriate society.

Trading interests in India were run by the British East India Company whose influence reached deeply into the lives of expatriate and Anglo-Indian populations. Sections of the English bourgeoisie and poorer ranks of the aristocracy began to see India as a potential sphere of influence and source of unattached males for unmarried daughters. Senior Company officials began to marry white women while the lower ranks continued their Anglo-Indian alliances. However, there was a creeping tendency towards disparagement of Anglo-Indians and a growing observance of English class mores. Anderson[19] captures the scene with humour in his portrayal of lifestyles of 'Tropical Gothic' whereby those aspiring to social mobility could ape aristocratic discourses of 'breeding' and live them out in the colonies. This new emphasis on class codes relied on the existing demarcation between white and Indian populations but also sought the exclusion of the Anglo-Indian population whose presence rather questioned the validity of the white/Indian division.

By 1833, when the East India Company sought the renewal of its charter, mixed race had already begun to be constructed as an undesirable and systematically marginalised state. The new charter, which enabled parliament to dictate its terms, barred Anglo-Indian children from entry to their fathers' professions and to the top grades of company employment. As more white English women began to marry and settle in India, the mixed marriages and Anglo-Indian children became increasingly stigmatised and pushed into the lower ranks of society. Additionally, Anglo-Indians, who had traditionally shown loyalty to Britain in disputes with local rulers and traders, were censured for alliances with Indian employers (where these were available), so work prospects were considerably reduced.

Migratory opportunities were also reduced. The former enthusiasm for, and explicit encouragement of, race mixing was bad for business in the developing context of British rule since it seriously compromised new codes of separation premised on notions of innate difference. As Stonequist succinctly comments: 'No doubt the Indian caste system on its side favoured the growth of the English caste system' (p. 12). Appearance, speech patterns and social aspirations of Anglo-Indians came to be negatively constructed and the loss of caste was effectively managed through the definition of Anglo-Indian 'problems' in terms of group inadequacies – a familiar strategy in the history of the mixed race condition. Even the term 'Anglo-Indian' was appropriated by the white elite who spent much of their working lives in India.

Caplan,[20] in a consideration of the extent to which colonial experience shapes discourses of present-day Anglo-Indians, examines the development of this group from its colonial origins. There are attempts to explain the group's preoccupation with its Englishness (actively encouraged during its early formation) and long-standing resentment at disenfranchisement. As part of the conclusion, Caplan suggests:

> The British helped to create and, for a time, accommodated a population of Eurasians in their midst. For a complex of reasons this willingness on the part of many Europeans to disregard ethnic boundaries – implied in their own creolized lifestyle – along with a readiness to acknowledge responsibility for and filiation with Anglo Indians, ceased in the early part of the nineteenth century. The British in India – taking their cue from metropolitan discourses – soon delineated a notion of racial purity, which in no uncertain terms excluded Anglo Indians.
>
> Whatever the hybridised realities of their own society and culture, Anglo Indian leaders insisted on biological and cultural affiliation with the ruling group, and vehemently denied kinship with 'mother India'. They therefore came to expound rhetoric of purity every bit as vigorously as the British, but the outcomes were, of course, different in each case. As the dominant power, the British were able to erect barriers to distinguish an untarnished image of self as culturally pristine, and at the same time designate the Anglo Indian other – against the latter's own self definition – as hybrid. (p. 758)

This struggle over self-definition and the power to define and assign others is pertinent to our enquiry. What Caplan does not perhaps sufficiently emphasise is the influence of changing socio-economic circumstances on the social careers of the Anglo-Indians. Changing socio-economic circumstances are critical for many Creole populations (such as those in the post-slavery Southern States) whose social careers involve sudden and radical fluctuations.

Where trading links were being established, mixed marriages were encouraged and Anglo-Indian children educated to perform vital work in the Company. When British interests moved into a more established and imperialistic phase, it became favourable to reverse the social construction of mixed race and to subsume Anglo-Indians with the 'native' population who were increasingly constructed as a childlike people under the benevolent guidance and protection of the British (as opposed to trading partners). Once white wives could be regularly imported for white administrators, the expatriate community was able to facilitate the further exploitation of India through its reconstruction of British forms of race, class and gender divisions. Mixed race was socially redundant and so demoted, deskilled and excluded as a by-product of colonisation.

Group Consciousness

As Shibutani and Kwan[21] note, it was not until the Anglo-Indians became aware that they were to be defied as being alike (in spite of their differences) that they began to develop a consciousness of shared interests and culture. The authors also make the point that once groups are identified and accept commonality of interests, etiquettes develop for maintaining social distinctions. Violation of such etiquettes is often dealt with through the use of social sanctions such as ridicule and gossip. This addresses the Anglo-Indian experience. Ridicule was used frequently in order to discourage further mixing, and served to reduce the status of existing Anglo-Indian families and individuals. On the other hand, the Anglo-Indians were outside the Indian religious and cultural mores and formed a distinct and socially excluded group.

A position paper submitted to the Hearing Committee on Fijian Unity[22] describes a comparable situation in post-colonial Fiji. In this case the 'part-European' Fijians are campaigning for recognition as full Fijian citizens:

> On the local scene, we the Kai Loma/Vasu are known to be the descendents of early European settlers and Fijian women ... Under the colonial system the Kai Loma interracial identity proved problematic for imperial administrators. Their caste-conscious classificatory system followed a divide-and-rule policy, designed to maintain social control and keep group interaction to a minimum. Invariably the Kai Loma child proved a disruptive

challenge to the colonial system. Kai Loma's hybrid identity high-lighted the contestations and hypocrisies associated with empire building. It exposed issues of concubinage and miscegenation (forbidden sex) between coloniser and subjugated natives and was deemed an unspeaksable act by Whites. The early products of such liaisons were strongly condemned and ostracised by Europeans. Fijians on the other hand, were more sympathetic to their half siblings.

We should observe here the way the Kai Loma are made scapegoats of the would-be-pure. Yet, prior to the colonial era children were born of traders and local (often high born) women, and absorbed into the Fijian population with little comment. They grew up and married within the Fijian population. Under colonial rule, a stan-dardisation of racial groups was imposed and the Kai Loma relegated to the fringes of Fijian society. The Fijian 'half-caste problem' was invented. Kai Loma are currently campaigning for choice of regis-tration as full Fijian citzens rather than individuals of barely acknowledged provenance who lack rights and privileges of belonging.

Métissage

A further example of the inconvenience of mixed race in colonial practices concerns a comparison of *métissage*[23] in French Indochina with the Netherlands' Indies, presented by Stoler.[24] The very different circumstances of the mixed race populations of these two areas make the discursive similarities remarkable. The Netherlands' colony had been settled since the seventeenth century and had a large and established mixed population whereas French Indochina had few *métis* and had been settled only since the 1870s. What first interests Stoler are the particular problems that the mixed race pop-ulations presented to the *colons* (settlers):

> What is striking is that similar discourses were mapped onto such vastly different racial and political landscapes; that in both the Indies and Indochina, with their distinct demographies and internal rhythms, *méssitage* was a focal point of political, legal and social debate, conceived as a dangerous source of subversion, a threat to white prestige, an embodiment of *European* degeneration and moral decay. I would suggest that both were so charged in

part because such 'mixing' called into question the very criteria by which 'Europeanness' could be identified, citizenship should be accorded and nationality assigned. *Métissage* represented the dangers of foreign enemies not only at external national borders, but the more pressing affront for European nation-states, what the German philosopher Fichte so aptly defined as the essence of the nation, its 'interior frontiers'. (p. 130)

Inevitably a '*métis* problem' (not dissimilar to the 'half caste problem') was identified in Indochina. This hinged on the question of 'abandonment' of *métis* children to an upbringing outside the norms of European society. This is to say that mothers consistently refused to allow their chidren to be raised under the protection of state institutions and a cultural upbringing as 'European'. The children were, thus, said to be 'abandoned' to a non-European background. At the same time, a panic over poverty among Indo-Europeans was brewing in the Dutch Indies and the claims of European paternity of mixed race children called into question. The question of full 'natives' (as opposed to *métis*) infiltrating the ranks of Europeans was considered a serious dilemma. For a fee, some European men were said to be prepared to admit to paternity of a child and so to admit that child to European privilege. This long-term anxiety over holding the borders is apparent in most racially ordered societies, particularly amongst the lower classes. The *Metis* population itself was an indication of failure to do this. A subtle problem was to engage the mixed race population's loyalty to Europe without offering the full privileges of belonging, which again may be seen as a fairly generally perceived problem with regard to race mixing. A further fear was that the European fathers would 'go native' and, therefore, lose their superior European cultural bearing.

An interesting line was drawn between the mixed race families that accepted European cultural ways and those that looked to the Indies and Indochina for cultural reference. Racism was expressed through discourses that focused on the cultural affiliation and social-isation practices of this choice and targeted particular arrangements that threatened European superiority. Inevitably, women became the channel through which social demarcation was to be effected. European women marrying non-Europeans were considered beyond the pale for inclusion within definitions of true and loyal Europeans (and the willingness to mix race was proof of their inferiority and waywardness). European men, on the other hand, were able to marry at will and their *méstis* children were automatically considered European, irrespective of their mothers' wishes.

Stoler's study is well worth reading as an example of the complex manipulation of race, class and gender divisions to the preservation of (in this case culturally defined) purity. The *métis* population were pawns in this enterprise. Interestingly, the arguments and actions were couched in terms of the *welfare* of the mixed race population. Pauperisation amongst part-Europeans, and the control of race mixing through family and social sanctions were pressing issues. Solutions were the separation of children from their 'native' mothers and the inculcation of loyalty to Europe with the prospect of economic and social reward. Marriage laws were tinkered with to this effect. Enormous quantities of state resources were made available for the 'rescue', surveillance and rehabilitation of the *méstis* population. Stoler notes:

> The fear of 'mixed bloods' may not have been about their burden to the state as so often claimed, but about the *empowerment* that cultural hybridity conferred; about groups that straddled and disrupted cleanly marked social divides and whose diverse membership exposed the arbitrary logic by which taxonomies of control were made.
>
> *Métissage* was so heavily politicised because it threatened to destabilise both national identity and the Manichean categories of ruler and ruled. (p. 143)

It is important to begin to note some commonalities between historical mixed race conditions. The unique forms of ambivalence displayed towards groups racialised as mixed seem to be linked to the dependence, of some social and economics systems, on constructions of social inequalities structured by class, race and gender in the distribution of wealth and power as well as status. Ambiguity is conveniently 'blamed' on the group itself and tends to be expressed in portrayals of the group as being unclear about its viability, identity, social position and so on. It is a pervasive matter.

The example of *métissage* in French Indochina shows how family and culture can be manipulated for the convenience of populations claiming superiority of race. Present-day discourses employing notions of 'cultural heritage' carry, in similar ways, intimations of race thinking. The discourses of propriety, morality and national loyalty may be observed to impact to a far greater degree on women than they do on men. Women and children are readily separated in the interests of socialising children into the requirements of the dominant group. Struggles over classification and inclusion, currently familiar in the United States and Britain through respective census surveys, have their precedents in other times and other places.

What, though, have the realities of life been for those considered to be mixed or mixing race? Surely at the level of 'ordinary people' a blending and borrowing has happened between all the cultural possibilities present. An informal 'creolisation' of day-to-day life born of pragmatism and human empathy has occurred. 'Ordinary people' are the weak links in the chain of racial purity.

Divide and Rule

The population classified as Coloured[25] in South Africa has been similarly adjusted to facilitate the acquisition and exploitation of territory through colonisation. Apartheid was not the first response of Dutch and British settlers wishing to control rich mining and land resources in South Africa. The Dutch East India Company had, from the seventeenth century, begun to penetrate the Cape territory through armed attack. Subsequently, the Company imported slave labour from Malaya, Madagascar, Sri Lanka, India and parts of Africa. (Slavery was later abolished under British Rule.) Local, indigenous Khoikhoi cattle traders, although not enslaved, were considerably weakened by warfare, disease and reduced access to land. Many moved from the area or intermarried with the Asian and white populations.

By the eighteenth century Britain was intent upon its 'civilising mission' and fought both the descendants of Dutch settlers and Xhosas for control of the Cape territory. Eventually, the Cape became a British colony, although, this was by no means the end of fighting in the area. A striking percentage of the land was claimed by white settlers and, by the time of the Natives Land Act of 1913, Beinart[26] estimates that around 77 per cent of available land was reserved for white settlers with some 8 per cent reserved solely for African occupation.

The Cape Coloured population was a very mixed group and there were few restrictions on intermarriage or concubinage between the different groups. However, the civilising mission carried the inevitable import of British class codes and the expectation of a 'natural' social hierarchy which included formalised statements about racial difference. Early in the twentieth century, an attempt was made to encourage the development of a white working class by attracting white women to even the male–female ratio in the Cape. What did not form, however, was a political solidarity based on both race and class among the English-speaking whites, which were in any case a very divided population. There was considerable anxiety and tension over group demarcations and a growing movement towards segregation between white and black. This was also so for the Afrikaner population who carried a strong sense of group identity and defensiveness towards both the British and African populations. Their national identity did, however, seem to make for a greater social cohesion within the group. Beinart explains the situation:

> Rapid migration by women both from Europe and the country-side reduced the preponderance of white men in the cities to negligible levels by 1921. To the great relief of those enforcing segregation, the incentive for white men to marry or cohabit across the colour line was reduced. In 1902, at a period of heightened racial anxiety, the Cape Parliament outlawed the sale of sexual services by white women to black men (but not vice versa); the Transvaal had already done the same. The legislation was extended in 1927. Surprisingly, marriage between whites and others was not made illegal. Such marriages were rare and segregationists believed that public opprobrium would be an adequate safeguard. (p. 73)

In fact, this same race optimism proved short-lived and from 1948, at a time when other colonies were seeking independence, a Nationalist Afrikaner dominated political leadership and introduced legislation based on notions of segregated development for black and white populations – apartheid. This was premised on racial variation and the perceived need for different races to develop their cultural identities and potential in separate ways. Social Darwinism dominated rhetoric, and fear of race mixing was articulated as concerns about social decline (as, of course it often is). This was the background to the 1949 Mixed Marriages Act and the 1950 Immorality Act which forbade marriage and less formal mixing between black and white South Africans. It was also a time of rapid industrialisation.

The position of Cape Coloureds is of particular interest to us here. The 1950 Population Registration Act required every person in South Africa to be racially classified. Many Coloured families had members classified in different ways on the basis of their perceived lightness or darkness. Although sometimes privileged over blacks, for example in job allocation, the Coloured population were never given full political rights under apartheid. (Again, this was so for the Anglo-Indians and Eurasians and for many other mixed race groups.) The main preoccupation of the racial classification system was to protect white interests, for classification defined rights, entitlements and freedoms in apartheid South Africa. Lelyveld,[27] a journalist, writes of the labyrinthine classification system, which has parallels in complex British class codes and behaviours imported into colonial ex-patriate communities to establish rank:

> Apartheid never concerned itself with mixed marriages between browns and blacks. They remained legal. It was only the white race that had to be preserved ... Viewed even on its own terms, South African racial law is the opposite of elegant. It is not a body of law really but a tangle of legalisms designed to maximise the power of officialdom and minimize the defenses of the individual, a labyrinth of words the meaning of which [is] determined by the white functionaries who administer it. (p. 86)

'Ethnic' awareness was encouraged and formed the rationale for regulating African residence and movement, and The Natives Land Act of 1913 effectively divided South African land and restricted the black population to reserves. The Cape Coloureds had no traditional 'homeland' (or Bantustan) to which they could be dispatched. They did not originate from a single area, nor from a single ethnic group, and by and large they were, and remain, urban dwellers. The emphasis on ethnic group awareness did force the Coloureds to realised their common situation, but this was not based on any ancient claim of cultural heritage. Rather, it was a growing awareness of, and protest at, their social positioning. This social detachment in the highly racialised apartheid regime was manipulated by the Nationalists who, whilst giving them slightly greater privilege, reduced the overall capacity of Coloureds to participate.

A report from the Inter-Press Service[28] gives a glimpse of some after-effects of racialisation on the Coloured population. Ironically, it seems that the Rainbow Nation continues to discriminate against its mixed race citizens. The report concerns a rent and rates boycott in Johannesburg on 10 February 1997:

'During the Apartheid era we were not considered white enough and now, under a legitimate government, we are not black enough' said Martha, one of thousands of coloureds who took to the streets on Thursday to protest against the massive rent and rate bills in the former Coloureds-only suburb of Johannesburg.

Martha was echoing the growing feeling among people of mixed race that the discrimination they suffered under white regimes before South Africa's all-race elections in 1994 has given way to marginalisation at the hands of a mainly black administration.

The population of Coloureds in South Africa is officially acknowledged at around 12 per cent. This is prior to any speculation about the numbers that have passed into and been counted with 'pure' groups, including whites. Within the Coloured category are subgroups such as Malay, Chinese and Griqua Coloureds. It is a major classification in a highly differentiated population, and this may account for the tendency to toss scraps of privilege to the group while seeking to ensure its restricted political and economic power.

As guest editor of the Interracial Voice web magazine,[29] Jayne Ifekwunigwe shares some impressions of a visit to Cape Town. In particular, she writes that the dispersal of the inhabitants of District Six now warrants a museum for the remembrance of a Coloured community. District Six was a poor suburb at the foot of Capetown's Table Mountain which was inhabited mainly by Cape Coloureds. It was emptied of Coloureds as it was felt to be too close to the white areas of the city to enforce segregation.

The interests and the rights of the Coloured population are not secure. Although many fought apartheid, others voted with ultra-conservative nationalists. The ambivalence in which the group is held makes the future uncertain. Parallels with the Anglo-Indian experience are evident. The Cape Coloured population has been and remains socially detached and, in the racialised climate of South Africa, constructed in terms of ambivalence and ambiguity. Where race informs political strategy, ultimately, mixed race groups have rarely succeeded. Perhaps it is in the deconstruction of race and in campaigns for social equality for *all* that their true interests and strength may lie.

The Mixed Race Condition and Genocide

So far, we have observed constructions of mixed race experience through rape, economic exploitation, social exclusion and the devaluation of racialised people and relationships. These processes engage articulations of gender, class and race with the particular aspirations and convenience of powerful social groupings. In the Australian version of the mixed race condition all five of the characteristic features of mixed race which I suggested earlier are demonstrated. Created in circumstances of extreme inequality and induced economic dependency, mixed race has been variously constructed as integral to the Aboriginal populations, as a separate 'problem' for white Australian society to solve and as being assimilable within the white population.

A bold solution to the Australian version of the 'half caste problem'[30] – a recurring phenomenon in racially ordered societies – has been the attempt to assimilate those of mixed descent into the lower ranks of the white population. This would have furthered the decimation of the Aboriginal groups available to contest ancestral land rights. The strategy was implemented through the forced removal (frequently by police; often under duress) of children considered to be of mixed descent to homes in other parts of the country.

The complexities of logistical detail move through several political and ideological phases, which cannot detain us here. It is, however, necessary to comprehend the expediency of family separation in the racial ordering of Australian society. A report into the death in custody of an Aboriginal of mixed descent, Malcolm Charles Smith,[31] engages with the quality and outcomes of this particular episode in the history of the mixed race condition. The report finds:

That stage [extermination of Aboriginal people by murder, starvation and disease] gradually passed away as it came to be comfortably assumed that Aboriginals would die out anyway and some kindly disposed Europeans sought to 'soothe the dying pillow'. While in southeastern Australia full blood Aboriginals tended to fulfil this expectation, there was an embarrassing resilience and ultimately increase in the number of mixed blood Aboriginals. The policy of attempting to separate children from their parents and merge them into the white community was seen as a solution to the 'Aboriginal problem' and it was on this policy that the Aborigines Protection Board embarked. (p. 96)

Between Aboriginal protection agencies, the 'welfare', the courts and the police, the planned disruption of Aboriginal cultural ties was attempted during much of the first half of the twentieth century through the removal of children of mixed descent. Estimates from New South Wales[32] indicate that well over 5000 children from that area alone were taken to alternative homes and that these were often not disclosed. The Australian Human Rights and Equal Opportunity Commission report sums up its estimation as lying between one in three and one in ten in the period between 1910 and 1970.[33]

The social legacy[34] of this policy of disruption continues to affect families.[35] The policy underlined the manner in which women and children in situations grounded in extremes of subordination, easily become divested of basic human rights. Van Krieken[36] makes the point that, contrary to the self-image of European civilisation, particularly during the twentieth century, the realisation of the 'best interests of the child' is far from intrinsic or automatically sought. He writes:

> The latest in a series of profound challenges to this conception of European civilisation, and the role of children within it, was raised in the Australian context in May 1997, when a report issued by the Australian Human Rights and Equal Opportunity Commission (HREOC), *Bringing them Home*, stressed that the treatment of Indigenous Australian children falls clearly within the terms of the UN definition of genocide. The definition in the 1948 UN Convention on the Prevention and Punishment of the Crime of Genocide includes 'forcibly transferring the children of the group to another group' committed 'with intent to destroy, in whole or in part, a national, ethnical, racial or religious group'. (p. 298)

The sterilisation of Aboriginal women was also seriously discussed by the various protection boards. This is significant in the light of moves to control the fertility of black and poor women in other parts of the world.[37] An attempt to collapse race into a class ordering of society – with a recycled mixed race group forming the lower strata – appears to be one explanation of events and was particularly expedient where racial differentiation signified a contest over valuable land. It is a strategy distinct from the more usual attempts to enforce racial segregation through assimilation of mixed race into least privileged groups. The maintenance of inequality through induced dependency of Aboriginal people was, in any event, a highly expensive undertaking and this may have contributed to the plans for the detachment of a generation of part Aboriginal children from their relatives for whom ancestral rights and duties remained significant.[38]

The Purposeful Concept of Mixed Race

The versatility of the concept of mixed race is becoming evident. Genocide, economic exploitation, social exclusion and rape as social control may appear extreme for inclusion as features of the mixed race condition. However, the tides of nationalistic and ethnic hostility in parts of Europe since (and, of course, during) the Second World War suggest that such acts are never too far from home. Mixed race, through its ideological association with ambiguity and social detachment, is capable of meeting various social purposes. Race mixing may be a weapon of war – as in inter-ethnic or inter-racial rape – or it may be a means of eliminating an inconvenient group. It may be encouraged as a means of settling new territory or used as a 'buffer' between absolutely separate groups, or forbidden as a means of underlining social divisions. At root, it is always a highly exploitative construct and its dishonest association with ambiguity has unsettling consequences for those so racialised. Their construction as 'intermediate', 'neither one thing nor the other', 'mixed' or 'half castes' attempts to suspend their social legitimacy in ways that enable those defined as mixed or mixing to be redefined for alternative social purposes.

5   Behind the Facade:
Race Mixing

He: I don't want a one note Samba ... I think my life is enriched
by having black friends and white friends, and Chinese friends or
gay friends or bisexual friends, or transracially adopted friends,
mixed race, people with disabilities, people who are going through
mid-life crises, people who have abandoned their children ... my
life is enriched by those people. And part of the reason is, part of
the reason why they have enriched my life is that I cannot have
those experiences, except vicariously. You know, I can't *know*. I'm
thinking probably of the male menopause. I've no idea what it's
like to be a woman who's going through the menopause, where
she is not going to be a mother ever again. I could ... I could always
become a father. Charlie Chaplin did when he was 73 ... so I can't
experience it. Of course I could ... I could always become infertile
... but I'm saying I can't have the experience of it ... so the only
way I can have some sense of it, however faint, is by association
and communication ... in a way it's different and I want that
celebrated. So often it's just about toleration. I can say difference
is good.
Jill: Difference is good because ... ?
He: Because the opposite is a bland homogeneity.[1]

Enough, then, of broad résumés of mixed race history and ideology;
where there is ideology there are myriad experiences in the lives of
ordinary folk living out or contesting their designated social
positions. What were the day-to-day social realities of those Anglo
Indian people who were ridiculed for their appearance, accent or
manners? What was the quality of experience of the Aboriginal child
snatched from mother and family and placed in an unfamiliar home
or institution? What matters were important to the many families
and individuals defined in terms of race mixture down the years?
How did they get by and who were their allies? How did they explain
their worlds?

Earlier chapters have suggested something of the temperamental
and capricious background to a racial definition of 'mixed'. This and

the following chapter move to a closer examination of the subject. On one level, the details of experiences appear to vary. Much depends on location, national politics, individual wealth, media exposure, personalities and beliefs within the surrounding population, and a whole range of minute but significant features of the individual's day-to-day environment. These chapters contain material concerning some experiences, observations, complaints and analyses from people associated with mixed or mixing race in the present. These are matters nominated as important by those involved.

It would be almost disingenuous to enquire why the problematic nature of race mixing is continuously reconstructed and forms the focus of much attention to mixed race. It would be equally disingenuous to enquire why race, which ranks with the tooth fairy as an ideology explaining human difference, should persist. We have sufficient evidence to debate the question coherently.

As Tizzard and Phoenix,[2] Root[3] and others begin to show, the interests, priorities and perceptions of the group defined as mixed or mixing race may be significantly different from the agendas of research, politics and psychology. So what are the priorities and common features of experience within this group?

The relative absence of reiteration of familiar political posture may surprise the reader, since in the interviews, discussed below, people were reflecting on personal experience which had not always been organised into a political view. The material is broadly arranged into the twin faces of race mixing and race separating – motifs often present concurrently, within families and amongst individuals associated with race mixture. In this chapter, people viewed to be mixed race or to be in a mixed race relationship consider positive aspects of social difference and identify some of the issues they have faced. Chapter 6 deals with some frequently reported social sanctions and the strategies used to deflect or confront these sanctions.

Neither chapter attempts to reduce mixed race experience to a single 'cause', nor is the complexity of individual circumstances misunderstood or ignored. However, the slide into individualism, which denies commonality and pattern in social life is also to be resisted. There are patterns in mixed race experience, and these sometimes span time and place. The discernible patterns here are based on different people telling of similar experiences, some of which will be familiar to many within the group.

Throughout the research I was aware of a tension between the need to organise material in some way, whilst enabling individual voices to be heard. The organisational themes, therefore, are loosely woven in order that differences of opinion and experience may be made apparent.

Background to the Research Population

The information, collected in different parts of England during 1996, comes from two main sources. These are 35 interviews with people in various mixed race situations plus several which formed a pilot study, and two workshops which formed part of annual day conferences for women performing voluntary work in their communities.[4]

Those who agreed to be interviewed were recommended by others, recommended themselves as being willing and interested, wrote to express interest in response to an article published in *Adoption UK*,[5] or were encountered in the course of life's conversations. The workshops, billed as 'issues for mixed race families', were among a selection (covering topics such as 'after school care', 'domestic violence' and 'dealing with bullying in schools') available to conference participants.

Although this information was collected in England, those in the study were often either born outside the country, had parents born elsewhere or retained links with families in different parts of the world. Some features of the environment described may be unfamiliar to readers in countries other than the United Kingdom. It is a fair expectation, however, that the substance of the experiences will have a far broader resonance.

Despite the fact that it is becoming customary to introduce participants in qualitative research as renamed friends, I beg to differ on this matter. Very brief contextual details of the people involved are offered as we go along. The participants range from teenagers to those in their 70s and there are roughly equal numbers of men and women. There are people who have lived and worked outside Britain, and those who have never travelled far from their homes. Some are in well-paid work, others unemployed, in poorly paid jobs or living on pensions. The terminology of racialised relationships is not necessarily that used by people themselves, but everyone understood the definition 'mixed race' and their own association with it. The request for information was simply that people talked, in their own terms, about what the idea of mixed race has meant in their lives. For the most part interviews lasted between one and three hours and were in people's own homes.

Access and Understanding

The person quoted at the beginning of the chapter is a man in his early 50s of mixed race[6] who was speaking, during an interview, about the value he attaches to human difference in his life. Clearly this is not a person who stops at the edge of the water afraid to get his toes wet. His interests, outlined here, are in understanding human difference as a means of self-enrichment. These are personal choices which not everyone is sufficiently confident to make. And yet, it is clear from many other people I spoke with, that in comprehending personal encounters with social difference it is possible to apply insights to other human situations.

One of the most commonly expressed benefits (and often joys) of being part of relationships that encompass cultural, ethnic and other differences was the opportunity to gain access to more than one world-view. (Indeed, to appreciate that more than one world-view is possible.) This could be effected through partnership, close friendship, through parent–child relationships, extended families, or through the desire – sometimes later in life – to explore the background of an absent close relative. At times, this included access to families in different parts of the world, and to very different ways of life. Difference here is not based on people's acceptance of race ideology but on real differences in perception, language, philosophy, religion and similar attributes. That such differences sometimes coincide with racialised features is unfortunate and confuses the situation.

Enhanced access also, for some people, represented a way out of adversity; a means of seeking shelter in a less hostile social group. A man with a Scottish father and Nigerian mother, in his 60s, had spent his early life in Nigeria. He felt, as a child, discontent and thought that he was receiving poorer schooling than his siblings. It transpired that the people whom he thought were his parents were members of his mother's close family. As he recalled: 'I always felt I was different. I don't know why. I just knew there was a difference.' On learning his mother and father's identities, and finding his situation untenable, he decided to attempt to trace his father and to try his luck in Britain. At 14, after several unsuccessful attempts, he stowed away on a ship bound for Liverpool and has now been resident in Britain for some 50 years. In this case, it was the information about an absent parent, combined with discontent about his situation, which gave grounds for the decision to migrate and provided access to an alternative future.

For many people, enhanced understanding was a gradual outcome of making sense of their own experiences of a mixed race social definition. The substance of the reported experience was on occasion painful, but even when very negative it was sometimes counted a gain in understanding. One mixed race woman, whose white mother was expecting her to be adopted within the family, was put into foster care at birth, when it became clear that she was 'coloured', because the family withdrew support. She had been 'transracially' fostered and by her 30s had become a foster and adoptive mother herself. Her partner comes from a very similar background.

Like many of the people in the study, she claimed an ability to 'suss things out' on the basis of her own experience. Applying this ability to her foster work with children considered to be of mixed race, she said: 'Because I'm more flexible. And I can change ... I can suss out what they [the foster children] have come from, how it must ... so I can actually tailor myself to those children.' This kind of empathy claim was common. Those working in schools empathised with mixed race children, those in social services could, similarly, engage with discourses around the 'needs' (and pathologisation) of mixed race families. Where there was access to and acceptance from two cultural groups, often people spoke of the learning of different behaviours acceptable within each group and the ability to pass amongst each group.

Difference as Liberation

There was a profound awareness, raised by almost everyone I spoke to, about the employment of racialised social categories. The difficulty of placing mixed race within this tendency towards bipolar racial or rigidly defended ethnic systems was seldom overlooked, and could be the cause of humour or anxiety. Something of a sense of liberation sometimes appeared to come from being difficult to pigeonhole, and for some people, their differing family influences had led to rich life experiences and opportunities.

One such person, the child of a white London-born woman and a black American man (now in her 30s), who spent her early years in the United States and moved to England as a young adult, is particularly interesting here. She appears to have learned to trip lightly through what might have been experienced as difficult situations, and to exploit difference as an interesting facet of her life:

> She: I have been told I was mulatto since the day I was born. It stems from the Spanish word that means mule ... I know since I've brought it up in England with one or two people, they don't like the term ... Mulatto came about during slave days, you know, octoroon ...
> Jill: quadroon ...
> She: You got it. I guess my father just picked it up ... I've met my Big Momma who still lives in the South. My father traced his family back in time. My great, great, I don't know how many greats ... anyway, he came over from Madagascar as an indentured servant. And he married someone, and there was some Native American mixed in there ... I've just been fortunate. Although my mother was an alcoholic, we've lived in different countries and experienced different cultures ... different languages ... I'm very broadminded, very open-minded, and I love people. All nationalities. I've just been lucky I think.

This is not necessarily a typical account of dodging racialised categories, but it does illustrate rather well the liberating potential of difference. The speaker neither denies, nor is completely defined by, questions of race (nor for that matter by other circumstances such as parental divorce and alcoholism and constant uprooting during childhood). She enjoys difference, and other's perceptions of difference, in the present.

For others, the liberating potential of being perceived as 'different' lay in claiming release from cultural obligations. This was sometimes expressed as an awareness of the choice of adopting or rejecting a particular culturally derived behaviour or way of thinking. For some, insights into the illusory nature of race and the hostility of racially defined groups was considered valuable knowledge. Others questioned aspects of the cultural environments in which they were brought up and, at times the whole notion of culture itself. While there did not appear to be any single reason for entering into what are commonly perceived as 'mixed race' relationships, all those I spoke to felt they had been required to address particular aspects of their choices. For those for whom this choice was already made – those *born* into a mixed race social definition – the question of accounting for their history or genealogy was felt in a different way but was, nonetheless, present.

Bridging

There was also a high level of consensus about what might be termed 'bridging' activity, that is, the perceived task of making links between two or more cultural backgrounds of relevance to individuals or partnerships. One aspect of bridging refers to the task of negotiating the idea of a 'dual heritage' – of being seen as a combination of two different and racially defined 'things'. This might be as a person with parents from differing cultural traditions, or in close relationships where these differences are perceived as occurring. It was an area in which people I spoke to sometimes allowed themselves to take the moral high ground in describing the value of their 'inter-cultural skills'.

The point has been made earlier but is worth making again. What seems to be crucial is the drawing of a distinction between the ideological construction of racial or ethnic divisions and the day-to-day practices and interpretations of the world. The latter often contain very real differences which may be enjoyed or which may prove difficult to negotiate in daily life. A further point needs to be made here about the ideological construction of difference as opposed to 'real' differences. From recent world history, for instance the undertaking of the former Yugoslavia to ethnically 'cleanse' itself and the racial perceptions of Nazi Germany and apartheid South Africa, it is clear that 'bridging' is not generally sought out as a valuable talent. Indeed, those attempting it under these extreme circumstances have often been murdered. This is not to discourage, but to suggest the scope of the challenge, and the stakes.

Stonequist[7] makes a point about the lives of the 'mixed bloods' being a 'crucible of cultural fusion'. This, he suggests, fits those who have undergone a 'crisis experience' in coming to terms with their duality to be diplomats, ambassadors, or teachers working between groups (p. 221). There are difficulties inherent in this view. The first concerns the nature of difference. Groups identified on the basis of perceived (mono)racial colour or cultural criteria cannot be assumed to have a deep interest in mutual understanding and cooperation. They employ their own diplomats and negotiators, not primarily to remove barriers but to strengthen their own positions. Second, there is no reason to assume that those identified as being an amalgam of two racially defined groups should automatically wish to pander to the ideological contortions of groups who believe themselves to be unmixed.

Ijima Hall[8] makes a similar point to Stonequist:

> Most of the mixed people I know are able to interact with many ethnic groups. They, like me, despise the fighting among different ethnic groups in America. They are able to act as bridges among groups, fostering communication and co-operation. The future role of mixed people may be that of negotiators. Since they belong to many groups, they will be seen as insiders, with vested interests in making plans work for all sides. (p. 329)

Bridging is a concept that requires some careful attention. On the one hand, it is mixed race caught at its most vulnerable: *in between, neither one thing nor the other, running between two camps – across bridges*. On the other hand, it commits mixed race to interpreting between two 'sides'. In turn, this assumes that there are different 'sides' which cannot interpret for themselves. The ideology of mixed race can be made to exploit its iconoclasm in less restrained and respectable ways. Demolishing racially constructed walls, challenging racialised social divisions, spitting in the eye of race; these also seem constructive tasks.

A serious reflection on bridging was offered in the pilot study by a man in his late 50s. He was born to a white woman who was already married to a white man – his own father was from the Caribbean. He grew up never having met his birth parents because he was placed in a children's home as a baby (as frequently happened then, to save the marriage). He spoke about stages of self-realisation during his life, including a point at which he had needed to explore his father's background and to consider the implications of being mixed race. Speaking of these stages in his life as a journey he said:

> It's a precarious journey, a bridging journey ... there is the possibility of bringing people together. It happens in the self, and outside. You will be misunderstood, you will be trampled on, BUT, there is always the possibility of bringing people together. It's very disturbing.

No Positive Images

There was much reporting of a paucity of positive depictions of mixed race in books and illustrations at school, on television and in areas such as advertising, children's toys and games. Remembering the problem from her own childhood, one woman I interviewed (the person who was put into care from birth and is now a foster and adoptive parent) had photographs of her family displayed all around the living room at eye level. She drew my attention to this:

> She: If anybody asks me, I'm mixed parentage, and I'm very proud of that and that's like the way it is with my children up there [indicates photographs]. There's us standing there with all these children. When people come in they can see that. The first thing that greets them is that picture up there ...
> Jill: Yes that's what I noticed first.
> She: And that's what we've done it for. For them to be very positive who they are, because you certainly couldn't go to town and buy a picture of a mixed race child ... You can't get them ... and so what I did, I took all the pictures out of the albums, I took them out and put them on the wall ... I extended it and extended it, and that's the way I want it, and that's how people ... they don't have to ask me, they can just look at that wall and it tells them right away. And you can't buy a book, you can't buy a picture or anything to promote mixed parentage. It's just not put down as the word in a book.

This seems to be a generally understood problem. For some of the people I interviewed the solution lay in making attempts to compensate for missing images. Others, however, drew inference from the omissions, suggesting that information about mixed race was deliberately suppressed because it threatens the political plans of powerful ethnic interests (of all shades). Some pointed to the idea that where mixed race *is* used in imagery (and here we are talking of race-as-colour), it is used instrumentally. Examples cited included a light-skinned in preference to a darker-skinned person in advertising images and 'cute' mixed race children as the 'token black people' in multicultural story books.

Parents Must Prepare

Parents I spoke to tended to accept responsibility for offering support to their children, but had divergent views on what support might be best offered. Two views appeared to prevail. The first, that children should be taught that colour, and other racialised differences, should not act as barriers between people. The second, that children should be taught to regard each of the parental cultures, and differences amongst friends and neighbours, as valuable and viable. There tended to be little stress on the features of 'white' culture, however, families with links outside Britain appeared to be more conscious of specific cultural details to be kept (or set aside).

One (white English) woman compared her own and her husband's background (English of Jamaican-born migrant grandparents). She told me that they were each from 'working-class families' brought up in similar parts of town and with friends in similar black/white partnerships. She felt that 'well-to-do white people are the ones that can cause problems' and that similarities in class background gave her family its strength. Of her partner's background she said:

> Well he was born here. I would love to learn about Jamaica – that's where his grandparents are from. I do wish to go and see everything ... what it's like to live out there. That side of where he comes from. But his father was also born here. So he's as English as I am.

For their daughter:

> My hopes are that she will achieve anything she wishes to achieve. My main fears have nothing to do with colour or race. They are to do with the world itself. What it's going to be like for her.

Another white mother had a more explicit sense of cultural difference:

> They [the children] should have the best of both worlds and the support of both parents. They should be equally able to deal with both sides and I think that's for the parents to socialise and make sure.

Her partner (born in West Africa) had a similar view:

> He: For the children it's good. It's a different quality. They will have the full spectrum. We are taking them back home in July.

She: It's for the parents to socialise them. We tell them certain things we want them to know.

He: In anything you do you can look at things and decide what's best.

She: You can say, 'That is negative; ignore it.'

For this family, there is a geographical and cultural distance to cover. They wish to prepare their children to live in present-day Britain but also to know and be comfortable with people in their father's family in Africa. A major difference here is that the partner of the first woman is of the second generation of a family of migrants to Britain, whereas the second father was born in, and maintains an active contact with, a 'home' outside Britain. While the first mother stresses similarities of class and rights of belonging, the second concentrates on establishing an equality of difference. Much depends on the individual's conceptualisation of family and social situation and how they understand and deal with difference. One of the visible parental strategies is the assumption that each parent represents to the children a cultural blueprint, supplemented with travel and positive information.

Representing two cultures to children was sometimes portrayed to me as ideally requiring two parents as well as access to, or association with, two 'communities' or 'both sides'. For single parents, those with hostile families and for some adoptive families, this view of 'heritage' becomes more problematic, and especially so where grandparents or the local community are unable to offer support.

The mixed race child may not, it is sometimes asserted, know her 'culture'. 'Culture', in this line of thinking, is often associated with the black or minority parent. There is also a difference to be acknowledged between knowing something, and living it from day to day. And anyway, is mixed race entirely dependent on its constituent cultures?

Some parents considered ease of movement of people between their respective cultural groups to be a priority. Others regretted the lack of preparation that might have equipped them for careers as mixed race children and adults. What seemed to be generally valued (or missed) were opportunities to explore the implications of mixed race, both for partners and mixed race people. This was acutely so for those mixed race adults who lacked information about their birth families from which to build their self-explanations.

Individuals and families defined as 'mixed' have been managing for generations in racially ordered societies. Each with a tale to tell of how they responded, got by, hid where necessary, formed their views, lived their lives and raised their children. These are histories in need of collection because they concern the contingencies of life from which we in the present might learn. Of particular interest here are the multi-generational histories of mixed race people marrying other mixed race people as has happened, for instance, in areas around British ports down the years.

Knowledge is Power

A common factor among people whose childhood was characterised by a sense of confusion was the lack of information available or opportunity to discuss their experiences of racialisation. Two people, adopted or fostered as children, were offered no explanation of their origins as children; the man who was given to understand that his near relatives were his parents, 'knew something was wrong'. Whatever the 'cover story' or strategy adopted within the mixed race family and by the mixed race person, sufficient and accurate information appears to be prerequisite.

In the case of the two transracially adopted people (both mixed race and in their early 30s), one is a man who was adopted as a baby by a 'religious' couple who lived in a very isolated country area. They sought to protect their children by physically distancing them from activities such as watching television, dancing and music and made religion the centre of family life. The family met exclusively with other members of their religious group. Race was never discussed and the man said that he was 'completely unprepared' for the taunting and racial abuse when he went to school: 'I just did not know what they were on about.' He knew nothing of his birth mother nor of the reasons for his adoption. A combination of this and the corporal punishment administered by his adoptive father brought forth an aggressive reaction during his teens. He has since traced his birth parents and has met with individuals from similar backgrounds to share experience and support. The opportunity to explore, talk through, make sense of and, ultimately, to be in control of his life experience has taken a circuitous route, mainly because of the lack of parental openness and information.

In a comparable way, the woman quoted above as being able to 'suss things out' had information withheld about her original parents. It was not her foster family who were responsible for this, but the social workers dealing with her case. She too had gaps in her information which she found intolerable as a young person:

> She: There was a lot of not knowing ... even though I told you at the beginning that I was taken into care ... at that time I didn't know.
> Jill: You didn't know you were in care?
> She: I didn't know until I was 14 *why* ... I knew I was fostered. But I didn't know anything about why or who was my mother. I was brought up where there were no black people at all. There was ... at school time a bus used to come from where the black people lived and they were shipped into school ...
> Jill: Like a sort of integration attempt?
> She: Yes, yes. And then I actually had black friends and Asian[9] friends, but I still knew there was a lot of difference.

Of her long-term foster parents she said:

> She: They were very open about talking but they felt they couldn't answer a lot of the questions. They just were not told. Still they never got any help off the department. My social worker, who was black, he never covered the issues either ... And my dad used to talk to me a lot about it and tried to make me very positive about being black. And we've always talked about it and we still talk about it to this day. It's always an issue.
> Jill: You're still in touch with them?
> She: Oh yes I'm closer than their own children. So yes. We've a very good rapport. I talk to my sisters. They did have an understanding, we all did. And they suffered a lot of racial abuse as well. My sisters did at the school because they'd got, you know, a black sister.

This woman still does not have a complete picture of her birth parents. She finds the lack of information tiresome and debilitating and counters it by building up a network of friends in similar positions. In this case, it was not unwillingness on the part of foster parents to divulge and discuss life details, but their lack of information about her biological father. It was also, for both these people, not a matter of 'culture' but of 'knowing'. The provision of opportunities for children to question and to be given information from which satisfying explanatory frameworks can be constructed is of fundamental importance.

A white English woman, whose ex-partner has an African father, considered the need to provide information for her son as a strategy against racial abuse. She was not at all clear about how to go about this and felt herself to be hindered in this by the limitations of the child's father's knowledge. She said of her ex-partner:

> She: No one ever really taught him about his race or owt[10] like that. He wanted to know. He wanted it to be different for his son ... but seeing as he's never done nowt about it ...
> Jill: You mean he wanted to know about his background?
> She: He just wanted to find out some stuff. You know, about his language and that ... his dad's country and stuff like that. His dad's died now. And [partner] doesn't know nowt to tell him [their son]. I mean I think it's good to teach your kids that anyway. They shouldn't be ashamed of that part of them should they? It's either that or pretend that they're white.

This was presented as a rather perplexing problem, the notion of partly belonging to another 'race' with language and secrets without having access to any member of the group from whom to learn the group secrets. Summing up the problem, the root appeared to be fear of an inability of her child to place himself and to protect himself from racial abuse:

> He won't know what he is. He won't know if he's Asian or black or what. It's hard because if he plays around here he gets 'black bastard' ... he's going to get all that when he goes to school ... so that's hard cos it's not his fault is it?

Information here is seen as a form of protection against racial bullying that is anticipated as inevitable. In this last example from the same conversation anxiety that the child might not even be dark enough to be considered mixed race became evident. Coupled with the lack of background information the mother seemed to feel that this could be problematic:

> She: They're light [the children] but they're not, because standing next to somebody else's kids that's white, nobody would say they're white because they're not.

Jill: Is that a problem?
She: It is really because he gets confused. He can't understand [the conversation is now relating just to her two-year-old son]. He tells anyone that he's black like his dad ... but he thinks he's white sometimes. Got other friends that's got mixed race kids but they're all a lot darker than him. He sees himself as being like us. Which is hard.
Jill: He *is* like you.
She: He thinks he's white.

Part of the problem here is that no recognised social category exists that the parent can understand on behalf of her child. The same thing is apparent in the child's father's background. There is considerable work to do in claiming a social space for mixed race in which people may explore, contest and define their realities. In many ways, this is not an area that parents can define, although they can help, as every generation of mixed race must resolve the issues for themselves.

The Wrong Parents

Another issue, commonly cited as an aspect of mixed race experience, concerns the suspicion that members of mixed race families do not belong together. This is identified and underlined in myriad ways. In this section extracts from interviews illustrate the point. The fostered, mixed race woman introduced above told of her white foster mum's experiences:

My foster mum ... she's my mum now ... they had lots of abuse. They fostered a number of black children because there were so many of us black children. Especially mixed parentage children. They've been told to get off a bus because they've got a black child with them. What they were called on the streets is nobody's business. So they've had a lot of racial abuse. Things were written on the doors and that. So they suffered a lot and they knew what was going on. And my mum and dad used to try and stamp it out, you know?

A woman, now in her 40s, with Cypriot and white English parents was first pregnant at 16 and the baby's father was Caribbean:

I got a bit frightened. I don't know what the reason was, but I was only 17, you don't ask questions do you? And you know, I did feel, that I had done something wrong. Not only being pregnant at 17, pregnant at 16, having her at 17, but also having a black child. I mean I was continually made to feel as though I had done something evil.

A woman in her 30s with a white English mum and Jamaican dad (who returned to the Caribbean when the short marriage failed):

There were issues around, like, my mum was bad, you know, like because she had coloured children. And I had this thing about people, you know because people used to think my mum was bad, I got into a thing about telling people I was adopted ... and that was about stopping my mum being hurt. Cos people used to say only prostitutes and bad women go with black men. And have black kids.

... I was called 'jungle jump' and all sorts of stuff like that, like friends that you went to school with said all sorts ... like: 'My dad says only prostitutes and bad women go with black men. Decent women don't.' That kind of thing. Very hurtful. And that was my way of coping with it.

The woman with a white English mother and black American father who went to school in the United States:

She: One of my memories I have is of dreading my mother coming to school. It was one of those days, you have them where your parents have a conference with the teachers ...
Jill: Open evening?
She: Right, but this was the whole day. Open day. And she came to my class and she brought my brother with her. And I thought, 'Oh no, what are they going to say?' I was just so worried.
Jill: Why were you so worried?
She: Because she's WHITE [loud]. We lived in a white area. And I never, never knew what to tell them ... why my mother was white.

A Caribbean woman, aged 70, speaking with her darker-skinned daughter about their experiences:

Mother: They said, 'She's white.' I said, 'I'm from the West Indies. I'm black because you see everything as black or white ... so I'm black.' 'Oh' they say, 'you look white, you're white'. I said, 'that may be the way I look, but look at my children. We were brought up in the West Indies and I pass it onto them. I don't think there's a difference in us.'

Daughter: ... And there were little things like walking up the road with Mum. And when they'd look at us ... I mean obviously I'm a lot darker than Mum. Even though there's a facial resemblance, what people first notice I think is skin colour. They think she must have been with a black man. Look at her children. And they would treat her differently because of that.

A mixed race woman speaking about a good friend who is white and has a mixed race child:

I've got a friend who lives over the road, white woman ... and the other week I was in the hospital. Her daughter had an asthma attack and I'd gone over. Now her mum was sitting at one side of the bed and I was sitting at the other. The doctor came up to me and said, 'We're going to discharge her today, Mum.' And I looked at him, and I said, 'You've jumped to the conclusion. I'm not her mum. That's her mum over there. A ginger-headed woman.' And when we go out all together, everybody thinks I'm her mother. We laugh about it but underneath it must hurt.

A woman of Jewish parents whose son's father is African:

I think white women with mixed race children are often assumed to have adopted their kids. When my son was a baby people used to talk to me and be all friendly and to admire the baby in his pram. If they said anything about being a foster parent I just used to say, 'No, he's mine.' You could see their faces change as the full horror of me having slept with a black man slowly dawned. Then they'd get embarrassed and hurry off. It just is not supposed to happen.

A Ghanaian woman whose partner is a white English man:

And these ones who say, 'Hey sister, why you with that one?' Well sometimes women say things too, but I think, 'And do you speak like this to your sister?' ... but I pass by.

I have chosen to illustrate this issue in this manner as it needs little interpretation. The question of being made to feel that one's parents, children or partner are 'inappropriate' appears to be at the very root of the way in which the mixed race condition is socially constructed. These notions are introduced and reinforced through abuse from strangers, through the reasoned arguments of parents, even through the exclusion from positive portrayal noted above. Discussion of these appears in the next chapter. The issue here is that, on the basis of appearance, assumptions and judgements are being made which point to perceptions about the inappropriate mixing of difference. The extent to which blame is successfully inscribed upon individuals or relationships depends on the level of support and self-confidence achieved.

Being challenged, in some cases routinely, over primary relationships has the effect of questioning and reducing social legitimacy. That some people assumed blame or responsibility for such difficulty shows us something of the power of social definition on lived experience. For mixed race children there are not only the issues around access to cultural group to consider, but the racialised day-to-day consequences of difference.

Set Up to Fail

The notion that mixed race is, in some way, a temporary or aberrant state was frequently reported as emanating from close family and kin in the context of advice-giving. Thus, there are several examples of which two will serve to convey the point. The first is from a Nigerian man and his white wife (who has a minor disability), both in their late 20s, who now live in Yorkshire with their children:

He: My relatives are not living around. The reaction was, as expected very, very, negative. I have the impression from my brother in America and my sister that the relationship won't last ... initially friends were not going to cooperate.
Jill: Why do you think that was?
He: If you look at my wife, because of her condition, she is different. Because of this they think ... they don't realise I have made the right decision. They think it will die quickly. But it will soon be the seventh year we have known each other.
She: We've had comments about my disability.
He: People commented that because of this she cannot have children.

The second example comes from a man of Pakistani parents who was born in Britain and spoke about opposition from friends to his partnership with a white woman in this way:

> One or two of them have said, 'Why don't you leave her? She's no good for you. She'll leave you in years to come.' Like, going back five or six years, you know what I mean, they said, 'Well why don't you leave her? In a few years time she'll probably go off with some other bloke or summat.[11] And then you're going to be left on your own. So why don't you just leave her now and just ... do you know what I mean? Get your life sorted out.' I've had people come up to me in the street that are from the same village back home or cousins or friends of my father, and they've said to me, 'Leave her. Take the kids, forget her, just take the kids and go.'

The other side of these expectations of failure was the difficulty some people expressed in ending relationships, partly as a result of the lack of support they initially received. A white woman who took part in a workshop discussion made this point about her former marriage: 'You can get so isolated ... we clung onto what became an abusive relationship because there was simply not the support for getting out of it. We were together long after the relationship should have been discarded.'

The expectation of failure was often expressed as an extra pressure on family life and this was sometimes the 'last straw' when compounded with other difficulties such as unemployment or low income. The elderly Nigerian man, for example, told me about his first marriage which had been undermined by his need to travel away from home for work. While away, his wife, who was estranged from her family because of the marriage, was unable to cope alone with their children, who were taken into care. On returning home to find both wife and children gone it took several years to trace the children and to convince the social services to release them from care. In this process he entered, rather hastily, into another marriage which was also short-lived.

Terminology

The question of terminology was an issue raised by almost everyone in the study and was frequently closely tied to attempts to locate a social space for people and relationships considered to be 'mixed'. One or two people retained the term 'half-caste' as a descriptive term, but in general it was a term that caused distaste. The difficulty in naming and in identifying social location ties readily with other categories of experience such as the lack of positive imagery and inclusion. Whilst many Western countries *may* be considered to be pluralist societies (and how often do equal opportunities and other statements of fairness begin 'We live in a multicultural, multilingual, multi-ethnic, multi-faith society ... '?), the convenience of ethnic grouping is considerably threatened by mixture and disruption of these homogenised units. While a country may be multi-ethnic at the level of describing 'communities' by ethnic labels, there is a lack of adequate terminology in place for *inter*-ethnic individuals and relationships. There is limited scope to *self*-define.

Through language we classify and discuss the world. Without a terminology, we deny a class of experience because it cannot be named or can only be understood within existing classificatory groups. (Jayne Ifekwunigwe terms this phenomenon 'bi-racialisation'.)[12] One man – late 40s, mixed race – spoke about his childhood realisation that being 'ethnically visible' (his term) was an issue for him:

> I realised, aahh, there is an issue about it, I was then 11, and I thought of myself then, and I would say for the next 15 years more as non-white, and 'half-caste' is the term. Well, there were two things, one was 'half-caste', which didn't actually have any negative stuff, except by implication and inclination. Even as a child, 'half-caste' clearly wasn't full-caste, or fully fledged ... and then the non-white.

He went on to talk about the significance of this negative ascription. In presenting race awareness training to white professional groups he has made use of the device 'non-black' to illustrate the feeling of negation such exclusive terminology carries.

The imprecision with which the racialisation of mixture is handled evidently brings personal dilemmas in which terminology is intimately bound up with rights to a social space. Speaking of her developing awareness of race, a mixed race woman explained:

> I don't think anybody had to tell me. I was the only black person around. I wouldn't have used the word 'black' in those days, it was the word 'coloured' in those days. I don't know, I think it was

being mixed and realising I was different ... And then the issue of when I was growing up of people not recognising a mixed parentage child. It was always a black child. And I used to say, 'No I'm black *and* white.' A lot of people couldn't take that. You're black. And I used to say, 'I've got two nationalities.' My mother was Welsh.

Naming exercised almost everyone, even where attempts not to deal in racial labels were made. The struggle, like that above, was always over attempts to self-classify. Looking at alternatives to bipolar racial categories, one man entertained the idea of developing a mixed race discourse which deliberately set out to blur either/or distinctions and gave examples of what he called 'integrationist language and ideas'. His idea was to emphasise the provisional and complex nature of events with phrases such as 'mixed feelings', 'everything really' and 'both'. In fact, there are many examples throughout the interviews of the positive use of the word 'mixed'. Many people spoke of areas or gatherings as 'well mixed' connoting a sense of social ease.

Perhaps the most contentious point surrounding racial terminology was its implied exclusion or splitting. This is compounded by those who challenged the importance of adopting a racialised identity of any description. As a woman in her 20s, of Indian parents and married to a white partner said:

Even that word 'mixed race' .. it's horrible isn't it? It sounds as though we're from different species ... there's only supposed to be one race ... humans ... and we're all supposed to be part of it ... mixed race sounds as if we really don't fit anywhere ... like we're doing something really terrible ... as if we shouldn't be here ... I don't use it and I don't want [daughter] to think she's got to use it either ... it's better than 'half-caste' ... but why do you have to call yourself by how people see your parents ... why do ... all the richness that we've got ... that we are passing on ... all the good things ... mixed race makes you think it's unnatural to live like that.

Rather than suggesting that the mixed race person or black person in a mixed race relationship 'wants to be white' (which appears to be a regular form of challenge or insult), this indicates an unwillingness to abide by ascribed racial categories. This unwillingness is particularly evident where inhabitants of those ascribed categories cannot be relied upon to offer acceptance and recognition. In the case of the woman above, her own family have completely cut her out of their lives and her husband's family maintain an uneasy contact. They make their lives amongst like-minded friends.

Another possibility considered was the hyphenated system of naming parental ethnic groups: 'English-Jamaican'; 'Korean-American'; 'Sudanese-Scottish'. These may serve a purpose in one generation of a relatively uncomplicated family genealogy but may increase in complexity with subsequent generations. How many grandparent generations back does one trace these titles of origin? At what point does 'mixed' melt away into the general slush of 'unmixed' normality?

Not Black/White Enough

The issue of being insufficiently black/white (here, being 'black/white' relates to having the appearance of mixed race) highlights the biological underpinnings of the social and political (and under these, economic) constructions of the mixed race condition. It seems reasonable to assume that there are many people of mixed origins who are invisible within racially identified social groups. An example of this was apparent on the release of the Disney film *Pocahontas*, which fictionalises (beyond recognition) the story of the marriage between a native American woman and an English man. Many white English people of some renown, including Viscountess Mountbatten, claimed, via the news media, to be descendants of this couple, even whilst maintaining successful racial identities as high-caste white people.

The same must be true of the many descendants of famous and less famous 'mixed' relationships which have occurred through the centuries. Apart from the 'stars' of history, the hundreds of thousands of anonymous migrants who have settled and merged with already well mixed indigenous populations of Britain, America and other Western states make up what eugenicists have referred to as national 'stock'. It seems we are more of a stew than a stock. This begs the question of how many generations of ancestry need to be traced in order to arrive at a 'correct' ethnic or racial identification.

The not-black/white-enough category of experience gives indication that appearance is taken as a reliable indicator of politico-racial affiliation – or at least ascription. It offers grounds for inclusion or exclusion. One white woman, speaking of her youngest daughter's experiences of friendship at school, considers options to be limited on the basis of colour:

> It's strange at [youngest daughter's] school. She's not accepted by black girls and most of her friends are white, bar one who is completely ostracised by the black girls in school because this girl, to look at her, you would definitely say she was white. She looks white. She looks as though she might be slightly Malaysian, but to look at her, she looks white, and they absolutely refuse to believe that her father is black.

Another dilemma for the mixed race community: who can be admitted and who is to be ostracised on the grounds that they do not 'look' mixed race? Or worse – that they do not 'think' and 'act' mixed race.

In the context of a discussion about anti-racist initiatives in schools, the same woman said of her older children's experiences of school:

> My children's experiences, in spite of that input, have still been very negative. Their experiences of being mixed race have been bad in relation to being at school and they've ... you know ... however they've *wanted* to define themselves, other people haven't allowed them to.

During a discussion of her work as a foster parent, a mixed race woman suggested:

> She: Listening to my friends who are black, who are social workers or work in colleges ... some have got white wives. This means that the attitude of ... what some of their colleagues are saying to them, black colleagues and white colleagues ... that they're mixed up, and, you know, you can't bring up your children positively ... there's a lot of hate-ness ... the issues have changed since I was a child. And I think the thing is that people will always come up to you to see if you're white or black.
> Jill: You mean to sort of test you?
> She: It's very much a testing ground to see what you are.

These examples are not indications of anxiety about cultural unfamiliarity but about a particular political rhetoric based around notions of 'unmixed' biological belonging and 'inherited' cultural blueprints.

The not-black/white-enough theme was of practical significance among those in the study and seems to rest upon essentialist notions of possessing an 'appropriate racial identity'.

Two white women with mixed race children felt themselves to be at a particular disadvantage in the area of applying to adopt or foster. An excerpt from a letter, written to me by one of the women (Jewish parents, West African ex-partner) prior to our meeting, serves to illustrate this. Having lived in West Africa with her African partner, she returned to England with their son after the relationship ended. She wanted to adopt a child of mixed parentage who was younger than her son (then six) but was unsuccessful within the local area. She wrote:

> I then tried to look elsewhere after waiting six months. BAAF[13] would not let me apply for children of mixed parentage in *Be my Parent*[14] nor be on the BAAF exchange for such children, though I could apply for white children. I argued with them but they were adamant that families such as mine were not suitable for black children. Barnardos[15] were unable to help as they say they have to follow BAAF's line. [Local authority] would not look elsewhere for me. I wrote to every authority in the country but with little success. I enquired about every child in the PPIAS[16] newsletter and was considered for few, not even considered for most. It was because I was white, or a single parent or too poor, I lived too far away or the child was too close in age to [son].

It is very significant that this woman and her son *do* constitute a mixed race family. Further, they replicate the backgrounds of many of the children in care for whom they are not considered a suitable match. It is also worth noting that this woman considers her economic position to be a factor in her lack of success. Although she is unemployed and living on state benefits, she is also planning to study for a master's degree which might well enhance her future earning potential. Even being assessed as poor has not prevented her from undertaking trips to West Africa to visit friends and in order for her son to maintain contact with his father.

During a discussion of child placement policies in her social work team, another white woman, a social worker with three mixed race children, said:

It's interesting because it came up for me personally rather than professionally when some time ago I applied to foster. Because I don't live with the children's father, I was considered a white family. But, you know, how are white children going to fit in with my family? How are they going to identify? Part of the argument is that children can feel they belong, so that when you're out you're perceived as being part of this family unit. How can a white child placed with me feel that they belong? But my argument at the time was if … what they were saying to me was, 'Oh yes, we'd love to have you as a foster parent but we can only place white children with you.' In my paranoia, I thought, well if you place white children with me and we're all out together, it's *my* children that are going to be perceived by other people as not being my family.

It is noteworthy that this person considers *her* views to be 'paranoid'. Being diagnosed as an inappropriate family for a mixed race child, when the family already contains three such children, gives some genuine cause for confusion. That she assumes blame for thinking in this way, particularly as the implication is that she is not a suitable parent for her own children, shows something of the convoluted nature of the social construction of mixed race. This division between the children that people are able to produce for themselves and those they must rely on the state to issue them with is a striking feature of the whole transracial discourse.

Telling me about their experiences of being assessed as adoptive parents, two people (the wife was born in England to parents who had migrated from the Caribbean, the husband was a white English man) described the following experience:

He: By May she [the assessment social worker] said, 'There's a couple of things I'm worried about. I'm going to put your case to an intermediate panel.'
Jill: She was worried about you? On what basis?
He: Well one of the things was that she decided that we really weren't going to be able to look after a mixed race child and raise her in a … good manner … for whatever reason … no idea what she meant by that. I think basically she got stuck and maybe someone at the office said … I don't know, whatever. Anyway, she said we wouldn't know how to bring up a mixed race child and yet that's exactly what [wife] did for about five years …

Jill: Does that imply that mixed race couples don't know how to bring up mixed race children in some way?

She: I think basically she wanted us to have problems. To be battling within our relationship. To be unhappy, 'Oh dear what are people thinking about me ... ', and er ... we're just a couple of people. I did say that it's not colour when we are together that we think about. That is one of the things ... We know what things are like out there, if a child has any difficulties because of colour or whatever, then we would be able to cope with it. We would be able to help her cope with it and face up to it ... She just couldn't put herself into the position of another person's view ...

He: We pretty much fell out with her.

She: There was nothing about my experiences at school would help me ... help our children. She focuses on the fact that we don't live in a black community. Nothing about my family nearby, we've always lived around here.

He: We went to her boss and they weren't happy about changing social workers but when it comes down to it we weren't going to get anywhere.

In fact, they have now adopted through another agency but still feel upset by the first process of assessment and not particularly happy with the second. They have learned to take a pragmatic view of the process. What struck me at the time was the irony of a white social worker suggesting that people she was defining as mixed race were not performing according to the way she wanted mixed race people to perform. That the experiences of the wife, and her profound concern and analysis of racism through some bitter childhood experiences, were not taken into account seems to be of significance.

In the area of public policy more generally, not being considered black/white enough causes considerable angst. This may well be because such policy enshrines understandings from whatever settlements between ethnic groups are current. A more flexible and inclusive approach is called for that is able to accommodate the 'non-standard' in the way of family form, affiliation and other areas of personal choice.

In the end, being viewed as insufficiently black/white is a no-win situation for those of mixed race. Even where the subject *is* discussed, there are increasingly proscriptive statements about how to live and conceptualise mixed race 'correctly' and considerable problems for those who do not conform to understandings of what it is to 'look' mixed race. These are broad questions which could find mixed race being encouraged (yet again) to accomodate to racially defined positions which are sometimes – although not inevitably – constructed outside the group. The examples here are weighted towards adoption and fostering situations mainly because the impact of the same race discourse on mixed race life can be shown through experience in this area. In this area of policy, the challenges of needing to second guess and conform to erroneous racial definition had to be met in order to proceed.

Siblings and Step-Families

There are several accounts of siblings from different relationships living within the same family. A woman with children from Anglo-Indian and Caribbean fathers described her grandmother's discriminatory treatment towards the darker-skinned children:

> She didn't know [youngest child] but she knew [second youngest]. She was always horrible to him. So I wouldn't go and see her. She used to exclude him and only give him little things when she gave all the others decent things. And of course I wouldn't stand for that. So we ended up hardly ever seeing her because I wouldn't have [child] upset.

A man who was the only mixed race child born into a white family described how he became aware that difference was an issue for him on hearing a comment by his sister:

> Well I overheard my sister, all my siblings were white. I heard my sister, who is two years older than me, say, 'Oh people think it's funny we go to the same school as you.' ... That was when I was ten, coming up to eleven. And it took me a while to grab what she meant, and I don't have any recollection before.

A mixed race woman described similar tensions:

> I had a brother who was from a previous marriage of my mum's and he was very hostile towards me. Because he couldn't deal ... he couldn't fathom out why he had a black sister. So he got it as well and he took it out on me. And we fought all the time and we didn't really get on until he left home.

A white father of three mixed race children told me that all his children received 'some teasing' but that this did not escalate into serious bullying. He felt that they were, as a family, well protected by living in a small community and having relatives with children of similar ages and backgrounds. He also thought that the continuity in the children's friendships had helped them. These had developed over a long period of time spent living in the same community.

Conclusion

While the above examples do not represent the whole spectrum of issues facing people in mixed race positions, they do serve to suggest that much energy is expended in considering responses to definitions imposed from 'outside'. These definitions arise in dominant political discourses (such as essentialist views of culture, race and difference) or behaviour from friends, family or strangers and challenge the personhood and integrity of mixed race. The mixed race condition is constructed as a problematic state, often on the basis of very little knowledge. Some people have evidently been more affected by this than others and in very different ways. Most often individuals and families wanted to be able to express their difference positively and to move freely within their different cultural groups. The extent to which this was possible often rested with the groups themselves and the views expressed there about race mixing.

The next chapter shows some of the social sanctions identified by those who took part in the study and some of the strategies of resistance employed by mixed race families and individuals.

6 The Balancing Act: Race Separating

> The mixture of bloods and affinities, rather than confusing or unbalancing me, has forced me to achieve a kind of equilibrium. Both cultures deny me a place in their universe. Between them and among others, I build my own universe. *El Mundo Zurdo*. I belong to myself and not to anyone else.
>
> I walk the tightrope with ease and grace. I span abysses. Blindfolded in the blue air. The sword between my thighs, the blade warm with my flesh. I walk the rope – an acrobat in equipoise, expert at The Balancing Act.[1]

The last chapter opened up some issues raised by people reflecting on their situations. It is ordinary stuff; the complex fabric of everyday life. Ordinary voices raise questions about difference, social alliances, paucity of social space. They want to understand why there are so few books about mixed race, why there is a lack of clarity about what mixed race 'looks' like and what it should be called, why binary opposites fail to encompass and adequately describe their lives. Then there are observations about crossing social divisions and conceptualising difference as a part of daily life. There are also the self-constructions of skills and values and a querying of the responses of others to what is perceived as the mixing of race. These 'insider questions' are in sharp contrast to the usual questions asked of mixed race.

Historically, race mixing has often been a managed affair – the prerogative of the powerful, instrumental in the projects of the race thinker, a means of appropriating or consolidating business or territory. Meanwhile, ordinary people, with less ambitious projects on their hands, have continued, down the years, to mix. Sometimes, what they are considered to have mixed is race.

In this chapter, some of the common sanctions aimed at race separating, as described by people in the study, are presented. To counter this opposition, strategies have inevitably been developed and these are also presented here.

Sanctions

Rejection

The rejection, by close family, of relationships and children defined as 'mixed' is possibly the most debilitating and widespread of the sanctions reported. It is also an important area for investigation of the numbers of mixed race children separated from their families of birth at different times and in different places. Some people in the study had been completely cut off by families of origin, others rejected in less explicit ways. The two people I interviewed who had been fostered and adopted each said that they had been placed into the public care system at birth because they were perceived to be mixed race. In one case, the mother was not in a strong position herself and received no support from her own mother and family until she had given up her baby. A mixed race man, whose white mother was married to a white man when he was conceived (one of two in similar positions), told me:

> He: Well they didn't throw her out as such, well she was already married when I was born, so she wasn't living at home ... they would always have started from the premise that a child was first a child and accepted as innocent and that all other things were not the child's responsibility, if you see what I mean. So my mother would experience racism, and I, by association. I don't remember it specifically.
> Jill: Did you have much of a relationship with your relatives or ... ?
> He: Well I did, but there were complications. I know my mother would be told by some members of the family, 'Don't bring him round here, you're a shame on the family.' And they were Roman Catholics so there was that as well.
> Jill: Did your father ... ?
> He: I didn't know my father. My mother had a fleeting ... [dismissive hand gesture].
> Jill: So, I mean, where did the support come from?
> He: Well, well, well. I think it's of interest that. Because she had ... well someone from work had told her how to ... how she and this other work colleague could arrange an abortion. So my mother accumulated what was probably a vast amount of money for her and turned up at the place, but the person to whom she had given the money didn't turn up. And I think that somehow after that ... One of the things I said was that I very much doubt that I would

have had the courage to keep me ... faced with some similar kind of pressure, I would not have had the courage to keep or to deal with something like that. Because undoubtedly it would have taken enormous strength of character, which isn't, never was, my mother's conscious way of dealing with things, she would adapt to the family pressure because it was very close knit and intense.

It is interesting that adoption was apparently not considered by the mother. The family were portrayed as a close, working-class network of people and at the time (during the 1930s) adoption may well have been a middle-class option for concealing inconvenient births. Or, perhaps, not a solution available for women with mixed race children.

A couple (white and British Pakistani), who have been together for 14 years and have two children, are not acceptable to the male partner's father and other men in his family of his father's generation. They explained their situation to me in this way:

He: They didn't like it. No no.
Jill: What reasons did they give?
He: It's colour isn't it? She's white. She's not a Muslim. But we're not allowed to go out with girls in the first place.
Jill: At all?
He: At all. Full stop.
Jill: Did that get better when the children came?
He: No. It's still going on now. 14 years later, still the same problem. My mum is alright with her ...
She: Yes his mum's fine.
He: Brothers, sisters, are alright with her and my children. It's just my dad. He says, 'No. She's white, she's not a Muslim, we don't want her'.
Jill: Would it make a difference if [name] became a Muslim?
He: Can't say for definite. It might.
She: I am going to change soon.
He: Because we want to get married soon. He sees the children all the time. They go down to my mum's house. He's with my mum at my mum's house, they go there. He's alright with them. He just doesn't do the things he would do with his normal grandchildren.
Jill: Such as?
He: Pick them up and talk to them and things like that.
Jill : How do you cope with that?

She: I think I cope very well actually. Sometimes I'll have a down day ... then I'll say things like, 'Why can't he be more ... why doesn't he kiss them?', you know what I mean? Some days, it's not very often, but some days I do say that. But that's the way it's got to be. His dad won't change.

He: My dad won't accept her I don't think. It's been 14 years. We've been together 14 years now. And he hasn't accepted her yet, I don't think he ever will.

In this account, it was suggested that the male speaker's father had two main reasons for rejecting the new family: that his son's partner was white and that she was non-muslim. Whilst neither was felt, by the son, to be acceptable to his father, the prospect of his partner's religious conversion was not seen as a guarantee of acceptability. The matter was further compounded by the man's marriage, within the family, to the daughter of his father's sister. Although he was married at 16 and has requested a divorce, the family has, so far, refused to allow this. They continue to accord the legal wife the privileges of belonging within the family.

Another woman described her family's rejection:

She: When my parents found out that I was going out with a black guy they gave me an ultimatum at 16 that I could either give him up or leave home. And I left home with hardly any notice. I think I was told to go and left within days.

Jill: What reasons did they give or did they just ... ?

She: I don't know whether it was that they just couldn't cope with the hassle or just that they thought it was a disgusting thing to do. I had nowhere to have the baby. And fortunately or unfortunately – whichever way you want to look at it – I became very ill when I was pregnant. So my mum actually did take me back and looked after me, and I was sick every single solitary day. So she did look after me but she made it very clear that once I'd had the baby I couldn't stay. I went to work every day, this is the late '60s, early '70s, they wore smock dresses, so nobody actually knew I was pregnant. And as I did begin to show my mum made it clear that I had to go. So I got a social worker and booked into a mother and baby home five weeks before the baby was born.

There are examples of different degrees of rejection by family members throughout the data ranging from discomfort with a chosen partner, to unfavourable or rejective behaviour shown towards children, to a complete cutting away of contact.

'Looks'

The anonymous gaze of strangers appeared to have great bearing on the construction of discomfort in public places. Everyone I spoke to mentioned an awareness of the 'looks' of strangers. For example, the woman above who is not accepted by her partner's Muslim, Pakistani father demonstrates the response she attracts when out with her partner or with one of her children. The couple live in Bradford in Yorkshire with a large population of Pakistani people:

> Jill: How do you think other people, you know strangers outside see you?
> She: As outcastes. Yes they do ...
> He: Yes they do. They give us funny looks when we walk down the street.
> She : They forever stare at us. Everybody has been staring at me today because I've been wearing my salwar kameez.[2] Everybody turns round and stares at you.
> Jill: Would it have made a difference if you'd been wearing an English-style dress?
> She: No. They'd still have looked ... It's something for them to gawk at.

Several people were made aware of looks during trips away from their home towns. One white woman in her 20s, with a former Anglo-Nigerian partner said:

> She: This happened to me in Scotland. Because Bradford has so many mixed race relationships ... it's just like an everyday thing for us, but in Scotland you just get a room full of whites and you get a lot of bad looks.
> Jill: Do you?
> She: Yes. And the first time in Scotland we went into a pub and it were like one of those old-fashioned Western films. You know like when you walk into a room and everything stops. That's just what it were like. They were all staring at us. Me and him we just had one drink and that were it. We went. We were there about two minutes.

Of the effects of looks, one woman (Anglo-Cypriot with a Caribbean partner) said:

> She: I'd like to be invisible. I'd like to go out for a walk with somebody and hold hands and not have people falling over themselves and walking into lamp posts staring at us. I'd like that very much. I'd like to be invisible.
> Jill: Is the answer a mixed area, a more cosmopolitan area where ... ?
> She: But it still happens there.
> Jill: Does it?
> She: Yes. It's not as though we're odd. I mean we're not the only mixed couple. I've never lived in areas where there were only white or only black people.

Looks are an important way in which perceived difference is registered and disapproval is conveyed. The matter of responding to looks was also introduced by several people. For example, the woman quoted above spoke about the looks when members of her family were out together. She said:

> She: I think it's mostly the stares. But I mean I still get that now. And I think I've learned not to look, not to feel the stares, whereas other people with me still see them. Certainly, [youngest child's Caribbean] dad was always conscious. And he stared back at people. But it still hurts. And I suppose, it isn't ... I definitely don't think it's something you get used to. I'm not used to it. I won't meet people's gaze in the way he does. He met people's gaze. I haven't the emotional energy to do that any more, because there's still a part of me that feels intimidated by people that stare and I know that other people who don't live with it every day, and are presented with it, they react in a way that I would never do.

Others said that they kept to parts of towns, or to particular pubs and other social areas, where they were least likely to attract looks. Two women moved their social life to different towns in order to avoid stares and other hostile responses. One young couple (she, of white and Jamaican parents, and he, with two Caribbean parents) compared the reception they have received as a couple who are not generally perceived as 'mixed' to relationships each has had with white partners:

She: With a white guy I seemed to get a different atmosphere. With a black guy there's not really that problem. People look at you and it seems to feel right. You don't get the same looks and stares that you did as a mixed couple. Although I'm not full black, it seems to satisfy people that I'm half black and he's full black.
He: We've had no reaction really. It's much easier than with white. More respect. If you're with a black girl it seems that's right. For a black girl you get more respect. It's like they're saying, 'Stick with your own kind.'

Another couple (white English and Nigerian), speaking of the suburban area where the wife's parents live, said:

She: We stayed in town most of the time. Where I come from you might get called names – let's put it like that.
He: The time I actually went to see [wife] it was a constant barrier. People were looking at me as if to say, 'What are you doing here?'

Certainly, there was an awareness of greater safety in certain geographical spaces. Several of the people I interviewed from the Bradford area,[3] for instance, were very aware of the parts of the city in which they were less likely to attract looks and other forms of attention. Others could pinpoint no-go areas where they would be more likely to encounter unpleasantness. Looks appear to be an effective strategy for confining those perceived to be mixed or mixing and also for conveying disapproval.

Abuse
As well as looks from strangers, many people also reported verbal, written and physical abuse. Name-calling among school children was a universal complaint and almost as widely reported was verbal abuse from passers-by. One woman told me about an anonymous letter she had received concerning her relationship with her partner and children. Another message of racial abuse had been written on the walls and door of her foster home. Two incidents, related by a woman living in London, will serve to represent some of the material in this category. She is a white woman living with children from Anglo-Indian and Caribbean former relationships:

Only recently, when I've been walking up the road with [youngest daughter], and it also happened to my other daughter, there's a man round here somewhere ... and it's not just me who's suffered. There's been an article in the *Guardian* about it. He gives abuse to anybody he thinks is mixed race. He has seen me with [youngest daughter] and he will swear at me and he will swear at her and she's only little. Somebody told me about this woman with a mixed race child and she had racial abuse. It must be the same man because she lives round here. He's a young white bloke. And another friend of mine, she is French-Algerian and her little boy has got tight curly hair, she has been walking up this road and twice she has been spat on. It is almost certainly by the same man because the description she gave tallies with what I remembered. Twice it happened. And her child was spat on. The man obviously thinks the child is mixed race.

She went on to tell me about an experience of one of her older daughters and her boyfriend:

She: [Daughter] was going out with a really nice African boy. They're still friends, and he was walking with her, it was near London Bridge and apparently there's a lot of racism near there. So I was told.
Jill: Would that be Bermondsey?
She: It might have been Bermondsey, and they were just walking, and a gang of white blokes came out of a pub and saw them walking together. Now he's a well-built lad. He can take care of himself. This whole crowd was egging him on and trying to pick a fight with him and threatening him. And of course [daughter], she's very outspoken and she was saying, 'Well look, all of you are cowards. You wouldn't pick on him if it was one to one, you know.' And she was calling them all cowards because if she'd taken them one by one and put them next to [boyfriend] none of them would have picked a fight. But it was getting pretty nasty ... But they managed to get a bus and get away somehow. [Daughter] was really shocked. She kind of didn't believe that kind of thing could happen. But [boyfriend], he took it in his stride. He'd seen it before.

Describing an area where her mother lives, one white woman, with a child from a Pakistani man, told me:

She: Well we've had a lot of trouble up there. And I used to get beaten up. When I was pregnant with [son], eight months pregnant, someone tried to run me over. They said, 'Get that Paki baby out of you.' And I nearly was run over. No kidding it's really bad up there. We used to get a lot of trouble ...

Jill: Has it been a police matter?

She: No I didn't really call the police.

Jill: Frightening though.

She: Oh it frightened me. Oh yes. Especially when I nearly got knocked over.

Jill: Were you on your own?

She: By myself.

Jill: How did they associate you with having a Pakistani baby?

She: Well they'd seen me around with him and I used to get hassled. When we went to upper school he went to the boys' school and I went to the girls'. So they'd seen us about. I wasn't friends with them. They're mainly guys who do this aren't they? They're mainly lads that do it. I wouldn't say there were any girls that did it. It was just lads.

This woman does not spend much time in that particular area now, although it is the place where she and her partner attended school and where the woman's mother still lives. It is an area where many Pakistani and a smaller number of Caribbean families as well as whites live. The schools in the area have a very mixed population of children.

Loss of Reputation

Loss of reputation was a sanction that was particularly important for the women in the study. It was a very well understood threat to the status of women in relationships or with children considered to be mixed. Experiences between white women and women of colour in the study differed somewhat, although, for each, the question of a perceived 'betrayal' often underpinned attacks on reputation. The racialisation of relationships is often arranged around attack on reputation. Cashmore's collection of English racist views[4] provides a quotation that can well be used to sum up this area of thought. This is from an interview with a young, unemployed white man in the Midlands:

But cos they can't keep to their own colour, they have to keep going for *our* [my italics] women. I'd shoot women who went with blacks. I class them as slags. And I'd shoot the blacks with them. It's because I think blacks should mate with blacks and whites should be whites and not half-castes. (p. 85)

A light-skinned Caribbean woman and her relatively dark-skinned daughter told me about the birth of a second, lighter-skinned daughter. The mother has been passed, by neighbours, as white because of her lightness. She has already been quoted speaking about the birth of a relatively dark daughter and the disapproval this evoked. This example shows a response to her second child:

Daughter: When my sister was born she was very very light-skinned. So light-skinned that they said things to my mum. Because they thought mum was carrying on with the greengrocer. Couldn't have been Dad's child because she was too light-skinned. With Mum, they all came together [the neighbours]. They got together behind my mum's back and decided she'd been carrying on ... and they ended up not speaking to Mum.
Mother: One day, I invited them all round for coffee. I said, 'I know what you're all going round saying.' They didn't know where to put their faces. But I said, 'I'm not angry but I thought you'd like to know that it's not true.' They didn't understand ... I'm not really very black, neither is my husband. So usually the children have a lighter skin. They started thinking well it has to be a white man. Well I'm used to all this from the West Indies. It's acceptable because if you're of mixed race ...
Daughter: Anything could happen.

This extract also conveys the very different definitions and under-standings of mixed race which occur in places other than Britain.

Talking about the response of people to their relationships two white women suggested:

First: They think that black and Asian men don't have no right to go out with white women and you know if you've been with a black man, you're a slag. They do.
Second: Nigger lover ... and with that kind of attitude ... yes. They think you're a slag, and that's all you get. When you've got kids

you can't lie about it. I've got used to it now. I don't have to lie anyway. You shouldn't have to lie anyway.
Jill: Do you think the reputation sticks?
Second: Yes it gets around.

Several women told me about their mothers' experiences of giving birth to mixed race children. One such story is from the white-Cypriot woman:

> The story that really sticks out in my mind is one she has said to me, over the years, hundreds of times. When she gave birth to one of my sisters, one of her first children, the midwife left the room because as the head appeared with an obviously big mop of black hair, the midwife said to her, 'You're married to a foreigner!', and left the room. The funny thing was, and the way my mum tells it, in a jokey way, because she wasn't actually married at the time, which would have been much worse.

There seems to have been a qualitative difference in abusive content between women perceived as white and those perceived as black. For black women in the study, the implications for reputation were somewhat different in focus, although the nature of abuse was regularly reported as sexualised and the women were sometimes depicted as 'exotic' objects of desire. There appear to be two strands of attack on black women in the study. The first is on their motives for entering into a relationship with a white man. One black woman expressed this by saying: 'It's like they're saying', "Oh you've done well for yourself." You know, with a white partner. "Oh she's really raised herself up in the world."' A second set of responses is connected with the notion of 'betraying' the race, community, ethnic or religious group which claims a woman's loyalty. This was sometimes expressed as being acutely painful, particularly as there was no desire (amongst those I spoke to, at least) to leave or to lose contact with family, friends and those in the neighbourhood. A version of this allegation of 'betrayal' is also brought on the reputations of black men, either in casual abuse or in more intimate contacts. There were several instances of this phenomenon whereby black men had been challenged by individuals about their motives and choice of a white partner.

Of all the sanctions identifiable within the study perhaps reputation is one of the more readily observable in historical constructions of racialised relationships between sexes. It has often been the threat to reputations of women perceived to be mixing which has helped to keep group boundaries in position. Even where boundaries have shifted, much has depended on the agreement or control of women in the group to 'do the right thing'. This, as black film director Spike Lee has pointed out to the cinemagoing public, entails 'sticking to one's own kind'.

Several of the white women interviewed said that their children were sometimes assumed to be adopted and that this was a relatively 'acceptable' explanation for being out with a mixed race child. The woman in the last chapter, who spoke about having pretended to be adopted because she judged that this would safeguard her mother's reputation, is a verification of this 'loophole'. It was, for a time at least, that transracial adoption was viewed as an acceptable way of mixing race, although not all such parents escaped abuse and attack. Conversely, Ceri Register[5] writing of the inter-country adoption of Korean American children in the wake of war, speaks of hate mail and other racialised abuses directed at families seen as transracial in the United States. The 'respectability' factor in transracial adoption has also been reversed in Britain during the 1980s constructions of transracial relationships as psychologically damaging to children.

Pigeonholing
Pigeonholing is a very serious sanction within the mixed race condition and it is one which continues to lead to allegations of confused identity and damaged sense of belonging. While the acceptance of a unitary sense of 'group identity' is possibly felt by some to be an expedient response to the conceptualisation of populations as a series of ethnic groups with separate 'needs', 'histories' and 'cultures', it is not necessarily a realistic picture of human behaviour nor of history. The processes of exclusion and counter-exclusion may well require the construction of ethno-nationalistic formulae to induce sentiments of group belonging and distinctiveness. Many of us, however, do not recognise the evocative mono-cultural and often mono-class constructions of ethnic or national identity. Ethnic stereotypes are devices, and must be understood as such, for they serve some sections of the population better than they serve others. It cannot, for example, be said that women and men of any group are served in the same way by group notions of female propriety. Nor are people of different ages and

economic classes likely to benefit equally. Perhaps those who stand to benefit least are those considered to be mixed.

Pigeonholing, in this study, refers to a tendency to place individuals within predetermined ethnic or racial groupings. Its seriousness, for those considered to be mixed or mixing, is linked to difficulties over naming and to other denials of social space and rights, such as the freedom to self-define. In societies where racial ordering first identifies white and non-white, and then further differentiates on the basis of an increasing range of factors which become drawn into projects of racialisation, it becomes imperative that boundaries are well marked. Individuals are made aware of their classification. Although whiteness is widely held to be synonymous with race privilege, it must be noted that such privileges are not evenly distributed among whites, nor have they ever been.

Pigeonholing of racialised individuals or families is anathema within the mixed race condition. It is a suffocation of choice about how and with whom one may live. At root it provokes a contest over self-definition. A woman of South Asian and white English parents remarked during a workshop discussion: 'People who want to live together can't just get on with it. Everyone has to be one thing or the other ... no middle ground ... and it has to be political ... you can't just get on with people.' This was by no means a way of denying the impact of racial definition on racialised lives. What was being contested was the notion that it is necessary to 'choose'. I have come to think of pigeonholing as a form of passing, or rather being passed, which is imposed on individuals, curtailing freedom to self-define.

It is here that mixed race seriously undermines race. Skip back a couple of chapters to the Indo-Chinese dilemma over covert infiltration into European ways for an example of the panic that this kind of undermining induces. If there is a challenge to the idea that choices must be made, disorder is imminent in a binary system of ordering. The struggles over United States and United Kingdom census categories are symptomatic of the pigeonholing requirement. Settlements over the inclusion of a mixed race option represent a complex and uneasy peace in this area. The underlying questions are, of course, around the need for racial classification of any sort.

Repatriation

'Where do you come from?', 'Was your father born here?', 'Are you planning to go home?' are the sorts of 'innocent' enquiries that efficiently perform the function of enabling those perceived in connection with mixed race to understand that they belong 'elsewhere'. As well as the obvious effects of 'psychological repatriation', almost universally noted by the people of colour in the study, there is also the indication of a 'splitting' of family interests which is much in evidence within the data.

Whereas the member perceived as black (or 'foreign') may be seen as having an option to 'go back home', for the portions of the family perceived as white, there is the dilemma that no such option is available to dispose of their presence. They are sometimes ignored or alternatively may have privileges of a white definition removed (as is evident from the forms of abuse cited by white women in the study, such as 'nigger lover', 'slag' and similar epithets). The problem becomes not one of race mixing but of race separating. Attempts at separating are by no means exclusive to white males. Already noted have been examples of men from different ethnic and religious groups forbidding intermarriage – particularly of women – with other groups.

'Repatriation' is a hostile motif in mixed race experience, implicitly excluding and pulling apart those perceived to have mixed and questitoning the legitimacy of those who are seen to be mixed. The phrases 'go back home' and 'go back to where you came from' are almost formulaic in their frequent repetition by people in the study. An example from an interview with a white woman, detailing her brother's experience in this area, also illustrates this category of experience. The excerpt is situated in a discussion of the effects of stares and negative reaction to her family from strangers:

> People who don't experience the being stared at, and the children being looked at as if they were freaks and all the shouting and everything don't always understand and then they get it with more intensity than if you're used to it. You know? I remember once my brother had my children with him, and he was in the post office, and somebody had a go at one of the children, and my brother had a go back. And the guy said something, either to my brother or the children about, 'Why don't you go back where you came from?' And my brother was absolutely outraged and wanted to kill the man. Even though he was a pensioner. You know, my brother said, 'I haven't, I just haven't ever felt that kind of rage in my life before. Not ever wanted to really hurt somebody. I wanted to hurt that old man', he said, 'I wanted to say "These

children were born in London. They have as much right to be here as you have" '.

A couple considered the effects of 'psychological repatriation' (the same woman, incidentally, who was considered 'racially unaware' by an adoption assessment social worker):

She: The fact that you are seen to be inferior affects what you achieve in your life. What people expect of you.
Jill: Perhaps what you expect of yourself eventually. What you can hope for ... ?
She: Up to a point, that's what we are trying to do with [daughter] ... to be aware of that. But it's not that simple ...
Jill: Not at all simple ...
She: I think when I was a child that's how people did think about me. What they expected. All this 'go back home to where you come from' and all these things, at the end of the day you begin to think that perhaps they're right. And it goes on from there and in the end you think, 'Why bother if I don't belong here?' ... If I lived in a house and nobody had anything, then that would be alright. But it's not like that. We're all struggling to pay our mortgages, but when they think you've got something they haven't got, and they've got a right to have it, then that's when the problems start. Where I used to work, a woman there said, 'You've come over here, you've taken our jobs.' I say, 'One, I didn't come over here and two, I haven't taken your job because in order for me to get anywhere I have to work twice as hard as you have. If you haven't got anything then what are you doing wrong?'

The refusal of the woman (quoted earlier) to consider her husband as anything other than 'as English as I am', when considered in the light of such 'repatriation' pressure, may be seen as a strategy for pre-empting any suggestion that he might belong elsewhere. During an interview with a couple (she is white and born in Yorkshire, he has parents who migrated from the Caribbean but was also born in Yorkshire), the question of repatriation and belonging was raised:

He: My first experience with the police was when I were young and I'd been fighting this schoolboy who were about nine years old. The police came down to the house and took me to the police

station ... At nine years old! ... Told me they'd deport me ... it was
his son I'd been fighting.

Further on in the interview:

> He: I was born here and I'm supposed to regard myself as an
> Englishman – which I do. On the other hand the establishment
> here don't regard me as English, they regard me as West Indian,
> which I'm not. I was born here so I am an Englishman. They call
> you everything in the book except what you actually are. They are
> ashamed of us, they want to be racist. They think that England is
> just white and it's not. It has never always been all white even
> from the seventeenth century there's been black people here.
> She: To be honest, if I want anything for my children I'd ask for
> them to come out of this country. They don't treat them as
> anything.
> Jill: They were all born here so ...
> He: Well I still don't feel a part of it. All the way through school
> and up to now, I mean you don't, I don't feel a part of it. I mean,
> I know I'm English, I'm a black Englishman, but nobody ever calls
> me that. You're a West Indian, you're a Jamaican, that's all they
> know and that's all they ever say, isn't it? That's all they know.

All through the accounts runs awareness that those perceived as
black, mixed or mixing are not only different, but that the difference
belongs elsewhere. Talk of repatriation is a way of underlining this
perception.

Suspicion of Unsuitable Combinations
This category, similar to the Wrong Parents category in the last
chapter, adds weight to the perceptions of those interviewed in the
pilot study that people considered to be mixed or mixing are not
seen as belonging together. The Wrong Parents material collects the
experiences of mothers who are identified as mixing through the
presence of their children. The group of responses here is identified
as a sanction mainly because the responses contain examples of,
what might be termed 'brushes with officialdom'.

There is an aura of suspicion that those constructed in terms of
mixed race fail to meet some universal imperatives for claiming
'normality'. The 'ought' statements, as they focus on the parenting
of a child considered to be mixed race, sometimes begin from the

notion that such children ought not to be conceived. One white woman told me of her grandmother's opinion on this subject:

> She: Well nobody said anything except my grandmother. I was waiting at the bus stop to come and see [Nigerian partner] and she said, 'It's alright to be married but do you think it's alright to have children?' That was the only thing at the beginning. Then there was something said at work by a person that I work with which I really just couldn't believe. It really did upset me. She said that it was one thing to marry but that I never should have had the children.
>
> Jill: How did you handle that?
>
> She: Well I disagreed with her but I wouldn't get into an angry confrontation.
>
> Husband: Well I think the children are beautiful. They are the best in the world. They don't have to look for faults.

This couple had an experience, with the minister who was to conduct their wedding ceremony, which illustrates another feature of this category:

> He: The problem came when we moved into actually getting married. Then we had to go and see the clergyman, the actual pastor who was to marry us. The man actually said to me, 'Do you want to become a British citizen?' And that I found very offensive to be quite honest. I said to him that no, I don't. I am nothing to do with that. I just love my partner. That is why I want to marry. He said that it was because he knew [partner's] mum, that was why he was marrying us. It was as if he was immediately seeing it as a matter of convenience. I think that there is no need for that.

A related set of reports from interviews casts light on the commonly implied view – acutely discernible in fostering and adoption literature – that 'some white mothers are racist'. This group of responses suggests that mixed race family members, and particularly mothers, are seen as being in some way harmful to their children through a failure to nurture healthy 'racial identity', or similar deficits. Critical perceptions of this sort are comparable to the accusations of 'abandonment' levelled at Indo-Chinese mothers because of their refusal to have their children removed to be brought up as European. One example of this was an incident with a neighbour who lives in the flat above in a two-storey block, told by a single white mother of two very young mixed race children:

> She: I've got a neighbour, she doesn't have children but a couple of occasions ... well you've heard [son] and [daughter's] got a loud voice ... well ... I came in one day from work and we got to the door and [son] started screaming. We got in and two seconds later it was my neighbour at the door. She said 'I'm very concerned, I could hear the children screaming.' I said they were fine and they went bounding out. She was looking. Really looking at [daughter] ... I thought it was a bit worrying because she's that sort of person, she knows I'm on my own ... I felt she was looking down on me. I felt angry because she was not listening to my explanation ... it was as if it didn't matter, she was checking up on me ... So I said to her, 'Look. It's really nice of you to be concerned about us and it's nice to know that you would come down if anything happened.' I could have just said, 'Oh silly woman' and slammed the door but then if she'd heard the children again, I might not have been so lucky, she might have called ...
> Jill: What, the NSPCC[6] or ... ?
> She: Exactly. That was my worry. I want to avoid that sort of situation.

This mother is concerned that her single status, coupled with the neighbour's disapproval of her former partner, will be more likely to bring her to the attention of child protection agencies.

Other examples involve aspects of 'essential' differences, constructed around those attempting to make lives together. The woman concerned that her son 'thinks he's white' is worried that she cannot provide a (nonspecific) knowledge for her son about 'who he is'. She is undermined in her confidence as a parent. Women, during the workshop discussions, told of experiences their children had of being teased at school because of their parents' relationships. This construction of difference within families is often very divisive, particularly where close family members are applying the sanction.

Strategies

Whilst no one I spoke to was unaware of some degree of antipathy to their particular mixed race condition, there was a range of responses and variations in the severity with which sanctions were experienced. In some respects, strategies devised to offset sanctions were influenced by available resources as well as social positions of individuals and families.

Hold Hands and Stick Together
Many of those living amidst racial ascriptions concerning their perceived mixed states displayed affinity with others in similar situations. This sometimes showed through membership of local and national organisations such as People in Harmony[7] but was mainly evident in less formal networks of people and opportunities for chance encounters. As one woman said: 'If I see another mixed race couple I always make a beeline for them. I always try and talk to them.' Another mixed race person told me of the support and satisfaction he derives from attending meetings with a group of mixed race and transracially adopted people. He described a programme of meetings at which aspects of mixed race experience had been identified for discussion and he had also made a study of some of the issues which have emerged among people who have been transracially adopted.

A further participant (Caribbean, married to a white woman) spoke about his friends: 'We don't look at ourselves as being mixed race, we're just us. Of my friends, they're the same. In mixed marriages with the same outlook. That's why we get on so well.' A more tentative assertion of the need for contact and discussion of racial issues came from a woman of Dominican and white Scottish parents who had spent much of her childhood in foster care. This example also illustrates some of the dilemmas for light-skinned mixed race people and the tensions between ascription and elective exploration of cultural background:

First friend: She's mixed race you know [indicates friend].
Second: My mum's Scottish and my dad's West Indian. He's Dominican. He's very light-skinned, that's why I'm light and people don't know I'm mixed race.
Jill: Did people make anything of it at school?
Second: ... If I'd have told anyone that I were having problems they'd have said, 'Pull yourself together and get on with it.' I'm lucky I've got good friends. You really know who your friends are. I lived with foster parents as well. I went to a thing in Liverpool a while back about black kids in care. I didn't receive any

consideration like that when I were in care. No. I could be placed with any family. No one talked to me about being mixed. They just treated me like as if I were white.

This gives an indication of the context in which contact with others in what are deemed to be mixed situations, along with opportunities to speak about experience, are considered to be a relief. The woman had been passed as white during her early life and appreciates the opportunity to speak with friends about what it means to her to be mixed.

Almost all the interviews contained examples of contact with others in mixed conditions, even where this was not particularly highlighted. For some, such networks were extensive. For others, they were a 'natural' part of the landscape ('all my friends are like me'). For those without a great deal of local support, there were examples of long-distance friendships and of making the most of the opportunities that did occur.

There appears to be a popular view that mixed race has no 'community' in the sense that the term 'community' has been appropriated to indicate ethnic or religious groups. While it is true that what has come to be identified as mixed race draws from a wide and varied constituency, the same variety is probably also found within designated 'pure' ethnic groupings, even where these are portrayed as homogeneous entities. Whether the networking will become a more coherent attempt to discover commonality among those defined in terms of mixture remains to be seen. Certainly, this has historical precedence. It would, however, be a great mistake for those of mixed race to make the same mistakes as those claiming to be pure in terms of exclusivity and proscriptiveness.

Challenge-Cure Ignorance

My research revealed a wide spectrum of ways and means of changing opinion about mixed race. Some people felt that negative responses were a matter of individual ignorance and that patient explanation or argument could, to some extent, contribute towards a cure for this ignorance. Others took the view that racialised hostility is more a matter of wilful and widespread intent and must be challenged. There were also a few instances of people suggesting that to ignore insults and bad behaviour might be the safest line of action in order to avoid trouble. Most people in the study could switch between all three perspectives depending on the context under discussion. One white man, whose partner is an African woman, in considering social interaction felt that it was by contact that people could begin to understand and to make positive assessments of himself and his partner:

> He: My personal experience is that I've never had comments. People, white or black, just look. It's facial communication for the first few minutes. Once they've had time to actually listen to your conversation and your body language and how you mix they tend to open up and think, 'Oh he's OK. Not the type of picture they paint white people to be.'
>
> Jill: And together, do you ... ?
>
> He: Yes, once they get to realise they can communicate with you they see ... it's like you're just another chap. You're accepted within the gathering. When you have the black in the majority, again one must mention this because its true in the West Indian set-up. There's this bother about the mix. Some are. Once they get to listen to [partner], how she communicates and so on. How she responds, body language, conversation, whatever, they accept. They think, 'Oh, alright.'
>
> She: And it's, 'He's OK. He's not just one of those ignorant white people.'

The distinction between 'curing ignorance' on one's own account and defending broad principles is in play here. This couple, along with other people in the study, set great store by their personal ability to convince others of their acceptability in spite of anticipated negative expectations. For others, 'challenge' had more of a crusading feel to it, as one mixed race woman made evident during part of a conversation concerning certain of her social work colleagues' attitudes:

> She: I certainly can't pick up everything. I'd be exhausted.
>
> Jill: It's quite a responsibility isn't it ...
>
> She: I think in recent years I've consciously wound down from that and where, maybe a few years ago, I would have felt that I had to pick up on everything, and OK, if I let one thing in ten go, that was OK, but it was my responsibility to do more. I don't feel that any more. I'm much more geared to protecting myself. I don't always do it now.
>
> Jill: On whose behalf were you doing it before?

She: Mine. Mine. That's why it was so bad. I would come home in the evening, having let a remark go by that I would then feel personally guilty about, and thought, you know, it's my personal responsibility to challenge these things. If somebody says something that I find offensive and I would feel worse about not challenging it than I would about the remark. Now I don't feel that. Now I feel that I have to look after me.

Jill: Do you think that was because of the children, you've got to change things to protect the children?

She: Yes, because I think that if people don't challenge they're colluding. And therefore if you're colluding, you're responsible for what your children are experiencing but also, you know, it's not just my children, it's society in general. I want things to change. And if I want them to change then I have to be a part of doing something about it.

This woman also described a situation at work in which she felt she was made responsible for 'policing' colleagues' racism. The two quotations above possibly represent the extreme ends of this category.

In between are examples of challenges to particular issues, such as school perceptions of the needs of mixed race children and the availability of an authentic category on ethnic monitoring questionnaires. One woman, using her experiences of having been fostered as a child, expended energy on challenging her local fostering and adoption unit's same race policy on the ways she felt it impacted on mixed parentage children. On the whole people saw themselves as a resource for those perceived to be in ignorance, as defenders of their own life choices and, sometimes, as challengers of broader matters of prevailing racial (and other forms of) inequity.

Hard Work and Rightful Expectations

A further strategy, most often emphasised in parents' discussions bearing on the prospects for children, was to work hard. It was a strategy apparently more available to people with fairly high levels of self-confidence and security which often included a supportive family and steady employment. One couple (white mother, African father) explained their position towards their children:

Mother: We expect for our children what any parent would expect.

Father: It's up to us to be positive. We've got to ... you just treat
them the same as everyone else ... expect the same.
Mother: You've got to work hard for whatever you're going to get
and we just teach our children that if you want something you've
got to work for it.

A very different perception was part of a discussion about
children's prospects in England. This is the Yorkshire-born son of
Caribbean migrant parents, a couple of more modest economic and
employment prospects:

To get anything we've got to be twice as good. I tell the kids,
'You've got to be twice as good.' If I go to school to look at the
kid's report the people start reading it for me as if I'm illiterate. I
think my children are first-class citizens on paper. I want them to
be first-class citizens in all respects. But I also know the level of
discrimination in this country. I have reason to believe that there
will be occasions where they will be perceived as second-class
citizens because they are black; they are not white. They are born
and bred here. They talk like the English people. It may be OK.
But there is a little disadvantage. But it won't be like ... How that
is going to iron out I don't know but it will depend on their own
choosing as well. What will come out of it I just don't know.

Education was often cited as a strategy for success, along with family
and friend's support. There is also the question of class position in
the structuring of access to higher education to consider here. The
man above and his partner have not received further education and
their perceptions of their children's life choices are of hardship and
the need to work extra hard to achieve. Other parents expect
education to have something of a levelling effect and that it will
enable their children to find success in their lives in spite of any
difficulty they may encounter from being perceived as mixed race.
This focuses attention on the interplay between race and class.

The Goodness of Mixture
There are many examples of people moving to spaces they perceive
as offering 'a good mixture of people'. People had moved home,
chosen schools, visited cities and made other life choices with the
motive of being part of the 'goodness of mixture'. Two women stated
that they had moved their social lives from a nearby town to

Bradford because they felt more comfortable with their partners there 'because you get a good mixture of people'. Others were very specific about which parts of a town they felt safest and most comfortable in.

A few comments from interviews will probably be sufficient to illustrate this strategy:

> Mixed race mother: I like it here. It's well mixed. I've had no bad experiences round here. It's alright to live in really because you don't get anybody calling you, calling each other really. It's good for the children.

White mother about a prospective school for her children:

> It's a lovely school. Really nice. It's got a good mixture of kids. I want my kids to go to a school that's all mixed.

Mixed race woman from the Midlands about visits to London:

> Actually we've had a lot of contact going down to London and it's been very eye-opening for me. To see the mix in London, we're nowhere near that. And the different nationalities you get there's Chinese and black, Chinese and Asian, and the mix of people walking round there is lovely, to actually see it happening, because we don't see it. Here you see some in the city centre, but in London it's so displayed. Everywhere you go you actually meet it. You're normal. In London. I feel happy, we've been going a lot and it's lovely to see.

This strategy, like that of 'hold hands and stick together', is not quite as uncomplicated as it may appear. It is not always clear whether people were advocating what is currently perceived as race mixing as a superior way of life in which people habitually cross racially construed boundaries or, as may be more likely, people were pleased to be amongst those whose relationships or person were also construed as 'mixed'.

Pass Amongst

I have dealt earlier with the concept of passing and find that it fits the sanction of pigeonholing, or being passed. All that there is to add to this information are more examples of people using their skills and knowledge to move, or to survive, in particular social situations. For example, one woman will wear clothing which she anticipates will be acceptable to her mother-in-law. An African father will leave routine school visits to his wife, although he will go into his children's schools if there is a particular problem to sort out. He believes that the teachers will find this the easiest arrangement and that this will benefit the children. A foster mother talked of adapting herself to the needs of foster children so that they will find food and surroundings familiar and welcoming. All these are assessments of ways to adapt to, or to withdraw from, aspects of life to maximise benefit or to minimise misunderstanding and tend to be temporary. One mixed race woman (married to a white man) was more diffident:

> She: If you do it properly [bringing up children as part of a mixed race family], it should be a benefit. I place my behaviour accordingly, depending on who I'm with.
> Jill: Is that a problem or a skill do you think?
> She: Well I suppose it's a skill, but I end up doing it without realising what I'm doing. It's only when it's pointed out to me and I've stopped and thought about it ... I think it is an ability but then ... sometimes ... see at work people say, 'If you're black, you're black.' And the way to go was to be true to yourself and always to be the same. Let other people fit in around you. Whereas I have learned to adapt. I do change with different people. There's no point deliberately getting on people's nerves by doing things to deliberately be different.

The fine line between deciding to get the best out of a situation and being made to feel awkward and inappropriate is sometimes difficult to draw. However, the skills and information which are considered to be a gain appear to be well used in passing amongst social groups and often with great delight. This seems an equivalent of what Root[8] terms 'situational ethnicity':

> This changing of foreground and background does not usually represent confusion, but it may confuse someone who insists that race is an imperturbable fact and synonymous with ethnicity. The essence of who a person is remains the same. Changeability is a familiar process for most people, if they consider the roles by which they identify themselves in different situations: child, parent, lover, employee, student, friend and so on.

Situational ethnicity is a natural strategy in response to the social demands of a situation for multi-ethnically and multi-racially identified people. (p. 11)

Imaginary Homelands

Mixed race family legends score highly in the richness of their travel and historical aspects. Where contact with relatives outside Britain was maintained, these places of ancestry were sometimes included in definitions of 'home'. Where such contact had lapsed, there was sometimes regret but this was not always an obstacle to claiming affinity. In the case of the mixed race woman who had pretended to be adopted during childhood, a claim of affinity was inspired – after a childhood of racial abuse and lack of opportunity to talk through her experiences – by a course in black history. As she explained:

> She: Left school. No qualifications or anything, then ten years later, I decided to go back to college and do some O-levels, then I ended up doing a degree. When I went to do these O-levels I was doing history. Black history – I went for that. And I found it absolutely fascinating. Cos I'd never read or seen anything about black people other than Roots and that kind of stuff. Then I was learning about the history of slavery and black consciousness and that. And then, when I did my degree, I did Caribbean studies for two years. It was like I didn't know that part of history. It was just like WOW, you know, finding another part of yourself and giving you an awareness.
> Jill: Did that change the way you thought about things?
> She: Well, to a certain extent. It made me feel right strong and right proud to think that black people were ... you know what people think about black people and drugs and everything.

I am using this account extensively because it illustrates so well the strategy of constructing imaginary homelands, particularly where there has been oppressive experience. (I think this might be the area in which the commonly termed 'racial identity' is situated.) The same woman also told me about her search for her father who had returned to Jamaica when she was still small:

> Jill: Are you in touch with your dad?
> She: No. I used to want to get in touch, and I did once. I wrote to this paper, the *Gleaner*, and I put a little piece in it asking him to

contact me and he did. I wrote back and then we lost touch. Apparently he'd gone to the States. Then he wrote me a card and I didn't write back any more. I don't know why. I think it was pointless really. That he thinks he can just pass in and out of my life and then disappear without a word. So I just sent him my graduation photograph and that was it. That was my cut-off point ... What exactly does roots mean? When I was growing up it seemed important. Why isn't he here and all that.

Moving on to her self-perceptions and her social movements, she noted some difficulties put in the way of mixed race children and drew on her own experience to illustrate this:

She: You get torn between the two, you want to be with white people and accepted and you want to be with black people and accepted. People put you in the position of ... where you have to choose.

Jill: Have you ever been challenged about that?

She: Oh yeah. Like, if we have discussions and it's about which side you're on; white or black, and I'm not on any side and someone will say, 'Ah, you have to choose.' And I'm not on any side. I say I'll be on the side of the underdog [laughs]. When I was growing up there was a lot of confusion – like about my hair. I decided, quite purposefully, that if people don't like me as black or as white then they can go ... I think, 'Oh to hell with having to keep justifying yourself all the time.' If people can't cope with it, that's tough.

Jill: That must have taken some doing.

She: Yes. It does. And it took a lot of time to get to that point. But I think you have to. It comes back on culture ... and I thought I had a problem. You end up thinking you are the problem, but you have to come to a point in your life where you think no, I'm not. It's all ignorance and that. Like me – I haven't done anything wrong. I'm me. Full stop. You know, you need to cap all that. You need to value yourself.

Imaginary homelands are a common device for exploring or claiming undervalued or suppressed aspects of the self or of a situation. They allow for the claiming of spaces in which to explore the fullest possibilities of self-identification, particularly where this has not been possible during childhood. The woman cited above moved through the familiar processes of finding out more about the history and background of her absent father. She contacted him and reclaimed 'missing' information through educational courses and was then in a position to make a decision about the way she would value cultural background and sources of friendship. This is a process requiring exceptional courage.

Although the mixed race people in the study were the ones most likely to undertake this process, mixed couples who had stayed together for any length of time also seemed to need to review their social placement as mixed race. This was particularly so in the case of rejection from one or both families of origin. They had often constructed their own stories about the world (for the benefit of the world and for their children). None of these stories of origins and of mixed race could contain elements of immutable or irreconcilable difference. Race just was not an explanatory option (although cultural practices were fair game). They were all stories of fitting in and seeking to acknowledge all elements of family history or replacing lost fragments: of reclaiming and owning. Judging by the current interest in tracing genealogy, this seems to be a widespread preoccupation – but so much more lively and interesting in the case of mixed race.

Keep your Distance
Many attempts to reassure parents and close relatives about chosen partners or children were evident in the data. There were, however, points at which individuals felt the need to keep away from their families of origin. One woman spoke about the rift between herself and her mother and the possibility of contact having a negative effect on her children. This was the person whose mother had asked her to leave home when she became pregnant by a Caribbean man:

> Now that she's an old woman, I think she actually admires the spirit in me, and she has said so over the years. But we aren't close and I haven't encouraged her to have a close relationship with my children because she's very racist, and I don't want ... in a way I felt when I was younger that I didn't want her influencing my children. I think she did a bloody awful job with me, and I don't want her to have any influence on my children. It's been a hard old slog. I haven't actually wanted them to be influenced by her.

Another woman, now living apart from her ex-partner with their children, had experienced him wanting to keep her, his parents and his children separate:

> She: Before the children came, he always used to say, 'You don't want to know my family. They're too nosy. They'll turn you against me.' This was his first thing. Yes? But then when the children came, he used them as an excuse for going down there without me. He never wanted me to meet his parents and I used to say to invite his mum up here or something.
> Jill: Did you ever approach her?
> She: I never had the nerve. I thought if they don't want to see me I really don't want to push it. She was never that friendly on the phone.
> Jill: You don't really know that they wouldn't want to see you then?
> She: Do you think so? Do you ... but why should he keep us apart?
> Jill: I don't know.
> She: I've always wondered. It really did wind me up and then I thought, especially during pregnancy, well they probably really don't want to know me. I'm inclined to leave it if that's the way it is. It is strange. I've never got to the bottom of it.

Speaking of his family's initial reaction to his choice of partner, one African man said:

> He: My sister was, my older sister, she was very resentful about it. And she thinks that the whole thing, because she's white. It might provoke political ... as time goes by her attitude is changing ... she has a long way to go ... In America [some of his family live in the United States] they are not sure ... they believe I should be closer to my sister in London. They want me to be closer because she's far away in London.
> Jill: Closer in the sense of distance or ...
> He: Exactly, closeness means interference.

I asked another mixed race man about his contacts with his adoptive and birth parents whom he has traced. He now is aware of three families and sets of siblings to whom he is related. He told me:

I do see them. But we don't meet up very often. I like it to be that I am the one left to make the contact. I feel more in control if that is left to me. I get in touch with them from time to time.

An elderly man who had been out of contact with his Nigerian family for nearly 50 years decided to visit them just a few years ago:

[Wife] persuaded me to go back and see Mama before she died. I'm glad I went. They all made a lot of me and that, you know, I remembered people and I was in their minds but I was right to go when I did. Things would have got worse for me. I have my own life and my own way of living now. But we made up some of the lost time and the regrets.

Sometimes putting distance between immediate family and families of origin was inevitable because of the levels of hostility.

Humour
There were some examples of people making fun of hostile and often racially abusive behaviour, perhaps as a way of reducing hurt and tension. Often this was in the form of pointing to flaws in the logic of racist thinking and socially inept behaviour. One white father told me about his daughter's experience:

It wasn't too bad. They were both in a strong group of friends at school. One time when [daughter] was taken home to meet a boyfriend's mother there was some awkwardness. She hadn't been told. [Boyfriend] hadn't told his mother about [daughter's] background so she was a bit taken aback when she first met her. It's alright now. They can all laugh about it now. It was that first time.

A woman who had received anonymous written abuse said:

Sometimes I have been called a 'nigger lover'. I think one of the ways in which I coped with that in the past is with humour. Because I remember the first time I was called nigger lover it was ... I was sent an anonymous note thing, and the nigger was spelt with one g. I felt it was hysterically funny, and that was the way I dealt with it. But obviously I was very young at the time.

Another white woman told me of the way she handled a situation in a pub:

> She: This white feller, he came up to me and he said, 'What are you doing with a black man? You could be with me. Why aren't you with me, not him?' And I just said to him, 'Have you looked in the mirror recently? Look in that mirror then you'll know why I'm not with you.'
> Jill: How did [partner] react?
> She: He just left it to me. He could see I could cope with that on my own.

Many experiences were singularly unfunny, but some could be diffused by making fun of the situation.

The sanctions and strategies, presented here in as transparent a manner as possible, go some way to indicating how mixed race families and individuals are made to understand their particular distinctiveness. Although there have often, in past times and places, been legislative sanctions placed on race mixing, it is evident that social sanctions are also a powerful means of structuring mixed race life.

7 The Foundation of Order: Social Origins of Mixed Race

Mixed race man: If you think about the actual mixing almost the whole of human history has been through regression, through wars and conquering and that almost all mixing was aggressive and a repressive activity whether it was colonialism or Ghengis Khan or almost all ...

Jill: Do you mean genetic?

Mixed race man: Just mixing, well genetic ... even pigmentation is not a good indication ... the whole notion of racism is a bit of a misnomer I think. We are a human race with rather superficial differences. I was meaning more that the history of the human race is a mix, almost all of it stemmed from oppression or war or conquest.[1]

Theorising Mixed Race

Much theoretical and discursive treatment has, as we have observed, relied on conceptualisations of race mixing as a route to physiological, psychological, social, cultural or political degeneracy. The task of refuting such notions is complex, particularly as these views have been supported in many areas of scientific research. As Kohn[2] has suggested, the opposition of biology and culture (and we must, most certainly, include the opposition of psychology and culture) are usefully challenged here. That biology or psychology could exist independently of (or in opposition to) the cultures in which they are embedded is absurd.

In a similar way, the proposition that there are races, and that these races can be classified in ways that suggest that they define discrete groups of people is also inadequate. It does not even satisfy rudimentary evidence of the eye and ear, let alone the experiences of those falling between racially defined groups. Yet the idea of race does seem to be on a par, as an organising principle, with both religious classifications of humankind (for example, the one people–one god idea) and political/national classifications (one people–one nation). Any kind of activity that challenges this kind of exclusivity is problematic.

What is also clear, in particular in the historical material of Chapter 4, is that racism is closely embedded in and expressed through culture and institutions such as the family and the ethnic group. Here I remain with the definition that racism is the operationalisation of race thinking. It is from within the intimacy of family, group and culturally-based alliances that some of the worst stings on mixed race are inflicted.

This chapter combines some theoretical material offered during interviews with relevant existing theory. Some individual views rely on prevailing political discourses of race. Others use personal experience and that of friends as empirical evidence, for example, naming categories of people in their environments perceived as being in positions to apply sanctions. The standpoint analyses are as important here as any grand theory of mixed race.

Ethnic Leakage

I have already suggested that the confusion over the mixed race categories in ethnic monitoring data points to an area of uncontrolled 'leakage' into groups which are more precisely defined. We have seen something of the struggles over classification and inclusion of mixed populations. It is possible to begin to understand the significance of these struggles for mixed race: failure to classify mixed race may signify social exclusion. On the other hand an overly rigid system of classification may exclude the range of possibilities inherent in mixed race.

The desperate measures introduced into the census forms of the new millennium in the United States and the United Kingdom hint at a policy of appeasement. Here, there are attempts to provide a level of choice for those claiming to be mixed. Anxiety over this may well be exacerbated by the claims of many mixed race families that they, having been given the opportunities to discuss their positions and to move among a range of family and friends, will be able to decide *for themselves* how best to identify. One African mother's views represent this point well:

> We support them at home by giving them the assurance, the moral support, and we try to build up their confidence to say 'Yes, you are who you are. What you are. People will have to accept you

for who you are. If they don't like it, it is really their problem. You just carry on with whatever you are doing. Do not feel belittled by either white or black. You go for the maximum achievement you can attain. Build that confidence up. Be independent.'

Writing about a future role for mixed race people prior to our meeting, one mixed race man covered several topics, including the need for those defined as mixed race to begin to develop what he called 'mixed race ideology':

> Ethnic groups buffer to and from each other which functions to reinforce ethnic solidarity within groups and the myth of the 'other', enemy group. The emergence of mixed race groups, however, serves to neutralise traditional hostilities by forcing monoracial groups to question their traditional motives ... The 'melting pot' effect will inevitably happen, since 'man's [sic] natural propensity is to integrate' (Jung) ... Thus mixed race people have a crucial role to play in influencing ideologies absorbed by future generations. The role of MR people is astronomical, but the worst mistake would be to side with any monoracial group.

There is also the question of deconstructing 'purity' and this was done with some relish by many of the people I interviewed. The construct was mocked, played with and generally dismissed. As one woman put it, in reviewing the Eastern European, Jewish, African and British influences in her family life: 'Look at hybridity in the animal world ...it's supposed to be a good thing, makes them tougher and better ... and look at all the diseases and genetic problems in pedigree animals.' Would it be fair to suggest that mixed race is appeased in this way in Britain and America at present to safeguard the practice of racial classification? Mixed groups in the past have been identified as weak links in the boundaries between racially defined groups. This matters mainly to those who derive benefit from the preservation of a racial status quo. Mixed race has been perceived, quite correctly, as a disruption to this.

There is a historical dimension also to ethnic leakage which goes way beyond the worst nightmares of ethnic statisticians. What of the descendants of the 'stars' of the mixed race condition – those who have entered the history books? This is to say nothing of the anonymous 'ordinary people': the soldiers and sailors and escapees from indentured servitude and slavery, the servants, factory workers and Anglo-Indian children who 'infiltrated' the whole range of social class groups. What of those who do not 'look' mixed race and whose children, and children's children have forgotten their ancestry and live amongst the un-mixed? What of the areas of migration, for example Britain's port areas, where mixed populations go back generations and have intermarried to the point of indistinguishable normality? Groups have all, most definitely, leaked alarmingly. The point at which 'mixed' ceases to be regarded as mixed is an interesting question. However, the point at which 'pure' begins to be constructed as a homogeneous entity is perhaps of greater importance in comprehending the social construction of mixed race.

Mixed race is naturalised in a way whiteness can only aspire to, and then only with massive expenditure of technical, military and ideological resources. This information, were it more widely disseminated, might form the main plank of any 'influence' to which the man quoted above refers. The white category, it might be argued, is hybridity successfully passing for white. And this is true for other groups defined and organised in terms of ethnic or racial homogeneity. Perhaps most pertinent of all are questions which gather around the salience of race as an ordering construct, and ways in which mixed race upsets this. This is so even to the point where its righteous claims to ethnic majority must be silenced and excluded from the language and from accounts of history. The project of rewriting history from a mixed race perspective is rather a radical notion.

There are, it also seems, in the post 2000 and 2001 census era, insistent arguments being advanced against *any* racial classification. News collected in the on-line United States' *Abolitionist Examiner*,[3] and an article in the United Kingdom's *Guardian* newspaper[4] illustrate the double-edged nature of this issue. A 'racial privacy initiative', introduced by Ward Connerly in California, is aimed at eliminating race from government forms, and would make it impossible to maintain statistics on area, school and employment statistics. The counter-arguments by the American Civil Rights Coalition are in the form of a challenge that alternative ways of pinpointing and addressing discrimination will need to be devised and implemented. Whilst we shall await the outcome of this with interest, the argument does little to deconstruct the idea of race – it privatises it.

In the *Guardian* article, written in response to an outbreak of inter-ethnic fighting in Bradford, Faisal Bodi suggests that the tension is not helped by a policy emphasis on ethnic particularity:

> Much of the blame lies with race relations policies that have promoted ethnic insularity at the expense of integration. Money for ethnically exclusive centres and language support projects has poured into Bradford. Muslim critics say that this has done nothing but create a whole [stratum] of people whose livelihoods depend on being linguistic intermediaries between linguistic communities and local authorities. But on the contrary, it has helped bigots for whom Asian and Muslims should not and can not be British and therefore should not speak English. And it has helped the race sector employees stay in work.

So much of the tension in cities across the world can be traced, as it can in Bradford, to unfair distribution of resources such as jobs and decent housing. As the American Civil Rights Coalition suggests, the challenge is to promote fairness and absence of discrimination by means other than racially divided statistics.

The Slimy Category

The absence of a suitable naming system for what has come to be identified as mixed race is frequently perceived as being connected with a fundamental aspect of social exclusion – a lack of legitimate social space. It performs the same essential function as the exclusion of mixed race from equal citizenship. Examples of exclusion from popular images, texts, language, families, cultural and religious communities were cited by people interviewed to illustrate this point. There is a need to account for such an apparent deprivation of legitimate social and semantic space. Many people quarrelled with the term 'mixed race' on the grounds that they found 'race' to be an unsatisfactory way of classifying human beings; others disputed the use of 'mixed' as signifying elements of difference they regarded as superficial.

Bauman[5] and Douglas[6] both discuss the concept of 'sliminess' as a property of certain categories of things because of their ambiguity in relation to particular ordering systems. For Douglas, the identification and tabooing of the slimy originates in the human desire for clear classificatory guidelines. The individual, as she/he represents the cohesive body of society, fights disorder through symbol and ritual in order to avert fears of wider social chaos. Bauman speaks of slimy states as those with the potential to disrupt the classificatory criteria which are the outworking of human ordering praxis – ordering praxis being the prerequisite of human culture and society. In this understanding, the slimy is not necessarily fought through ritual and symbol, but causes anxiety as it clouds clear criteria of difference. In the context of a discussion of European Jews at a time when some were becoming indistinguishable from their fellow Europeans[7] (as opposed to the 'safer' Jew who maintained distinctiveness of dress, lifestyle and recognisable clan boundaries), Bauman[8] illustrates his use of 'slimy':

> They belong neither here nor there; they trespass the boundary whose unambiguity is the very foundation of order. They share this treacherous quality with foxes or mice who belong in the 'wilderness' but foist their commensality upon us; or with strangers who try to reconcile the irreconcilable: to be aliens and natives at the same time.

The concept of sliminess appears to be very pertinent to an analysis of the mixed race condition in so far as mixed race is capable of interfering with the racial ordering of society and de-stabilising structural divisions. Race mixing is regularly constructed as 'unnatural' and its people, as we have observed, defined in terms of physiological, 'racial' or cultural composites (half-caste, mixed blood and so on) rather than as unified entities (Scottish, African, human). That these 'pure' designations are also social products rather than 'naturally occurring' phenomena is an essential point here. However, it is the projection of sliminess or *ambiguity* which may be responsible for the popular view that mixed race children need to know 'both halves' or may suffer from confusion over identity, or that families defined as mixed race may not find a welcome from 'either side'. To maintain order, ambiguity must apparently be reduced either through its exclusion, its incorporation into the non-ambiguous, or else its extermination.

This overwhelming concern over negativity appears to take precedence over any benefits felt to accrue from being at ease with social difference and the ability to view questions from more than one perspective. Whilst those involved in being and living mixed race frequently prize such abilities and opportunities, their negative experiences frequently come from social sanctions applied from *outside* the group. Moreover, much investigation (and speculation) originating outside the group has begun from the premise that mixed race is inevitably a problematic rather than a multi-skilled condition. Added to this is evidence of struggles that individuals and families have undertaken in order to be able to say 'I am who I am' or 'we are who we are'.

The pressure to 'choose' an ethnic or racially defined group renders any ability to live comfortably and creatively with difference a liability. Racial ordering has reached something of a social contract with clearly delineated boundaries and rules of engagement – at least in the minds of majority populations. The disruptive mixed race category indicates people who are out of order, who blur standard criteria of racial difference, who defy religious and cultural norms and even challenge the category 'race'. However wrong the classification of humankind into races may be shown to be, it has assumed a salience and a convenience in social organisation.

In considering the origins of the perceived need to construct the demarcation lines of racial difference, Bauman[9] writes of a dilemma over the decline of racially constructed difference. This also begs the question of for whom the maintenance of such difference is important:

> It was proposed as early as 1815 by Christian Friedrich Ruhs that 'solche Allerweltmenschen, die ma ... Juden nenny' (expression coined by Ernst Moritz Arnt) should wear a yellow patch on their dress. The idea was to be made the best of by the Nazi law makers, who decreed that the Jewish star was to be placed both on the dress of Jews and on the entrances of their houses ... The method looked like being foolproof, but not the most convenient and not always practicable. The alternative is a sort of 'psychological marking' which consists in cultivating deliberately – in fact whipping up to hysterical proportions – the instinctive fear of ambiguity. (p. 136)

Part of the general ambivalence over mixed race, it may be argued, is worry over the certainties of criteria which serve the same purpose as these 'yellow patches'. *Could mixed race be race without its yellow patch?* Racialised distinctions, such as differences in dress and lifestyle, become less reliable or less reverently adhered to where mixing is involved. The 'signs' of race such as colour, features or naming systems are confused by mixing (and this is particularly so for those who are considered not to 'look' mixed race). As for 'psychological marking', almost all the recent research has conceptualised and investigated mixed race as a psychological rather than as a social phenomenon. Pathology is thus located in the group rather than in the social structure which employs race as a main axis of division and mixed race as its unnatural adversary.

Mixed Race Undermines Black and White: It Derecognises Race

The question of the derecognition of race as an organising principle was linked, amongst those I interviewed, to an acute awareness both of its inadequacies and its power in structuring life chances. Many people expressed the view that race mixing is seen as a betrayal or undermining of 'one's own kind'. An English-born man of Caribbean parents discussed this point:

> Well there's a portion of black people who think I shouldn't have ... that I should be ... who think I should be with my own. And there's a portion of whites who think that [partner] should be with her own too.

A mixed race woman elaborated on this:

> I've heard a lot of comments from black and white, they feel threatened by people mixing. It's weakened down the black race, that's very popular. There's enough black women to go around, so why have they gone for white? And I think the two sides feel very happy separated because it's protecting them. And now there's more mixed parentage children around, it's more disliked. And I've heard, 'Well we'll have more coffee coloured children than there'll be white or black.' That's been said over the white side. I mean they don't always pick the word coffee ... but I've heard it from black and white. So there's a lot of reasons within the two races why they don't like it.

Is the need to maintain distinctiveness simply a human need for clear order and the avoidance of ambiguity or slime? If the sanctions, identified as discouraging aspects of the mixed race condition are to be explained as anti-sliminess campaigns alone, then two questions emerge: why do people continue to mix if slime is intolerable to humankind? And do some sections within officially designated groups stand to benefit more than others from the maintenance of boundaries through the ferocious application of anti-mixed race sanctions? It is in vested interests that we may discover the reasons why race and gender are so intractably enshrined as essential differences. It is also vital to understand the possible outcomes of these ideologies.

There were many examples of people deciding to derecognise race within the private spaces of their lives. Doing so was not, however, a guarantee of escape from the attentions of those who evidently *do* recognise race as significant. One person from a large household of children and step-children told me:

> Well, in this house we have black people and Indian people, mixed race people. This house is full of people. It's a bit of a madhouse at times really with people coming and going. I mean my daughter's friends, they don't worry about colour. And my son ... well all the children, they don't worry. They all have friends of different ... in fact I would say the majority of their friends round here are black. We've never had any problems.

However, she went on to describe incidences of verbal and physical attack, spitting and discrimination she and members of the family had experienced 'out there'. Another person explained his view of the importance of 'attitude':

> There's always summat. In my situation my parents taught me different. If you meet with someone, at someone's house, they expect this black person to come in with a chip on their shoulder. My parents taught me it doesn't matter if you're white or black or whatever. When you first meet somebody ... it's how you portray yourself that's important.

These views, and many others, were not without acknowledgement of attempts to curtail opportunities for self-definition. Indeed, ignoring the impact of skin colour was never an option for most people in the stufy. They were frequently reminded of perceived 'difference' and its social implications. There were, however, attempts to derecognise or limit the scope of such curtailments. These attempts were, no doubt, mediated by class, gender and other factors. An important economic factor seems to have been the ability to move away from adverse environments and towards more congenial (often 'well mixed'), self-selected environments.

Women and the Reproduction of Own-Kind

The concept of one's 'own-kind' (i.e. unmixed) is powerful. Own-kind benefit from the privileges of belonging, of family and the familiar. Own-kind tends to trace its history through glorious struggle to the dawn of time, whilst offering the comforts of the familiar in the present. Own-kind is a way of progressing aspirations amidst competing claims from other-kind. Mixing can only be regarded as a threat to those who are seduced by the narratives of own-kind-as-essentially-different. Yet within own-kind, women are invariably constructed in different ways from men; poorer yield to wealthier and more powerful. Differences exist, and these are not neutrally nor evenly constructed. A man of Caribbean parents and his partner whose mother is white and father Jamaican discussed this matter:

> He: Well I've been out with both black and white women. And, like, with white some of my friends asked me what am I doing with her. I thought to myself that it's got nothing to do with them. It's like you don't need to talk about people's colours. Everybody's the same inside.
> She: White friends are less bothered. Black friends say, 'Don't touch white.' To me, I don't care. I'm both, I'm either. White people class you as Jamaican. That's what they know. A lot of people are ignorant. You have to tell them if you're actually mixed race. White friends wish they were black because black people look as if they're enjoying themselves. And they want to be part of that. You know, 'every black person's got rhythm'. That's not true, but they see something very positive there. ... My mum's in the same position, her friends are in the same position. People who didn't care about colour, mixed. I can't be racist to black or white people because I'm from both. I'm more broad-minded. I will look at the person not the colour. I argue the point: 'Why is it such a difficult thing for you? Why does it get you so uptight?'

These two people were very aware of the ease of (perceived) mono-racial relationships compared to those identified as mixed. They were not prepared to allow the existence of supposedly mono-racial unions to fully define their choices, however, the male partner did make the point that for women perceived as black, there is 'more respect' available in relationships seen as same race rather than mixed race. He did not analyse why this might be so beyond suggesting that relationships perceived as mono-racial are seen as 'right' and as part of keeping to 'your own'. It is possible that a more significant division exists between men and women than between black women and white women. Women are certainly racialised in different ways but it is often their sexuality and reproductive rights that are struggled over by opponents of race mixing.

We can see these differences where own-kind disputes with those perceived as mixed or mixing. There are attempts at conversion to, and exclusion from, various constructions of own-kind in the case of the couple above. The woman sees herself as 'both' whereas she is often seen as sufficiently black to 'satisfy' (a majority of) people that her relationship is same race. Where own-kind constructs itself as more powerful, more intelligent or more deserving of resources, it does so by relying on differences within its ranks. No one would wish to argue, for example, that white women had the same relationship to race and to privilege as their male counterparts in a plantocracy. Yet, their construction as faithful wives ensured the production of Master's legitimate heirs, and freed him for the coercive exercise of power over women designated as slaves. Sections of own-kind in this situation claimed the power to break ranks. The resulting production of children and their social location in relation to each parent provides a clear and amplified example of the social confusion, as opposed to individual pathology, around race mixing. In the act of sexual exploitation, black and white are both undermined and reinforced as meaningful divisions. Race is mixed and cannot be unmixed.

In more modern times, women and children were involved in the 'ethnic cleansing' of the former Yugoslavia through inter-ethnic rape. MacKinnon,[10] in a consideration of rape in expansionist war states, writes:

This is also rape as a policy of ethnic uniformity and ethnic conquest, of annexation and expansion, of acquisition by one nation of other nations. It is rape because a Serb wants your apartment. Most distinctively, this is rape as ethnic expansion through forced reproduction. African American women were forcibly impregnated through rape under slavery. The Nazis required Eastern European women to get special permission for abortions if impregnated by German men. In genocide, it is more usual for babies on the other side to be killed. Croatian and Muslim women are being raped and then denied abortions, to help make a Serbian state by making Serbian babies.

If this were racial rape, as Americans are familiar with it, the children would be regarded as polluted, dirty and contaminated, even as they are sometimes given comparative privileges based on 'white' blood. But because this is ethnic rape, lacking racial markers, the children are regarded by the aggressors as clean and somehow purified, as 'cleansed' ethnically. The babies made with Muslim and Croat women are regarded as Serbian babies. The idea seems to be to create a fifth column within Muslim and Croatian society of children – all sons? – who will rise up and join their fathers. Much Serbian fascist ideology simply adopts and adapts Nazi views. This one is the ultimate achievement of the Nazi ideology that culture is genetic. (pp. 191–2)

The author distinguishes between 'racial' and 'ethnic' rape, the latter being defined by a lack of 'racial markers'. I have some difficulty with this absolute distinction between race and ethnicity; however, with the view that women and children – defined as the 'property' of a group – are the means to group ends, I find no quarrel. Be it a desire for more sex, more land, more slaves or more Serbs, it is most unlikely that these acquisitions will benefit, or be shared equally within the conquering group. Women's cooperation (sought or enforced) is made instrumental in the ambitions of those who stand to gain most from the project of ethnic cleansing. The view of the children conceived under such circumstances is unlikely to be of unquestioning gratitude for their ethnic cleanliness. It is also most unlikely that culture will prove to be hereditary in this case or in any other.

Ahmed,[11] in examining the use, often sanctioned by states, of rape and the intimidation of women in the course of inter-ethnic hostility, finds that:

Because rape is so intimately tied to ideas of honour and disgrace people are reluctant to discuss it ... The woman is twice punished: by the brutality of the act and by the horror of her family. Notions of honour, modesty and motherhood are all violated. Rape strikes families at their most vulnerable point especially in traditional societies where, in certain tribes, illegitimate sexual acts are wiped out by death alone (Ahmed 1980). It is thus deliberately employed by ethnic neighbours who are fully aware of its expression as political power and cultural assertion to humiliate the internal other. (pp. 19–20)

It is possible to see, through Ahmed's approach to the subject, ways in which women, frequently given responsibility for a group's reputation, become a target through which group honour is attacked.

Race is an exploitative ideology which joins readily with other ideologies of human difference. Reports of sanctions, particularly where reputations are physically or verbally repudiated, tend to focus on behaviours perceived to be inappropriate (by the assailant) for members of the race or gender group in question. Whether this is a concern over classificatory confusion, an anxiety over loss of group status claims or loss of control over group members is a key question. Where race (or any of its derivative ideologies) is viewed as grounds for war – and really this must be a matter of degree since race is always constructed in terms of some level of antipathy – gender is in danger of similar exploitation. It is necessary to look very carefully at whose purity and ethnic superiority are being constructed through antipathy to mixed race. We can see, in the extreme progressions of ideologies of essential human differences, the cruelty and injustice to which such logic can lead.

Family

Family is not an inevitably hostile feature of the mixed race condition. Family members were, however, among people I spoke to, most frequently cited as having an opinion and as being in a position to transmit it. What people in the study meant by family differed considerably, particularly as some were in adoptive, fostering, step and other relationships. The more traditional definitions tend to put emphasis on factors such as economic interdependency and shared accommodation as well as lineage, religious, cultural and genetic inheritance. In doing so, relationships such as those created through adoption, as well as differences within families of phenotype, culture or sexuality are easily excluded from 'normality'. One mixed race man had a very clear analysis of ways in which families may limit their members' growth:

He: As Alice Miller said, the family is a conspiracy to keep us from knowing ourselves. And I think that's true, and I think it is more often true in adoption, because there are so many other factors.
Jill: Against knowing ourselves? Why?
He: Why do I think that? It's because a lot of people, the vast majority of people are dependent, that is, their sense of self, their mood, their state of mind, their behaviour depends on other people. They live within ... not as autonomous beings. Often as grown-ups they do not function as if they are inherent grown-ups, where their emotions are mature. Almost invariably they hold other people responsible for their relationships, and that is how they have lived their life. The basis of those marriages or partnerships ... because they believe that they are not responsible ... that you are cause and I am effect, prevails on marriages or relationships that start to demise. Now I think that often those patterns of thinking, feeling and behaving get in the way of people realising their full potential because in childhood ... well it's not just parents in childhood, but authority figures, in this culture certainly, saying, and saying explicitly, 'You do not have the right to be here.'

This certainly covers families who subject members to estrangement and other forms of coercion over choices of partners and lifestyle. It also has much to say about ways in which children, and adults too, reported having been unable to explore their full range of options for developing selfhood. Often, however, families of people I interviewed were themselves under pressure over a member's choice to marry away from the social expectations of the group. The Pakistani-white couple, not accepted by the husband's father, for example, had disrupted a complex system of kinship marriage which operates within the man's social group. Where the family is seen to act as an agent of social control, mixed race sometimes represents the failure to socialise.

Those families who supported their members' race mixing often did so from within a strong ideological alternative, such as a religious or socio-political view, which underpinned their own actions. Forms of security, such as a professional status or being in the midst of like-minded friends also helped to free families to hold on to positive approaches. The family involvement in applying sanctions shows that families can offer support or can add to social stresses to the point at which contact is severed and support completely withdrawn.

It is an inescapable fact that families are the main conduit for cultural norms, and if those norms stress racial difference then opposition to race mixing may well feature on the family agenda.

Religion

Religion, in so far as it appears within the empirical study data, shows itself as a curious mix of ideological material. This is amplified in the material on history and on the stage of world events. It appears frequently as part of the fabric of people's lives and philosophies. But adherence to religious groups and the tenets of faiths are also used to justify behaviours and beliefs not always intended in the original scriptures. In some cases religion provides rationale for opposing the racial status quo, in others it insists on a highly conservative view of group boundaries reinforced (or excused) by religious doctrine.

I was once asked to speak on a local radio programme which set out to examine 'mixed marriages'. In fact, the programme was dominated by local male religious leaders (Sikh, Muslim, Jewish and Christian). Each offered initial assurance of their support for such marriages while underlining the extreme difficulties faced by such couples, and the wisdom of thinking carefully about marrying into a completely 'alien' lifestyle. Marrying 'out' was not considered a viable option, nor was the possibility of dual faith households.[12]

I remarked, during one of the off-air advertisement breaks, that it was interesting that religion was beginning to look like an agent of social control for keeping people in their separate spheres. This remark was not well received. The biggest problem appeared to be over the children of mixed marriages. This was well concealed under concern over children's religious 'identity'. There was no escaping the notion that being born into a group served as a reinforcement of lineage and tradition. This belief was framed in terms of the familiar 'best interests of the child'. The matter presents a challenge to all the faiths.

Several of the people in the study considered questions of religious difference or similarity to be crucial. Religion had provided grounds for rejection as well as for the support of relationships over other socially construed divisions. It also provided rationales for advocacy of marriage and particular family styles. During the course of an interview, in the context of a discussion of attitudes to mixed race children, one couple (Caribbean man; white woman) made the following observations based on their shared Roman Catholic beliefs about family:

> He: I think that a lot of the problems which used to occur with mixed race children was not having a stable background. That's got to be it. The sense of not belonging to this category or that.
> She: I think that's because over the last ten years a lot of mixed race children have been brought up by single mothers and I think that's now changing. There are a lot more couples, married or not, who are together and have been together for, like, ten or more years. They have stable relationships. So we're hoping that the view on mixed race children will change.

This appears to emphasise the popular view of mixed race children as being mainly from single parent (and, in this line of argument, therefore unstable) households. From this follows the notion that this perceived instability is responsible for the negative image of mixed race children. This tends to be rather a matter of blaming the victim. The pair refuted the view that race determines friendship and life choices by drawing upon their religious beliefs which emphasise the unity of humankind. They live in an area of cultural and religious diversity and most of their friends are in mixed race relationships, in similar lines of professional work and hold similar beliefs. In this instance it is religion which is used to define 'one's own kind'. Religion also, in the case of this couple, has overridden class differences in their backgrounds and underlines, for them, the crucial importance of a particular family form and of creating 'stability'. It does, however, point to divisions within the population defined as mixed.

The parents of the wife, who called whilst I was interviewing, were also very explicit about the part played by their religious beliefs in determining their views on life and their choice of friends. They were talking about their initial reaction to having a black son-in-law:

> Mother: We didn't have any bad reaction. I can't remember anyone who did have hang-ups. Over the years, because of the way we have been, our friends would not be our friends if they did.
> Jill: Is there any Catholic influence in this?
> Mother: I can't imagine not being influenced by my religion.

Father: I think the concept of the Communion of Saints ... everybody is a child of God and if we pray we should accept anybody who is a human being as a child of God the same as us. That is the religious aspect.

The extent to which the black and Pentecostal Churches in Britain might support or oppose race mixing is not clear from the data. I interviewed only one couple (white British and Indian origin) who were deeply immersed in Pentecostalism and who saw their position as members of a church family in a very practical and supportive way, not unlike the family quoted above. They expressed, however, a far greater emphasis on the power differentials accruing to particular social differences. They perceived a need to work, as a church family, towards a greater equality – this was not, for them, an already realised religious truth but a condition to be aspired to. Nor do I have sufficient data to explore any other religious faith in its attitudes to race mixing. One man, who felt particularly under pressure from racism and class prejudice did speak about his Rasta-farianism as a means of achieving balance and stability:

He: It's a conscious thing. I never wanted locks, but it's just one way ... I knew from the time I twisted my first piece of hair that my whole life got to change. The turning point ... I was a wild child. The locks on my head made me more conscious. I was thinking about what was going on around me. I try not to have no prejudiced views or anything. I deal with everybody up front, the way I feel about them. Trying not to touch anybody, and nobody seems to be touching me.
Jill: What about whites? How does ...
He: White or black. If you're a white man they move you on and call you a gypsy. They make everyone feel like a second class citizen. I don't know but it's to do with the locks. It makes you more aware of yourself.

The 'they' refers to what this person identifies as a small elite of powerful people who exploit the rest of society (both black and white are subject to exploitation in the conceptualisation). He speaks from a class position in which his parents moved from being teachers in the Caribbean to doing labouring jobs when they migrated to Britain, a position from which the family has not been able to regain its former social prestige. This, he feels, affects the opportunities available to himself and his partner and children. It is worth noting that by adopting a Rastafarian religious outlook and appearance, this man is attempting to reduce ambiguity over his social position. He is aware of the stereotypical connections between locks, black men and drugs and prefers to 'draw out' racism in order that he can face it 'up front' rather than in its covert forms.

It is also apparent that some religious movements are targets of racialisation, as the long-standing experience of anti-Semitism by Jewish people attests. Irish Catholicism, Islam and Sikhism have become bound up in expressions of racial difference. Dress, food and hygiene regulations derived from religious practices are singled out as differentiating factors and sometimes used to identify and exclude some groups.

Professionals

On the question of who applies sanctions which contribute to the mixed race condition, there is evidence that close families are particularly able to influence the thinking and experience of their membership. The comments and stares of strangers and passers-by also have an effect on the comfort and feelings of legitimacy of people perceived to be in a mixed race condition. Perceptions of 'safety' of some geographical areas over others are often reported as marked by the ability to move about without attracting stares and comments. Another set of people frequently mentioned in interviews are those whose work enables them to make statements or take action based upon racialised assumptions about individuals and family groups. I refer to this group broadly as professionals and they include teachers, police, social workers, medical workers and those in various benefits agencies.

Speaking about teachers, the Rastafarian man above explained his experience:

> After the middle school[13] I found there was a lot of racist teachers telling us we was good for nothing and a waste of space. It was hard. I just had to fight my way through it. Teachers have that influence on you. So when you leave school for work you think that things are not what they are.

A white woman who had worked as a non-teaching classroom assistant prior to the birth of her children told me of the following experience concerning a mixed race child:

There was a kid in my class called [child's name]. His mum must have fell out with his dad and she were with this English man. And he used to pick [child] up. And [child] used to call this man 'Dad'. And they were sat there in the classroom discussing it ... and one of them says, 'Oh he's a bit of this and a bit of that, no one really knows.' The staff! And I thought what kind of attitude is that? He were out in the playground and we were playing, you know when them ninja turtles were out? So they were all kicking each other and three of them started fighting. [Child] and these two white boys. And I had to take them in because that's what I had to do and I told their teacher that it were all three of them and that it had started with an accident. Anyway I saw [child] inside with no shoes on and I said, 'What's he done?' And they said, 'Oh it's not because he's coloured, it's just because we thought he was the instigator.' And I said that I'd told them it was all three kids.

Suspicion of schools ran high. There were reports of overtly racist behaviour and language as well as more subtle forms of differentiation, for example, within procedures for making complaints about racial harassment. During a workshop discussion about supporting mixed race children who experience bullying of this nature, a mother explained that in the school her children attend the complainant is required to fill in a form which requires personal information. This includes the status of parental relationships and country of origin of mother and father. Further, it is the bullied child who is monitored rather than the alleged bullies and this, it was generally agreed, was particularly difficult for a child who was already being singled out for unfair treatment. This group of women (who may, incidentally be described as being from very mixed backgrounds in terms of class and colour) were highly sensitive to the portrayal of mixed race families in their children's schools and willing to supplement schools' awareness if enabled to do so.

Individuals without steady work, support from their families, decent housing and other markers of security tended to find schools particularly daunting. Inevitably, these factors also tended to cluster. For example, being a single parent of a mixed race child might be combined with reduced access to work opportunities and, therefore, to prospects of owning accommodation and being sufficiently mobile to move home to be close to schools of choice. Other factors such as parental support and level of education also, as might be expected, contributed to security and confidence in making demands of education professionals. Social class divisions within the mixed race population are very evident in the area of dealing with professionals such as teachers.

A similar pattern emerges with regard to the police, politicians and the medical profession. The data contains examples of racialised abuse and incorrect assumptions on the basis of perceived racial origin as well as analyses that people in professional jobs work more for their own interests than as public servants. Discussions of racial factors in policing are adequately discussed elsewhere.[14] One example may be taken to represent a feeling that police officers discriminate and offer racist treatment to those they recognise as black or 'not white'. The interview excerpt quoted below concerns an attack on the white partner of the speaker:

> He: The police never do nothing.
> She: I don't think they take it seriously.
> Jill: Why do you say that?
> He: Because the police are only for white people. The amount of us that get stopped by the police is unbelievable, you know what I mean? You get stopped in your car. 'What's a black bastard like you doing in a car like this?'
> Jill: And do they use words like that?
> He: Yes. Yes. 'You Paki this, you Paki that.' Unbelievable. Even now with me being a taxi driver. It exists. Of course it exists. They stop you and if they can't do you for summat, they do you for summat else.

It is useful to note that both the people here perceived the police to be acting only in the interests of white people. The target of the attack, which was the initial focus of the conversation, was white. Interestingly neither she nor her partner appeared to expect what they saw as a white prerogative (police protection) in the face of a racially motivated attack.

Welfare Professionals

The social work profession was frequently cited as having the power to affect lives. Whatever view we may take of various kinds of welfare work in the enterprises of state surveillance or control, welfare services are sometimes employed to deal with fallout from our attempts at social organisation. The interest here in social welfare may be narrowed to the ability of social services in the United States and the United Kingdom, during the 1970s and beyond, to control discourses which impacted on public perceptions of race mixing. In this area social work attempted to act as a social policing force in matters of race, with very real implications for opportunities to *mix* race. We must also bear in mind the part played by 'the welfare' during earlier episodes of managing mixed race.

The same race placement discourse in fostering and adoption, which prevailed during the 1980s and 1990s was viewed, by people I talked to, as disadvantageous to all families perceived as mixed. Adopters, foster carers, the adopted and fostered people in the study, as well as those engaged in the practice of social work, discussed at some length their experiences in relation to social services from very different angles. One white woman, who has three mixed race children and who is also a trained social worker, had a particularly wide range of relevant information. Of practice relating to foster care she contributed the following information:

She: Well I suppose when I've been in a position of having to find a place for a baby or a child or an adolescent, the feeling has been, if it's a mixed race child, if you can't find a mixed race family, then the next best thing is a black family. And that has caused difficulties in our team, when a mixed race adolescent did not want to go to a black family. All of her experiences had been in a white family because the black part of her parents wasn't around and hadn't been around. So her family were white and she was really opposed to going to a black family because of her experience, and in her mind all she could think of was, 'I'm going to be surrounded by a family I don't know, who are also going to be black, which I'm not used to, and I'm going to be made to eat food that I don't like.' Well that would have been really difficult for that young person if that's what [Borough] had insisted on. Fortunately we found a mixed race family to take her on, but you know, that would have caused great distress. And, you know, she was already in a distressed state because of the circumstances, coming into ... being accommodated by social services. So to add to that would have been difficult and we would have had a battle on our hands ... I think you have to go ... when it's a young person rather than a child, I think you have to go with what that child wants at the point, but then do some real in-depth work with that young person about, you know, what it is that person wants. Because obviously that young person, that young woman was obviously having difficulty about her own identity. But how do we pick up that kind of stuff anyway?

Jill: When you say she was having difficulty, do you mean apart from ... ?

She: ... She couldn't relate to being black or mixed race. As far as she was concerned she was white. She was part of a white family. She didn't know her black father. Anyway, looking at her, she was mixed race.

There are some useful insights here into the capacity for social work to rearrange social events and to inject an 'ought' into association and self-identity. An absent parent is required to be represented to the child as, above all, a *black* parent. The child might fear unfamiliar food in a *black* household, but mixed race households are constructed (here) as being ideally suited and non-threatening, although scarce. Whether the perceived racial contribution of an absent parent should be a determining factor in the choice of alternative accommodation for the child requires scrutiny. Perceptions of 'whiteness' are pathologised and taken as an indication of 'identity problems'. (Are mixed race children's perceptions of themselves as black considered to be pathological also?) On a simpler level, are 'black' households very different from 'white' households in their abilities to meet the emergency needs of children they care for? And must mixed race families always have two parents of different sexes and cultural affinity?

It is quite likely that much, if not most, of the population of Europe, the United States and beyond are what would be termed, in this generation, mixed race. The numbers of people who have been absorbed into white, black and other communities is unknowable. And just how important is this? There are questions around the power of welfare agencies to define 'correct' identity, about what sorts of people belong together and how they 'should' think of their collectivity. Speaking to mixed race people who have acknowledged a time in their lives when they needed to explore the implications of their ancestral backgrounds, it seems evident that they, and only they, must be trusted with the task of defining the significance of their ancestry.

This direct power to disorganise or rearrange race mixing is limited to families who come within the remit of social welfare work. Often these are poor families with little social support. There are no longer any legal statutes *directly* prohibiting 'miscegenation' or requiring racial identities to be publicly scrutinised. There are, as we have seen from the information about sanctions, several less formal prohibitions available to those who are discontent with what they perceive to be race mixing.

Two white sisters, one of whom is a foster parent and the other who has mixed race children, independently questioned the prioritisation of racial criteria over other factors for children coming into care. They brought out a salient point about fostered children returning home:

> Foster parent: I mean I've had the argument ... if you're a single white mother with a black child, you are still a racist. But that must be the exact opposite of what is actually the case. If you are non-racist enough to have ... to be a white person having a black child, that must be the ultimate in non-raciality surely?
> Sister: What does this also say about reuniting the child with the mother or the natural family? You've said that the practice is to place a child very temporarily, but that often, if fostering breaks down, a child is moved and moved. I understood that fostering was about looking after a child while the parent or parents couldn't, with an aim of reuniting where possible ... where there wasn't a danger.
> Foster parent: Yes.
> Sister: So I mean, what does that thinking say? Does it really mean that in fact social services don't intend to reunite the mixed race child with the white mother?
> Foster parent: I would imagine so, yes.
> Sister: You really think so?
> Foster parent: Yes.

This is entirely possible given the ambivalence, within the profession, to white parents of black or mixed race children. The single white mother and her mixed race child pose a particular challenge to a discourse littered with terms of reference such as 'pathological bonding' and 'cultural genocide'. By and large it may be assumed that parents are 'entitled' to expect to look after their children. However this entitlement appears to be seriously jeopardised in the case of the poor white mother–mixed race child combination. In other times and places it has been different combinations that have been most vulnerable to welfare attention (Aboriginal women with part-European children; Eurasian women with white partners; African slave women and 'mulatto' children). At present it is the white–mixed combination that is the focus of these attentions.

A crucial factor, often missing from discussions which employ crude terms such as 'racial identity', is that there are many ways of acknowledging and exploring ethnicity or 'racial' sympathy. In the same way, there are many ways of living, subverting, or circum-venting, the social identities of gender, class, sexuality, age and disability. Local youth cultures, women's groups and many other elective configurations of people foster and struggle over new identities and values. Just as divisions are socially constructed, so the individual responses are constructed using whatever materials are available and found to be useful. We could hazard a hypothesis here, that what are commonly termed 'identity problems' among those considered to be mixed or mixing are a temporary victory of social sanctions over individual attempts at self-identification. This seems to boil down to ways in which human differences are perceived and ways in which difference is allowed to inform action.

Talking about her own foster mother's experience of racial abuse, the mixed race foster parent in the study told me about her own par-ticipation in a course for foster parents. She found a certain lack of subtlety in the case material which did not authentically connect with her own recollections of important issues as a mixed race child in care nor as a foster and adoptive parent:

> I went last year on a fostering course, and it talked about these issues of black children, and thinking and explaining to black children that they're black children. In a sense it was only just barely touched on. It was all about children scrubbing their knees to be white and things like that, and I thought, 'You've done it again, you've white stereo'd it.' Of what it was like. What they could see, or what case they could come up with ... yes it did happen, I'm not saying it never happened. But it wasn't the only thing. And a lot of things they jump on the band wagon and think they've got it right. But they haven't. You know it's like everybody's got a pigeonhole and because you're black ... and I mean I'm on about black as being mixed parentage or Chinese or whatever, you've all got to fit into that pigeonhole.

There is a sense in which professional statements of intent to be anti-racist, anti-sexist or generally anti-oppressive are self-defeating. I mention this because claims to act on behalf of, or in the interests of, a whole socially identified group of people (black people; women; the oppressed; the poor; the 'natives') are redolent of imperialistic declarations of intent. The shouldering of an imaginary burden on behalf of groups constructed as versions of the 'poor benighted heathen' enables no end of state interference. There is a kind of chauvinism which prevents the defined from exercising autonomy. As Gilroy[15] notes in his critique of forms of anti-racism which developed in local government, social service and other sites of British state employment during the 1980s:

> Anti-racism in this sense is a phenomenon which grew out of the political openings created by the 1981 riots. In the years since then, anti-racists have become a discrete and self-contained political formation. Their activism is now able to sustain itself independently of the lives, dreams and aspirations of the majority of blacks from whose experience they derive their authority to speak.

This is particularly relevant to the 'ought' claims made about a mixed race identity both in areas of welfare work and in some forms of psychology. On whose behalf and with whose authority are these people actually speaking? Is this more a strategy for claiming professional expertise than a genuine desire to address issues of race in the lives of their clientele?

Race Does Not Always Override Class and Gender

There is considerable evidence that experiences, particularly oppressive experiences, are by no means always determined by racial definition alone. Rather, they arise through complex combinations of circumstances. These include gender and class positioning as well as individual interpretations of personal situation. Two people, for example, spoke directly about class solidarity as overriding race as a source of support. One woman found her sense of 'community' amongst women in similar positions to herself *vis-à-vis* race and gender. Three women friends gave one another both moral and practical support based on their friendship and common experiences of having been associated with mixed race (through their relationships and children). More striking than racial divisions for an

American woman is what she perceives as an English preoccupation with class:

> She: And another thing I don't like about England – the class system. It's ridiculous. America – we're all the same. Some of us may have more money, more education but we're all the same. All of us. And it really ticks me off ... Did I tell you about that doctor? ... Did I tell you? He must think he's God or somebody, he just treated me like a piece of crap. I was supposed to take it. And now, because I didn't want to take it, I've been asked to leave the damned surgery. Did I tell you?
>
> Jill: No.
>
> She: Well I can't put it down to racism. It might not be racism [tells of an altercation between herself and the doctor over an emergency treatment for her son]. I've been in touch with the BMA.[16] I will be complaining about that doctor. The last thing I need is for someone to be telling me what to do. I take offence to anyone telling me what to do, nobody has the right unless you pay my rent. That's how I feel anyway.
>
> Jill: Yes it's hard if you can't discuss things as equals.
>
> She: It's exploitation, exploitation, exploitation. There's so much exploitation that goes on. They take away your rights and it's just pathetic. I think they really do manipulate people here. It's ridiculous, the king and queen says and all that.

Personal stories were constructed through intricate negotiations between available social space and individual histories and sets of experiences. Everyone I interviewed was dynamically involved in the process of thinking about and acting from the range of possibilities available to them in their self-development.

The Need to Talk

The opportunities to think and to act free from sanctions and constraints were seen as being of fundamental importance by everyone I spoke to. The lack of these opportunities formed very negative aspects of life experience. In terms of providing analyses of the motives of opposing forces or rationales for their relationships or personal histories, the people I interviewed were highly adept. A constant complaint, however, was the extent to which individual assessments were hampered by more powerful orthodoxies demanding loyalty, compliance or silence. Those who as children had been impressed with feelings of shame or ignorance, had needed to busy their adult selves with information gathering and the making of adjustments to their historical selves and current outlooks. Those whose relationships were questioned or attacked had needed to review or rebut, to contest or depart from situations in which they were defined as unacceptable. This work is sometimes arduous and inevitably leads to casualties and drop-outs.

Of the parents I interviewed, most put forward views about helping their children to discuss any negative experiences and had strategies for imparting alternative positive views to their children. Those who had as children been unable to explore their histories and the cultural backgrounds of their parents tended to cite this lack of opportunity as confusing and debilitating.

People in mixed race situations appeared to be intent on finding one another and creating opportunities for self-exploration. One mixed race man is highly sensitive about the need to assure 'mixed parentage' children that there is nothing strange or 'wrong' with exploring their experiences and histories. He attacked 'colour blindness' as a conspiracy against discussing uncomfortable experiences:

'We won't mention it if you don't.' But if you don't see it, it's like saying, 'I don't see wheel chairs I just see people.' So we don't have to build ramps, we don't have to consider public transport. Because we don't see the wheelchairs, we can treat everybody the same. But to treat everyone equal you can't treat them all the same. To deny somebody's pigmentation is a denial of that person's experience and expectations and identity and reality, and it's patronising.

If there is a single factor which is universally acknowledged as part of mixed race experience, it is the necessity, and sometimes the lack of opportunity, to examine and draw inferences from the position of being seen as a composite of two or more quite different elements. This is a contest between self-definition and social construction and it seems to be to be addressed most effectively in the open and in like company.

In November 2000, the United Kingdom-based People in Harmony organisation organised a conference on mixed race experience.[17] The range of speakers, backgrounds and points of view showed a distinct determination to openly debate, define and highlight mixed race experience in Britain. The need to talk is inevitably a problematic provision to meet where race mixing is denied, forbidden or is the subject of shame. For this reason, if for no other, it is of paramount importance to deconstruct race and to expose its many fallacious claims. What is more, it is necessary to struggle to do this in very loud voices.

8 Communities to Conjure With: Concluding Remarks

> Don't be afraid to ask questions comrade!
> Don't be talked into things
> See for yourself!
> What you don't know yourself
> You don't know.
> Study the bill for it
> It's you who must pay it.
> Point with the finger at every item
> Ask how it comes to be there.
> It's you who will have to give the orders.[1]
>   Bertholt Brecht, 'In Praise of Learning'

We cannot deduce – Hume's celebrated dictum runs – how we ought to act from what we believe is. Neither can we deduce how anyone else ought to act from how we believe we ought to act. In the end, if the end comes, we just have to beat those who disagree with us over the head; let us hope the end comes seldom. In the meantime, being as reasonable as we are able to be, we ought all to argue.[2]

There is no end to the social construction of mixed race. The concept has bothered and gnawed away at the foundations of race thinking and has emerged in some unusual ideological attire: 'cultural difference'; 'mixed blood'; 'hybridity'. Drawing together some threads of ideas about human difference and mixed race experience, what does it mean (if it means anything) to be the product of this alleged human capacity to mix race? Is there any basis for the view that mixed race experience is patterned, that there are recognisable features that span time and place? Are there grounds for collective action and thought amongst those who are defined in terms of race mixture?

We can certainly lay claim to the view that ideologies of mixed race have been constructed and manipulated to meet particular purposes and desires, serviced through recourse to ideologies of race. This is so to such an extent that groups defined as mixed or mixing race are eligible for the description 'communities to conjure with', since there are clear patterns of use, abuse, denial and transformation to be discerned. Race mixing has been constructed as beneficial to the establishment of transnational trading, or as a 'perk' for men wishing to underline the power accruing to positions of sexual, class and/or racial dominance. Race mixing has been outlawed where race has been employed to achieve refinements in social stratification. It has been collapsed into one racial category – not necessarily, but often, the socially subordinate one. Its designated classificatory space, however, is not a space with clear guidelines as to history and ethnic affiliation, nor does it offer much room for manoeuvre. Mixed race has been pushed around a lot and so have the people to whom the term attaches.

Those wishing to organise their political activities in exclusive racial terms must inevitably formulate a response to those they perceive to be mixed or mixing race. Those who use race as an ideology to mobilise resistance, as well as those who claim racial superiority, can have no interest in an independent and freethinking mixed race group. Straddlers must either be isolated and expelled or they must be transformed and incorporated into one of the more clearly defined groups.

People who regard mixed race as symbolic of a desirable and generalisable social condition must also be mindful. Beyond what may turn out to be a political fashion, real lives are buffeted or stranded by changing social responses to their situation. They may well become the 'psychological misfits' or 'half-caste problem' of tomorrow, should the whims of political and economic expediency shift. This has happened throughout history to mixed race groups.

Those to whom the term 'mixed race' (or interracial, or mixed blood or any other term signifying a mixture of racial 'essences') is applied are well placed to show the negation of race. They are, indeed, neither one thing nor the other but both, either or neither – they represent a melting away of racial signifiers, be these cultural, physical or political. They provide a reminder that race is not a 'thing' but an ideology that may be actively disputed.

The salience of race ideology in lived experience cannot be denied. It must, therefore, be addressed. However, it is important to address it on the ground of its creation – the ideological. Whatever the social experiences arising from the social construction of mixed race, these are not intrinsic to the population but arise from social processes that create, enable and sustain race thinking and the racialisation of difference. Race is a state of mind, often a poor response to diversity. The struggle for a space and a voice for mixed race is, above all, an ideological struggle.

Mixed race threatens the idea of racial difference. It also threatens ethnic boundaries and this seems to matter when groups wish to espouse and protect their uniqueness (for various reasons). All that is claimed for race – that it is a means of dividing and ranking humankind; that it is 'natural' to keep to 'one's own'; that the consequences of mixing race are dire – is disproved by the very existence of mixed race. Race is not the only difference that mixed race challenges. Differences in custom and religion, geographical and class differences can all be shown to have been mixed without adverse effect.

Mixed race as a group in itself (and perhaps eventually a group *for* itself) is not necessarily a divided group, although it is diverse. (It would be a great pity for mixed race to fall at this hurdle and to begin to ostracise groups within its own ranks, showing an inability to accommodate diversity.) It has a history that spans its many constructions. It has forbears from ancient times when perceived human differences were used to rank and exploit sections of populations. Mixed race has been constructed in similar ways in very different circumstances. Where new outbreaks of race mixing are detected (and surely we must take the long view and agree that the population of the world is irredeemably mixed), mixed race dilemmas are invented anew. Parents are rumoured to differ essentially from their children and from each other in subtle and often undefined ways. Women carry the responsibility of sullying the purity of the group.

What slogan, then, should mixed race consider bearing on its collective tee shirt? It may be of value to revisit briefly the five suggested features of mixed race experience, and to review some of our evidence in the light of these before deciding on that matter.

Five Features of Mixed Race Ideology

An Ambiguous Social Location

Ambiguity and ambivalence are part of the fabric of mixed race experience. If the proposition that there are human races is taken sufficiently seriously as to be employed in ordering populations, it is unthinkable that the flimsy criteria for this task can withstand much of a challenge. In fact, mixed race groups often do not enjoy the protection of groups claiming a higher level of 'racial consolidation'. Where racialised groups come to promote or to accept their constructed differences as distinct and even absolute, there is no legitimate social space accorded to mixed race.

A mixed family or individual may be ostracised or embraced by the communities of origin, or may be pulled apart by social pressure, or lauded as emblematic of harmonious integration. The career of mixed race, as lived by individuals, is as unpredictable and capricious as the shifting and shiftless career of race thinking.

Mixing race is rarely portrayed as 'normal'. At best it is accepted as inevitable or even useful. The ambiguity lies not in the identity confusion of the mixed race individual or family but in the confused and self-interested thinking that has shaped the amorphous package of race ideology. If there is no legitimate space for identification with more than a single racially defined group, then the ambiguity is constructed through this social situation and not by those who are considered to be mixed or mixing race. There is surely no ambiguity in naming one's people, however different their origins.

Birkitt[3] argues a similar point, that our 'social selves' are reflections of wider social contexts:

> There is, then, no division between society and the individual, nor between the mental functions and the emotions, the mind and the body, or conscious and unconscious processes. What divisions and barriers there are between the different psychic functions are created within the matrices of social relations, reflecting the divisions and barriers within those relations. We are in every respect social selves. Even our psychological conflicts and dilemmas are a reflection of social conflicts and hostilities. (p. 215)

This view departs fully from any notion of intrinsic deficiency in mixed race populations. It points to the investigation of external social conflicts in the structuring of mixed race experience. This position effectively challenges the mainstream of research into mixed race that has tended to focus intensely inwards upon those defined in this manner rather than to investigate the surrounding social circumstances. It also supports the analyses of those in the study (and writers such as Kureishi and Walker)[4] who expressed the view that they were required to represent the ambivalence of the supposedly 'unmixed' towards race mixing.

We may be formed within social contexts, but are not without power and agency to resist and alter the society in which we live. Social change, and the elimination of limiting and redundant constructs such as race, require vision: how would we rather things were organised, by what means is this achievable and what obstacles might there be?

A Contested Site

That mixed race is a contested site is particularly manifest in the struggles to define mixed race. Problems, pathologies, identities, physical inadequacies have formed the substance for claims about race mixing. Contested mixed race constituencies have often been among the poor and vulnerable of a society. Looking back to the Australian experience and the contest in Indochina over the upbringing of children with 'European blood', it is clear that mixed race has been contested as a means of achieving desired social ends. In the example of the transracial adoption discourse, discussed earlier, children and families perceived as mixed race have been part of a contest over professional practice. The struggle by the social work profession (particularly in the United States and Britain) to redefine such children and their families in racialised terms is emblematic of this contest. Further, that any counter-argument resulted in the further definition of a damaged self-perception seriously curtailed the possibility of self-examination of meanings and identifications.

Whatever beliefs led to the orchestration of the anti-transracial adoption discourse that spread from the United States to Britain, it is evident that hegemonic status for this discourse was achieved for a time within professional social work.[5] This was not entirely about the welfare of children, but rather a separatist philosophy which selected the mixed race family (specifically transracial adoptive families) as its target. That such a highly racialised discourse could find any favour, let alone hold sway, in any professional culture gives some indication of the vulnerability of mixed race to this kind of attack. Mixed race became a battleground of claim and counterclaim.

The exclusive loyalty of mixed race populations has also been contested throughout history by unmixed groups. Sometimes through bribery such as slightly enhanced social benefits or through threats and social relegation. These contests have at times been born of fear that mixed groups have eroded lines of demarcation, particularly significant for those claiming racial superiority. At other times there has been interest in maintaining group numbers by including mixed race.

At the level of street abuse and family discourse, the loyalty of those who mix or who are mixed is contested. They are disloyal to the group; they are race traitors; they should identify in exclusive terms; they must reduce the area of their identifications.

Induced Dependency

If dependency is a condition required of certain groups, we must always ask what purpose it serves. For if social order rests on the perceived need for a small group of people to plan the welfare of others in the population without their active consent, this requires some rethinking. Induced dependency does not necessarily fit patterns of reality and nor is it the only means of social organisation.

The importance of welfare provision in the social organisation of mixed race is evident. Welfare agencies have been instrumental in defining and organising groups of people trapped by changing political strategies in relation to race mixing. The ascendancy of professionalised groups of health and welfare workers has increased control over processes of social definition and resource allocation in relation to mixed race groups. Many of the agencies in recent history through which mixed race experience has been managed have apparently benevolent titles: 'The Liverpool Assocation for the Welfare of Half-Caste Children'; 'The Aboriginal Protection Boards'; 'The Hanoi Society for the Protection of *Métis* Youths'. However, these, and many other welfare organisations in different times and places, have tended to run on eugenic principles and to take responsibility for the management of political problems perceived to arise from the mixing of race.

The discourses arising from such institutions construct mixed race in terms of inadequacy, ineffectiveness and menace. They propose strategies based on race separating (often mothers from children) or the prevention of further mixing. In either case, mixed race is made dependent on the paternalistic management of 'good government' to save it from its pitiable self. It is at the level of poverty that mixed race populations can most readily be managed in this manner.

A social milieu in which acceptance within a group of friends is dependent upon the suppression of individual history is another commonly reported area of dependency. An example of this kind of dependency occurred in the course of an interview with a woman of Pathan and white English ancestry who grew up in Yorkshire. Her father, a Muslim, had migrated alone from Pakistan and the family was isolated from the local Pakistani community by differences in language and background (as well as by their mixed condition). The local school, which this woman attended, was part of a scheme for 'bussing' (mainly Mirpuri) Pakistani children to schools in different parts of the town (the policy was stopped in the 1960s). There was, amongst her white contemporaries, considerable unfavourable comment about 'Pakis'. She spoke of her perplexity about being connected to the incoming children (she took Halal food at mealtimes with them although was not particularly welcome within their friendship circle). Looking back, she feels that she had no option but to pass for white at school. This she was allowed to do by white peers in exchange for silence about her own background. The whole of her school career was described as 'a nightmare'. As a result of this coercion and dependency, she waited until well into her 30s before finding sufficient confidence and safety to explore the implications of her full family background.

A Conditional State

The changing fortunes of mixed race (again the Anglo-Indian example illustrates this point well), may mean that it is tolerated or encouraged under some circumstances. It is also rapidly undermined when alternative strategies or circumstances come into play. This is a strong area to bear in mind in formulating a political response to mixed race.

If the administration of welfare has been a conduit for the management of difference, so too has the legal process. In the organisation of, for example, racially specific marital law to ensure the benefits of particular social groups and the exclusion of others (as was the case in apartheid South Africa or in the United States during slavery), legislation has identified and institutionalised race as an organising principle.

The very presence of mixed race has been dependent on changing social circumstances. For example, children of black American service men and white women born during the Second World War in Britain were constructed in highly problematic terms.[6] Welfare organisations met in 1944 to discuss the 'needs' of these children. There was serious discussion about exporting the babies to the United States where it was felt they would have a 'better chance'. While there was some dissent, at the level of government, around the prospects for children defined as mixed race in the United States, there seems to have been consensus that their white mothers would be socially compromised by their children. Further, the prospects for the children were deemed to be poor, with adoption and fostering being difficult to arrange. Bevan, then Minister of Health, opposed exportation plans but, as Harris writes, there was some newspaper reporting about the proposed export of mixed race babies:

> It is not clear if the refusal of Bevan to accede to the proposed solutions was final since a few months later the *Daily Mail* (5 April 1947) ran a story entitled 'Britain exports five thousand dusky "problem babies"'. These babies, observed the paper, were to be 'shipped to America in a specially chartered liner ... [to] save them from growing up social misfits and from possible stigma'. (p. 38)

The reputation of women, as suggested in Chapter 6, is sometimes conditional on remaining within the group. Women perceived to have mixed race are often judged severely. The position of women of high status groups, such as white wives of slave owners, has been dependent on them maintaining mono-racial affiliations. For poorer classes, race and class have sometimes been collapsed in expedient moves. A good example of this appears in Braidwood's exposition of the plan to export part of the poor black population of London during the eighteenth century.[7] The plan was to settle the territory that is now Sierra Leone with the exported black citizens. Reasons for this may also have been around concerns over racial purity, the drain on poor relief benefits and the desire for further territory.

As Braidwood suggests, many of those classed as black poor were white artisans and the white partners of black men who inhabited London. (There was some dismay as the scheme had been intended for black people only.) However, the whites on board were soon written off with condescension. Braidwood quotes a Mrs Falconbridge writing in 1794 who suggested that the white women included in the venture were likely to be mainly prostitutes if they had accepted mixed race liaisons. They were therefore not worthy of concern. This suggestion has resonance with the street abuse of today.

The empirical material of Chapters 4 and 5 also shows the conditional nature of group belonging. Families, religious groups and other institutions frequently make membership conditional on not mixing race. In particular, the not-black/White-enough group of issues shows ways in which compliance may be sought for a non-mixed lifestyle. Ways in which those perceived as mixed are required to identify in exclusive terms or are rejected for not sounding or (worse) looking sufficiently mono-racial are limiting. Where the condition of acceptance is silence, mixed race may have to endure lavish racism with the occasional assurance, 'not you, you're one of us'.

A Point of Articulation in the Ordering of Race, Gender and Other Divisions

Race, gender and class appear to meet regularly in conditions of poverty and induced political and economic dependency. This has certainly been so of the mixed race populations discussed in this study. For the most part groups perceived as mixed or mixing race have been dependent on more powerful social groups for allocation (or denial) of social space.

Stoler's exposition of the discourses of *métissage* in French Indochina and the Dutch Indies[8] offers an excellent example of this articulation. In particular, it shows a contempt and panic over the poorer elements of the more powerful racially defined group. The mixed race groups were required either to provide loyalty to European culture or to be socially demoted – relegated to lower ranks in the social orders. This is also an example of race thinking being expressed in terms of 'culture' rather than simply phenotype.

The recent 'discovery' that mixed race children are greatly over-represented in the British public care system is another instance of the articulation of race, poverty and gender. These lives and circumstances will no doubt, once the phenomenon is unravelled, reveal a complexity of factors. It is, however, most likely that these factors will include reduced access to education and thus to work, race thinking, lack of family support and the subordinating effects of gender.

I have tried to show that women and children have occupied, and continue to occupy, a crucial position in the conjuring of the mixed race condition for reasons not unconnected to their near universally subordinate status. It is the reputations and reproductive capacities of women as well as mother/child relationships which constitute the ground upon which struggles over purity and dominance are waged.

Sally Morgan's family biography[9] also shows the power of racial ascription in affecting economic and gender experience and life chances. The social experimentation that was forced upon poor aboriginal and mixed race women and children in Australia was a reminder *within living memory* of ways in which mixed race can be made to articulate changing social plans. Also in Morgan's work, another pressing need is clearly described – *the need to give voice to mixed race experience.*

All through the empirical data, experiences of a denial of social space for those considered to be mixing race are apparent. Whilst class often structures the experiencing of sanctions (for example better-off families in the study usually managed to avoid 'the welfare' since its traditional constituency is 'the poor'), it is through racialised constructions of women and children that the mixed race condition appears to be most consistently attacked. Their reputations, behaviour and social legitimacy are relentlessly undermined.

The experiences of poorer mixed race groups are readily contrasted with examples of wealthy mixed race liaisons that are well able to resist the power of racial and cultural ascription. The super-wealthy Dodie al Fayed linked to the former Diana ex-Princess of Wales is a recent example of class overriding race.

Emotional Subjects

Little has been mentioned of the conjuring of appropriate emotional responses in populations committed to the extraction of social benefit from mixed race conditions. The area of emotional response poses some interesting questions, not least about its relationship to ideology and self-identification as well as ways in which emotion is able to be shaped and altered. The functions that ideologies of mixed race can perform in a society appear to be connected to ways in which populations can be persuaded to *feel* about race mixing. Repugnance, aggression, guilt, protectiveness and possessiveness are emotional states commonly referred to in connection with race mixing (or separating). Any daily newspaper provides examples of the acting out of these states: the underlining of the rightness and normality of own-kind.

The power over emotion which can, to give an example, persuade a soldier to rape in the cause of racially or ethnically defined conflict, is power indeed. Emotional response to the victim and any child born of such circumstances is unlikely to reflect her status as one of a war heroine. Hers is a mixed race condition of extreme emotional ambivalence. This example has a translucent quality through which the construction of other mixed race conditions becomes discernible. It displays little in the way of human sympathy. Rather, it tells us much about what individuals may do in the interests of self-appointed leaders who have, by whatever means, been able to influence others' emotions on a grand scale. Any social construction of exploitative divisions of humankind must employ some form of emotional coercion. We must 'feel' that something is natural or unnatural.

What emotional condition can persuade a father to reject a once loved child planning to enter what he perceives to be a mixed race marriage? What feelings surround the decision to press a daughter into parting with a child perceived to be mixed race? What changes in family feeling can discriminate between siblings perceived to be racially different? These questions are about ways in which difference is both constructed and acted upon. Shudders and disgust at the idea of race being mixed have emotional origins in group aspirations and claims. Diversity is often, it seems, profoundly distressing.

Giving Voice to Mixed Race

I have already suggested that some of the experiences which constitute the mixed race condition might be referred to as forms of passing in the sense that they describe the processes of negotiating or being denied social space. At the positive pole of the mixed race condition are the (self-identified) opportunities to enlarge meaningful social relationships by moving easily with difference. Some people have expressed this in terms of acquisition of inter-cultural skills, others as the embodiment of interracial understanding. Bridge building is sometimes mentioned. Here the people of the mixed race condition construct their own stories; it is improvised drama – theatre in the round.

A personal observation about the already very capable articulations of the merits of the mixed race condition is that the ability to pass amongst racially defined groups enables the apprehension of what constructions of race, culture and ethnicity are *not* able to achieve. This is perhaps the most dangerous knowledge which the mixed race condition is rightly suspected of possessing. The imagined communities of the mixed race condition are richly endowed with cultural, linguistic and culinary artefacts. Left to blossom unchecked they are fine places of the imagination where dragons are slain and wrongs righted.

And that really is the most powerful message for the mixed race tee shirt. There are no races. Just an infinite range of major and minor differences between people of the same race. Some differences may be physical, most are socially constructed. Culture is no excuse for ostracism. There are no cultural 'essences' and very little is carried in the blood or genes that could be called race. We are social selves and how we negotiate and live out that selfhood remains a function of the profundity of our intelligence and willingness to use it.

It seems that negations of validity of lifestyles which challenge social divisions are repeated in finite patterns from which few lessons are retained. The continual recycling of oppressive strategies that promote race and other essentialist notions of difference must be studied in the trough of greed, desire for status and power in which those who benefit continually scavenge. Much depends on the strength and quality of counter-constructions among those whose lives are affected by social definitions of the mixing of particular differences.

During an interview with a mixed race man who had recounted some severe life experiences, he paused and said of his past experiences and of being mixed race: 'But I have decided to make it a good thing.' This decision to take responsibility for his sense of self was impressive. He was defined neither by his past, his parents nor by any of the political currents competing for his attention.

A similar attitude may be adopted to research questions just as well as to tee shirt slogans. While research questions may be formulated to investigate anxieties over the perceived mixing of difference, in this case – I have decided to make it a good thing. A final word, I leave to Alice Walker.[10] This is intended to convey thanks to the people who took part in the study as well as encouragement to those for whom the formulation of a mixed race response is now pressing:

> In a way, the whole book is a celebration of people who will not cram themselves into any ideological or racial mould. They are all shouting Stop! I want to get that petunia.
>
> Because of this they are made to suffer. They are told that they do not belong, that they are not wanted, that their art is not needed, that nobody who is 'correct' could love what they love. Their answer is resistance ... They do not measure themselves against black people or white people ... They are aware that the visions that created them were all about a future where all people – and flowers too – can bloom. They require that in the midst of the bloodiest battles or revolution, this thought not be forgotten. (p. 269)

Notes

Chapter 1

1. From Robert Frost's poem, 'Mending Wall' in Frost, R. 1955. *Robert Frost: Selected Poems* (London: Penguin).
2. Birkitt, B. 1991. *Social Selves: Theories of the Social Formation of Personality* (London: Sage).
3. Olumide, G. 1997. 'The Social Construction of Mixed Race. An Enquiry Into the Experiences of Those Designated Mixed Race and Into the Agency of Professional Cultures in the Production of Racialised Social Ascriptions' (PhD thesis. University of Bradford).
4. Day, B. 1974. *Sexual Life Between Blacks and Whites* (London: Collins).
5. Williamson, J. 1980. *New People: Miscegenation and Mulattos in the United States* (New York: Free Press).
6. Young, I.M. 1990. *Justice and the Politics of Difference* (Princeton: Princeton University Press).
7. Zack, N. 1993. *Race and Mixed Race* (Philadelphia: Temple Press).
8. Spickard, P.R. 1989. *Mixed Blood: Intermarriage and Ethnic Identity in Twentieth Century America* (Wisconsin: University of Wisconsin Press).
9. Root, M. (ed.) 1992. *Racially Mixed People in America* (London: Sage) also Root, M. (ed.) 1996. *The Multiracial Experience: Racial Borders as the New Frontier* (London: Sage).
10. Harding, S. 1996. 'Rethinking Standpoint Epistemology: What is Strong Objectivity?' in Keller, E.F. and Longino, H.E. (eds) *Feminism and Science* (Oxford: Oxford University Press).
11. Bell, C. and Encel, S. (eds) 1979. *Inside the Whale: Ten Personal Accounts of Social Research* (Rushcutters Bay: Pergamon).
12. Olumide, G. 1994. 'Good Fences Make Good Neighbours' (Unpublished postgraduate seminar paper. University of Bradford).
13. Birkitt, B. *Social Selves*.
14. Root, in *The Multiracial Experience* in the chapter 'A Bill of Rights for Racially Mixed People', discusses the practice of 'situational ethnicity'. She means by this that 'biracial and multiracial people' tend to identify themselves in different ways depending on which aspect of their ethnic backgrounds has the greater relevance in the situation. Although she also makes the point that most people behave in different ways according to the presenting situation and company, it is possible that placement and identification with distinct ethnic groups is very much a matter of how the members of the group receive the idea of mixture. This is an issue for all members of families defined as mixed.
15. Bradshaw, C.K. 1992. 'Beauty and the Beast: On Racial Ambiguity' in Root, M. (ed.) *Racially Mixed People in America*.

16. Nakashima, C.L. 1992. 'An Invisible Monster: The Creation and Denial of Mixed Race People in America' in Root, M. (ed.) *Racially Mixed People in America.*
17. The 'one drop rule' refers to the notion of hypodescent. Fernandez (in Root, M. (ed.) *The Multiracial Experience*) puts the notion in a historical context and discusses its significance for multiracial America. The colloquial 'one drop' version of hypodescent refers to the attempt, during slavery, to maintain children of slave and master within the 'black' category. Effectively, any person with 'one drop' of African blood was classified as 'black'.

Chapter 2

1. Allen, S. 1994. 'Race, Ethnicity and Nationality' in Maynard, M. and Afshar, H. (eds) *The Dynamics of Race and Gender* (London: Taylor and Francis).
2. Gramsci, A. 1972. *Selections from the Prison Notebooks.* Translated and edited by Hoare, Q. and Nowell-Smith, G. (London: Lawrence and Wishart).
3. Mouffe, C. 1981. 'Hegemony and Ideology in Gramsci' in Bennett, T., Martin, G., Mercer, C. and Woollacott, J. (eds) *Culture, Ideology and Social Process: A Reader* (London. Buckingham: Batsford and Open University Press).
4. Young, I.M. 1990. *Justice and the Politics of Difference* (Princeton: Princeton University Press).
5. Gilroy, P. 1987. *'There Ain't No Black in the Union Jack': The Cultural Politics of Race and Nation* (London: Hutchinson Education).
6. Goldberg, D.T. 1993. *Racist Culture* (Oxford: Blackwell).
7. Ibid.
8. Fryer, P. 1989. *Black People in the British Empire: An Introduction* (London: Pluto Press).
9. Modupe Oduyoye, a theologian, linguist and publisher of note who lives and works in Ibadan, Nigeria.
10. See Smith's discussion of this in Smith, A. 1996. 'Chosen Peoples' in Hutchinson, J. and Smith, A. (eds) *Ethnicity* (Oxford: Oxford University Press).
11. Dikotter, F. 1996. 'The Idea of "Race" in Modern China' in Hutchinson, J. and Smith, A. (eds) *Ethnicity.*
12. Hannaford, I. 1996. *Race: The History of an Idea in the West* (Baltimore: Johns Hopkins University Press).
13. Momoh, C.S. 1989. 'A Critique of Borderland Theories' in Asiawaju and Adeniyi (eds) *Borderlands in Africa: A Multidisciplinary and Comparative Focus on Nigeria and West Africa* (Lagos: University of Lagos Press).
14. Smedley, A. 1993. *Race in North America: Origin and Evolution of a Worldview* (Boulder: Westview Press).
15. Rowley, C.D. 1970. *The Destruction of Aboriginal Society* (London: Penguin).

16. Poliakov, L. 1996. 'The Aryan Myth and Biblical Universalism' in Hutchinson, J. and Smith, A. (eds) *Ethnicity*.
17. Goldberg, D.T. *Racist Culture*.
18. Anderson, B. 1991. *Imagined Communities: Reflections on the Origin and Spread of Nationalism* (London: Verso).
19. For example, in Sivanandan, A. 1990. *Communities of Resistance: Writings on Black Struggles for Socialism* (London: Verso).
20. Fox-Genovese, E. 1988. *Within the Plantation Household* (Chapel Hill: University of North Carolina Press).
21. For example, Truth, S. 1850. 'Narrative of Soujouner Truth, a Northern Slave' and Craft, W. 1860. 'Running a Thousand Miles for Freedom' in Bontemps, A. (ed.) 1969. *Great Slave Narratives* (Boston: Beacon Press).
22. Cohen, P. 1988. 'The Perversions of Inheritance: Studies in the Making of Multi-racist Britain' in Cohen, P. and Bains, H.S. (eds) *Multi-Racist Britain* (London: Macmillan).
23. The poem by Daniel Defoe in H. Nicholson, (ed.) 1944. *England: An Anthology* (London: Macmillan)) called 'The English Breed' pokes fun at the notion of the racial purity of the 'true born Englishman'. The poem contains the following lines:

> The Romans first with Julius Caesar came,
> Including all the Nations of that Name,
> Gauls, Greeks, and Lombards; and by Computation
> Auxilliaries or Slaves of ev'ry nation.
> With Hengest, Saxons; Danes with Sueno came
> In search of Plunder, not in search of Fame.
> Scots, Picts, and Irish from th'Hibernian Shore:
> And Conquering William brought the Normans o'er.
> All these their Barb'rous Offspring left behind,
> The Dregs of Armies, they of all Mankind;
> ...
> These are the Heroes who despise the Dutch,
> And rail at new-come foreigners so much;
> Forgetting that themselves are all deriv'd
> From the most Scoundrel Race that ever liv'd.
> A horrid Crowd of Rambling Thieves and Drones,
> Who ransack'd Kingdoms and dispeopled Towns:
> The Pict and Painted Britain, Treach'rous Scot,
> By Hunger, Theft and Rapine, hither brought;
> Norweigian Pirates, Buccaneering Danes,
> Whose Red-hair'd Offspring ev'rywhere remains;
> Who join'd with Norman French compound the Breed
> From whence your True-Born Englishmen proceed.

24. Anderson, B. *Imagined Communities*.
25. Although, as Fiona Devine shows, differences in social class between the UK and US are perhaps not so great as might be imagined, depending on the criteria for evaluation. Devine, F. 1997. *Social Class in America and Britain* (Edinburgh: Edinburgh University Press).

26. Zack, N. 1993. *Race and Mixed Race* (Philadelphia: Temple Press).
27. Biddiss, M. (ed.) 1970. *Gobineau: Selected Political Writings* (London: Jonathan Cape).
28. Frankenberg, R. 1993. *White Women, Race Matters: The Social Construction of Whiteness* (London: Routledge).
29. This was a workshop on mixed race families which formed part of a conference entitled 'Women's Stand for Community Action' which was organised by Susan Hyatt and held in Bradford in 1994 and 1995.
30. Max Weber, for example, found: 'The concept of the "ethnic" group, which dissolves if we define our terms exactly, corresponds in this regard to one of the most vexing, since emotionally charged concepts: the *nation,* as soon as we attempt a definition' (from 'The Origins of Ethnic Groups' 1996 in Hutchinson, J. and Smith, A. (eds) *Ethnicity*).
31. A good introduction to the breadth and complexity of meanings attaching to the term 'ethnicity' is found in the introduction to Hutchinson, J. and Smith, A. (eds) *Ethnicity.*
32. Cohen, P. 'The Perversions of Inheritance'.
33. Bauman, Z. 1973. *Culture As Praxis* (London: Routledge and Kegan Paul).
34. Vail, L. 1996. 'The Creation of Ethnicity in South Africa' in Hutchinson, J. and Smith, A. (eds) *Ethnicity.*
35. Furedi, F. 1998. *The Silent War: Imperialism and the Changing Perception of Race* (London: Pluto Press).
36. See, for example, Gailey's exposition of Lugard's military and administrative career in Nigeria in the second decade of the twentieth century (Gailey, H.A. *Lugard and the Abeokuta Uprising* (London: Frank Cass and Co. Ltd)). In Chapter 4 Gailey's account covers the development of the colonial and imperialist thought and activity of Lugard's career.
37. Anthias, F. and Yuval Davis, N. 1994. 'Contextualising Feminism: Gender, Ethnic and Class Divisions' in McDowell, L. and Pringle, R. (eds) *Defining Women: Social Institutions and Gender Divisions* (Cambridge: Polity in association with Blackwell and the Open University Press).
38. Ware, V. 1992. *Beyond the Pale: White Women, Racism and History* (London: Verso).
39. hooks, b. 1982. *Ain't I A Woman?* (London: Pluto Press).
40. Engels, F. 1845. *The Conditions of the Working Class in England* (London: Penguin).
41. Wells, I.B. 1895. *A Red Record* (Chicago: Donohue and Henneberry).
42. Rich, A. 1979. *On Lies, Secrets and Silence* (London: Norton).
43. Brah, A. 1992. 'Women of South Asian Origin in Britain: Issues and Concerns' in Braham, P., Rattansi, A. and Skellington, R. (eds) *Racism and Anti-Racism: Inequalities, Opportunities and Policies* (London: Sage in association with the Open University Press).

Chapter 3

1. Gilman, S. 1995. *Difference and Pathology: Stereotypes of Sexuality, Race and Madness* (Ithaca: Cornell University Press), pp. 27–8.
2. Provine, W. 1973. 'Genetics and the Biology of Race Crossing' *Science.* Vol. 182. No. 4. 114.

3. Graves Jr, J.L. 1993. 'Evolutionary Biology and Human Variation: Biological Determinism and the Mythology of Race' *Sage Race Relations Abstracts*. Vol. 18. No. 3. August.

4. See, for example, the discussion of news reporting of the discovery of a 'gay gene' in the US and UK. Conrad, P. and Markens, S. 2001. 'Constructing the "Gay Gene" in the News: Optimism and Skepticism in the US and British Press' *Health*. Vol. 5. No. 1. July.

5. Steven Rose has done considerable work in refuting tendencies towards genetic reductionism, pointing instead to the social nature of difference and inequality. See, for example, Rose, S. 1987. *Molecules and Minds: Essays on Biology and the Social Order* (Buckingham: Open University Press) and Rose, S., Kamin, L. and Lewontin, R. 1984. *Not In Our Genes: Biology, Ideology and Human Nature* (London: Penguin). Feminist analyses of the enterprise of the natural sciences have challenged understandings of science as a 'neutral' and unbiased activity. See, for example, Harraway, D. 1991. *Simians, Cyborgs and Women* (London: Routledge), Harding, S. 1986. *The Science Question in Feminism* (Ithaca: Cornell University Press) and Rose, H. 1994. *Love, Power and Knowledge: Towards a Feminist Transformation of the Sciences* (Cambridge: Polity).

6. Steinberg, D.L. 2000. '"Recombinant Bodies": Narrative, Metaphor and the Gene' in Williams, S.J., Gabe, J. and Calnan, M. (eds) *Health, Medicine and Society: Key Theories, Future Agendas* (London: Routledge).

7. See Biddiss, M. (ed.) 1970. *Gobineau: Selected Political Writings* (London: Jonathan Cape).

8. Gobineau quoted in Biddiss *Gobineau* (p. 98).

9. Davenport, C.B. 1911. *Heredity in Relation to Eugenics* (New York: Holt).

10. Zack, N. 1993. *Race and Mixed Race* (Philadelphia: Temple Press).

11. Galton, F. 1883. *Inquiries into the Human Faculty and its Development*. (London: Macmillan) 1892. *Hereditary Genius: An Inquiry into its Laws and Consequences* (London: Macmillan).

12. We have to assume that the term 'Englishman' covers the motley group that were passing for white, in spite of the additions and subtractions referred to in Defoe's poem cited in the last chapter.

13. As discussed, for example, in Furedi, F. 1998. *The Silent War: Imperialism and the Changing Perception of Race* (London: Pluto Press).

14. Defined by Galton (quoted in Hannaford, I. 1996. *Race: The History of an Idea in the West* (Baltimore: Johns Hopkins University Press)) as 'the study of agencies under social control that may improve or impair the racial qualities of future generations either physically or mentally'. Here concern is for the quality of the 'white race' which, in turn, is equated with definitions of nationhood. From 'the Nation' national character could be constructed.

15. See Rich, P. 1986. *Race and Empire in British Politics* (Cambridge: Cambridge University Press).

16. The 1927 Immorality Act was a cornerstone of the racial division upon which apartheid rested. For the Cape Coloureds its implications were unambiguous. As Sparks explains in his discussion of the demise of Cape

Town's District Six (Sparks, A. 1997. *The Mind of South Africa* (London: ArrowBooks):

> And before they were done the apartheidists inflicted on the 'coloured' peoples the ultimate in human insults. They passed a law called the Immorality Act, outlawing sex across the colour line. It was a statutory declaration that the 'coloured' people should never have existed, that their procreation was a sin and a crime which should have been prevented. (p. 87).

17. Spickard (in Spickard, P. 1989. *Mixed Blood: Intermarriage and Ethnic Identity in Twentieth-Century America* (Wisconsin: University of Wisconsin Press) p. 374) provides an appendix summarising, by state, the different laws and punishments for interracial marriage prior to the *Loving* v *Virginia* case in 1967 tha overturned all surviving anti-miscegenation legislation in America. Such laws have tended to be introduced (and harshly applied) to shore up the underlining of 'racial' difference and have often had (sometimes quite local) implications for differential freedoms for white men and women and black women and men.
18. Hannaford, I. *Race*.
19. Furedi, F. *The Silent War*.
20. Stonequist, E.V. 1937. *The Marginal Man: A Study in Personality and Culture Conflict* (New York: Russell and Russell) and see also Park, R.E. 1928. 'Human Migration and the Marginal Man' *American Journal of Sociology*. Vol. XXXIII No. 6. May.
21. Hughes, E. 1941. 'Social Change and Status Protest: An Essay on the Marginal Man' *Phylon*. Vol. 10.
22. There was considerable discussion of the concept of Marginal Man in the United States. See for example Antonovsky, A. 1956. 'Towards a Refinement of the Marginal Man Concept' *Social Forces*. Vol. 35. A good deal of this makes reference to Jewish settlement in the United States and very little attention is diverted to the persistence of 'marginality' and ways in which it might be structurally reproduced.
23. See, for example, Little, K. 1954. *Negroes in Britain* (London: Routledge). Little (and those with similar views on 'race relations' such as Park) was amongst those consulted by UNESCO with regard to its Statement on Race.
24. Wilson, A. 1987. *Mixed Race Children: a Study of Identity* (London: Allen and Unwin).
25. See Clark, K. and Clark, M. 1947. 'Racial Identity and Preference in Negro Children' in Newcomb, T.M. and Hartley, E.L. (eds) *Readings in Social Psychology* (New York: Holt). This is critically evaluated in Katz and Zalk. 1974. 'Doll Preferences: An Index of Racial Attitudes?' *Journal of Educational Psychology*. Vol. 66.
26. Khan, Y. (In preparation.) *Beyond Black or White: Mixed Race Britons* (London: Routledge).
27. Tizard, B. and Phoenix, A. 1993. *Black, White or Mixed Race?: Race and Racism in the Lives of Young People of Mixed Parentage* (London: Routledge).

28. Song, M. and Parker, D. (eds) 2001. *Rethinking Mixed Race* (London: Pluto Press).
29. The National Association of Black Social Workers in the US and the Association of Black Social Workers and Allied Professions in the UK are the two main professional bodies through which the 'same race' argument has been produced and disseminated. However, local authorities, adoption agencies and advisory bodies have come to accept the principles. The British Central Council For Education and Training in Social Work has enshrined the ideas in its educational packages to develop anti-racist skills and competencies.
30. Bartholet, E. 1994. 'Race Matching in Adoption: An American Perspective' in Gaber, I. and Aldridge, J. (eds) *In the Best Interests of the Child* (London: Free Association Books).
31. Allen, S. 1994. 'Sociological Perspectives on Adoption: The Policy Implications of the Transracial Discourse' (Unpublished paper. University of Bradford); Macey, M. 1995. 'Same Race Adoption Policy: Anti-Racism or Racism?' *Journal of Social Policy*. Vol. 24. No. 4. Autumn; Hayes, P. 1993. 'Transracial Adoption: Politics and Ideology' *Child Welfare*. Vol. LXX11. No. 3. May/June.
32. BAAF. 1995. Practice Note 13.
33. The connection between welfare work and the poor is (and has always been) significant and provides a means of organising and experimenting with these constituencies. A wry comment on this disparity is found in the journalist Simon Hoggart's writing. Hoggart has long maintained that the British royal family are dysfunctional. In one piece he discusses the possibility that Princess Anne's second marriage is failing: 'If Princess Anne's marriage really is in trouble (and the denials have been slow in coming) we could be looking at four divorces between the three older children. I sometimes think that if the royal family lived on a sink estate, social workers would need a case conference about them every week.' Simon Hoggart's Diary. *Guardian*. 7 April 2001.
34. Larson, for instance, provides a good sociological account of the development of professions and the status of professional knowledge. Larson, M.S. 1977. *The Rise of Professionalism: A Sociological Analysis* (California: University of California Press).
35. Cohen, P. 1994. 'Yesterday's Words, Tomorrow's World: From the Racialisation of Adoption to the Politics of Difference' in Gaber, I. and Aldridge, J. (eds) *In the Best Interests of the Child*.
36. Bebbington, A. and Miles, J. 1989. 'The Backgrounds of Children Who Enter Local Authority Care' *British Journal of Social Work*. Vol. 19. No. 5. October.
37. Barn, R. 1999. 'White Mothers, Mixed Parentage Children and Child Welfare' *British Journal of Social Work*. (pp. 269–84).
38. Barn, R. 1993. *Black Children in the Public Care System* (London: Batsford) and Banks, N. 1995. 'Children of Black Mixed Parentage and Their Placement Needs' *Adoption and Fostering*. Vol. 19. No. 2 each discuss the over-representation of mixed race children in the public care system. Folharon, G. and McCartt Hess, P. 1993. 'Placement Considerations For Children of mixed African American and Caucasian Parentage' *Child*

Welfare. Vol. LXX11. No. 2 show additional family pressures on mothers with children considered to be mixed race.

39. A few examples of research into the outcomes of transracial adoption are: Gill, O. and Jackson, B. 1983. *Adoption and Race* (London: Batsford); Feigleman, W. and Silverman, A. 1984. 'The Long Term Effects of Transracial Adoption' in *Social Service Review.* December; Ladner, J. 1977. *Mixed Families: Adopting Across Racial Boundaries* (New York: Anchor Press/Doubleday); Simon, R. and Altstein, H. *Transracial Adoptees and Their Families* (New York: Praeger); Tizzard, A. and Phoenix, A. 1994. 'Black Identity and Transracial Adoption' in Gaber, I. and Aldridge, J. (eds) *In the Best Interests of the Child.*

40. Bartholet, E. 'Race Matching in Adoption'.

41. Quotations are taken from Bagley, C. and Young, L. 1979. 'The Identity, Adjustment and Achievement of Transracially Adopted Children: A Review and Empirical Report' in Verma, G. and Bagley, C. (eds) *Race, Education and Identity* (London: Macmillan). See also Bagley, C. 1993. 'Transracial Adoption in Britain: A Follow Up Study With Policy Considerations' *Child Welfare.* Vol. LXX11. No. 3. May–June.

42. Rose, N. 1985. *The Psychological Complex: Psychology, Politics and Society in England 1869–1939* (London: Routledge and Kegan Paul).

43. Banks, N. 'Children of Black Mixed Parentage and Their Placement Needs'.

44. I would like, at this point, to add to Jayne Ifekwunigwe's attribution to me of the argument that since a majority of mixed race children in the UK care system are taken from white mothers, then a white foster carer would more adequately reflect their circumstances (Ifekwunigwe, J. 1999. *Scattered Belongings: Cultural Paradoxes of 'Race', Nation and Gender* (London: Routledge) p. 66).

   Whilst it is certainly the case that many mixed race children with white single mothers do survive outside the attentions of the state, this is perhaps the most vulnerable of all groups (particularly) *vis-à-vis* the public care system, and one in serious need of investigation. Certainly, should we be intent on a continuation of 'colour matched' adoptions, a white foster mother would replicate the 'ethnic background' which the child has most recently left, but this is hardly the point. What needs to be investigated is why this particular permutation of mother and child is found to be so woefully inadequate and so frequently disparaged and disrupted. Why are (usually poor) white women constantly criticised (with state sanction) for their inability to parent their mixed race children? Perhaps more pressing, what support is offered to such families?

45. Shaw, C. 1998. 'Latest Estimates of Ethnic Minority Populations' *Population Trends.* Spring. (London: HMSO).

46. Aspinall, P.J. 2000. 'Children of Mixed Parentage: Data Collection Needs' *Children and Society.* Vol. 14.

47. Charlie Owen provides a coherent account of the collection of data in the UK mixed race census category in 2001 *Mixed Race Matters: Conference Report* (Slough: People in Harmony). See also www.pih.org.uk.

48. Bebbington, A. and Miles, J. 'The Backgrounds of Children Who Enter Local Authority Care'.
49. Rowe, J., Hundleby, M. and Garnett, L. 1989. *Child Care Now: A Survey of Placement Patterns* (London: BAAF).
50. Charles, M., Rashid, H. and Thorburn, J. 1992. 'The Placement of Black Children With Permanent New Families' *Adoption and Fostering*. Vol. 16. No. 3.
51. Fernandez, C.A. 1996. 'Government Classification of Multiracial/Multi-ethnic People' in Root, M. (ed.) 1996. *The Multiracial Experience: Racial Borders as the New Frontier* (London: Sage).
52. Lucy de Bruce, who is from a Fijian Kailoma family. The extract is from a position paper prepared by Lucy de Bruce for her brother, William, to deliver to Fiji's Constitutional Review Commission on Fijian Unity. Part of the text of the paper is reproduced in an article by de Bruce in the *People in Harmony Newsletter* (Issue 27, April 2001).
53. Root, M. (ed.) 1992. *Racially Mixed People in America* (London: Sage); Root M. (ed.) *The Multiracial Experience*.
54. Folharon, G. and McCartt Hess, P. 'Placement Considerations For Children of Mixed African American and Caucasian Parentage'.
55. Ifekwunigwe, J. *Scattered Belongings*.
56. Small, S. 2001. 'Colour, Culture and Class: Interrogating Inter-racial Marriage and People of Mixed Racial Descent in the United States' in Song, M. and Parker, D. (eds) *Rethinking Mixed Race*.
57. Frankenberg, R. 1993. *White Women, Race Matters: The Social Construction of Whiteness* (London: Routledge).
58. Hoyles, A. and Hoyles, M. 1999. *Remember Me* (London: Hansib Publications Ltd and Ethos Publishing). This is a collection of short biographies of mixed race people past and present and includes information on Booker T. Washington, WEB Du Bois, Bob Marley, Ellen Craft and others.
59. Equiano, O. 1789. 'The Interesting Narrative of Olaudah Equiano or Gustaus Vassa the African: Written by Himself' in Edwards, P. (eds) 1967. *Equiano's Travels* (Oxford: Heinemann International).
60. Sayers, W.C.B. 1915. *Samuel Coleridge Taylor, Musician: His Life and Letters* (London: Cassell and Company).
61. Kureishi, H. 1986. *My Beautiful Launderette and The Rainbow Sign* (London: Faber and Faber).
62. Arnold, S. 1996. *A Burmese Legacy: Rediscovering my Family* (London: Hodder and Stoughton).
63. Morgan, S. 1988. *My Place* (London: Virago).
64. Rich, P. 1986. *Race and Empire in British Politics* (Cambridge: Cambridge University Press) and Fryer, P. 1989. *Black People in the British Empire: An Introduction* (London: Pluto Press), for example, show something of local reports and plans for mixed race in local areas of the UK.

Chapter 4

1. Walker, A. 1988. *Living By the Word: Selected Writings 1973–1987* (London: The Women's Press).

2. Anderson, B. 1991. *Imagined Communities: Reflections on the Origin and Spread of Nationalism* (London: Verso).
3. Stetson, E. 1982. 'Studying Slavery: Some Literary and Pedagogical Considerations on the Black Female Slave' in Hull, G.T., Scott, P.B. and Smith, B. (eds). *All the Women Are White, All the Blacks Are Men, But Some of Us Are Brave* (New York: The Feminist Press).
4. Williamson, J. 1980. *New People: Miscegenation and Mulattos in the United States* (New York: Free Press).
5. James, C.L.R. 1980. *The Black Jacobins* (London: Allison and Bushby).
6. Fox-Genovese, E. 1988. *Within the Plantation Household* (Chapel Hill: University of North Carolina Press).
7. Frankenberg, R. 1993. *White Women, Race Matters: The Social Construction of Whiteness* (London: Routledge).
8. Roberts, D. 1994. *The Myth of Aunt Jemima: Representations of Race and Region* (London: Routledge).
9. Lerner, G. 1972. *Black Women in White America: A Documentary History* (New York: Pantheon Books).
10. James Baldwin's play *Blues For Mr Charlie* explores, with characteristic sensitivity, this and related issues (Baldwin, J. 1964. *Blues For Mr Charlie* (New York: Samuel French)).
11. Wallace, M. 1990. *Black Macho and the Myth of Superwoman* (London: Verso).
12. Cox, applying a Marxist analysis to questions of race, challenges the importance of sex in relations between black and white in America finding socio-economic factors to be of far greater importance in understanding race thinking (Cox, O.C. 1948. *Caste, Class and Race* (New York: Monthly Review Press)).
13. Davis, A. 1982. *Women, Race and Class* (London: Random House).
14. Brownmiller, S. 1975. *Against Our Will: Men, Women and Rape* (New York: Simon and Schuster). Brownmiller argues that rape is a defining male ideology.
15. Firestone, S. 1970. *The Dialectics of Sex* (New York: Bantam Books). Firestone argues that the oppression of women stems from their biological inequality with men based on their position in the reproductive division of labour.
16. Cleaver, E. 1991. *Soul on Ice* (New York: Dell Publishing).
17. Wells, I.B. 1895. *A Red Record* (Chicago: Donohue and Henneberry).
18. Henriques, F. 1974. *Children of Caliban* (London: Secker and Warburg).
19. Anderson, B. *Imagined Communities*.
20. Caplan, L. 1995. 'Creole World, Purist Rhetoric: The Anglo Indian Cultural Debates in Colonial and Contemporary Society' *Journal of the Royal Anthropological Institute*. Vol. 1. No. 4. December 1995.
21. Shibutani, T. and Kwan, K. 1965. *Ethnic Stratification: A Comparative Approach* (London: Macmillan).
22. Presented by William de Bruce on behalf of the Kai Loma Interest Group of Fiji.
23. '*Métissage*' refers to interracial unions, and '*métis(se)*' to the children born of such unions (in this case, in French Indochina and the Dutch Indies at the beginning of the twentieth century – although the term is widely

used, particularly in French-speaking areas). See a discussion of these terms in Ifekwunigwe, J. 1999. *Scattered Belongings: Cultural Paradoxes of 'Race', Nation and Gender* (London: Routledge) (pp. 17–22).

24. Stoler, A. 1995.'Mixed Bloods and the Cultural Politics of European Identity in Colonial Southeast Asia' in Pieterse, J.N. and Parekh, B. (eds) *The Decolonisation of the Imagination: Culture, Knowledge and Power* (London: Zed Books).

25. As Sparks explains: 'They (Khoikhoi) and the slaves and the occasional descendants of the San and other bit-players who don't fit neatly into any of the more precisely definable race groups in South Africa's labelled and compartmentalised society have all been lumped together into this hold-all category called the 'coloureds'. It is a sort of 'miscellaneous' category of the ethnically undefinable, a prenumbral group in apartheid's stark world of light and shade' p. 85. Sparks, A. 1990. *The Mind of South Africa: The Rise and Fall of Apartheid* (London: Arrow Books).

26. Beinart, W. 1994. *Twentieth Century South Africa* (Oxford: Oxford University Press).

27. Lelyveld, J. 1987. *Move Your Shadow: South Africa, Black and White* (London: Abacus).

28. Inter-Press Service 10 February 1997. 'Coloureds Complain of Marginalisation'.

29. Ifekwunigwe, J. 1999. 'Passing Through: Preliminary and Partial Meditations on the Fate of Coloured Communities in "New" Capetown' *Interracial Voice* (www.webcom.com/intvoice).

30. See, for example, Harris, C. 1988. 'Images of Blacks in Britain: 1930–1960' in Allen, S. and Macey, M. (eds) *Race and Social Policy* (Surrey: Economic and Social Research Council) and Rich, P. 1986. *Race and Empire in British Politics* (Cambridge: Cambridge University Press) for discussion of the British versions of this.

31. Wootten, Commissioner J.H. 1989. *Royal Commission Into the Aboriginal Deaths in Custody: Report of the Inquiry into the Death of Malcolm Charles Smith* (Canberra: Australian Government Publishing Service).

32. Rowley, C.D. 1970. *The Destruction of Aboriginal Society* (London: Penguin).

33. Van Krieken, R. 1999. 'The "Stolen Generations" and Cultural Genocide: The Forced removal of Australian Indigenous Children From Their Families and Its Implications For the Sociology of Childhood' *Childhood*. Vol. 8. No. 3.

34. For example, see the Wootten report *Royal Commission Into the Aboriginal Deaths in Custody* and Morgan's family account (Morgan, S. 1988. *My Place* (London: Virago)) for the qualitative effects of this policy on lived experience.

35. There have been newspaper reports in UK newspapers in recent years of 'stolen children' pressing for action to redress their situation. The *Weekly Journal* 17 August 1985, for example, reported the setting-up of an inquiry into the situation. The *Guardian Weekend* supplement of 25 May 1996 carried the story of Archie Roach who was taken, aged four, by representatives of the Aboriginal Protection Board and the police, to an orphanage and on to a white family who had been led to believe that he

was an orphan. The *Guardian* supplement, *G2*, for 16 April 2001 has a portrait of Edna Walker similarly removed from home and family and placed with missionaries on Croker Island prior to adoption.
36. Van krieken 'The "Stolen Generations" and Cultural Genocide'.
37. See, for example, Anthias, F. and Yuval Davis, N. 1992. *Racialised Boundaries: Race, Nation, Gender, Ethnicity and Class and the Anti-Racist Struggle* (London: Routledge).
38. Patrick Brantlinger (in Pieterse, J.N. and Parekh, B. (eds), *The Decolonisation of the Imagination*) writes of the nineteenth-century rationalisations of genocide of 'primitive people'.

Chapter 5

1. Part of an interview during fieldwork for doctoral research.
2. Tizzard, B. and Phoenix, A. 1993. *Black, White or Mixed Race?: Race and Racism in the Lives of Young People of Mixed Parentage* (London: Routledge).
3. Root, M. (ed.) 1992. *Racially Mixed People in America* (London: Sage) and Root, M. (ed.) 1996. *The Multiracial Experience: Racial Borders as the New Frontier* (London: Sage).
4. These conferences were organised in Bradford by an American researcher, Susan Hyatt, who was investigating the work of women active in their own communities.
5. Olumide, G. 1994. 'Mixed Race: Defining the Indefinable'. *Adoption UK* May 1994. No. 69
6. It is unsatisfactory to reduce his, or anyone else's personal description to such a meaningless term. However, it is a term of identification currently understood (and much disputed) to refer to those whose perceived difference is racialised in this manner. It also has the merit of maintaining awareness that people who attract the definition 'mixed race' are the subject of race thinking.
7. Stonequist, E.V. 1937. *The Marginal Man: A Study in Personality and Culture Conflict* (New York: Russell and Russell).
8. Hall, I. 1992. 'Please Choose One: Ethnic Identity Choices for Biracial Individuals' in Root, M. (ed.) *Racially Mixed People in America*.
9. 'Asian', in the British context, tends to refer to people from India and Pakistan.
10. 'Owt' and 'nowt' are Yorkshire words meaning 'anything' and 'nothing' respectively.
11. 'Summat' is a term sometimes used in Yorkshire for 'something'.
12. Ifekwunigwe, J. 1999. 'Passing Through: Preliminary and Partial Meditations on the Fate of Coloured Communities in "New" Capetown' *Interracial Voice* (www.webcom.com/intvoice).
13. British Agencies for Adoption and Fostering.
14. A magazine that advertises children in need of new homes.
15. The children's charity.
16. Parent to Parent Information and Advisory Service – a support group for adoptive families.

Chapter 6

1. Anzaldua, G. 1983. 'La Prieta' in Moraga, C. and Anzaldua, G. (eds) *This Bridge Called My Back: Writings by Radical Women of Colour* (New York: Kitchen Table Press).
2. A dress consisting of wide trousers and long top often worn by Pakistani women.
3. Bradford is a very cosmopolitan city having experienced successive waves of migration from Eastern Europe, India, Pakistan, Ireland, the Caribbean (particularly Dominica) and West Africa. It is also, like many cities, a much divided space.
4. Cashmore, E. 1987. *The Logic of Racism* (London: Allen and Unwin). Studs Terkel provides an American view of a similar area of life in Terkel, S. 1992. *Race* (London: Minerva).
5. Register, C. 1991. *Are Those Your Kids? American Families With Children Adopted From Other Countries* (New York: Free Press).
6. National Society for the Prevention of Cruelty to Children. An organisation that is called upon to investigate allegations of child abuse.
7. People in Harmony is a UK-based charitable organisation, founded almost 30 years ago to support mixed race families and individuals.
8. Root, M. (ed.) 1996. *The Multiracial Experience: Racial Borders as the New Frontier* (London: Sage).

Chapter 7

1. An excerpt from an interview for PhD research.
2. Kohn, M. 1995. *The Race Gallery: The Return of Racial Science* (London: Random House).
3. www.multiracial.com/abolitionist.
4. Bodi, F. *Guardian*. 24 April 2001.
5. Bauman, Z. 1973. *Culture as Praxis* (London: Routledge and Kegan Paul).
6. Douglas, M. 1984. *Purity and Danger: An Analysis of the Concepts of Purity and Taboo* (London: Ark Paperbacks).
7. The many mixed Jewish-German families with their Mischlinge children, of course compounded this state of 'slime'. In a review of Soltzfus' book (Soltzfus, N. 1996. *Resistance of the Heart: Intermarriage and the Rosenstrasse Protest* (London: Norton) Wilcox makes a very valuable point – possibly the most valuable point of all – about mixed race families. She writes:

   The long Nazi campaign against Rassenschade (racial shame) and intermarriage failed because, within families, people valued each other as individuals and the ties between them proved stronger than the ties or demands of community or state, even when backed up by the threat of imprisonment or death. It seems difficult to suppose that rabbinic denouncement of mixed marriages will prove capable of preventing intermarriage, where the Nazi authorities failed.

8. Bauman, Z. 1989. *Modernity and the Holocaust* (Cambridge: Polity).

9. Bauman, Z. *Modernity and the Holocaust.*
10. MacKinnon, C.A. 1994. 'Turning Rape Into Pornography: Postmodern Genocide' in Stiglmayer, A. (ed.) *Mass Rape: The War Against Women in Bosnia-Herzegovina* (Lincoln: University of Nebraska Press).
11. Ahmed, A.S. 1995. 'Ethnic Cleansing: A Metaphor for Our Times?' *Ethnic and Racial Studies* Vol. 18. No. 1. January.
12. An unpublished paper Wilcock, E. 1990. 'The Half Jew and the Synagogue: Jewish Failure or Jewish Future?' deals with some issues for Jewry around the escalating numbers of 'mixed' marriages which tend to occupy a somewhat ambivalent position in the thinking of the faith group.
13. Middle school takes pupils up to the age of 13, when they move to secondary school.
14. For instance, with regard to policing in the UK: Hall, S. *et al.* 1978. *Policing the Crisis* (London: Macmillan) and the more recent *MacPhearson Report* on the death of Stephen Lawrence.
15. Gilroy, P. 1987. *Problems in Anti-racist Strategy.* Runnymede Trust Lecture 23 July 1987 (London: Runnymede Trust).
16. British Medical Association – the professional body for doctors in the UK.
17. 2001. *Mixed Race Matters: Conference Report* (Slough: People in Harmony). See also www.pih.org.uk.

Chapter 8

1. Brecht, B. 1987. 'In Praise of Learning' from *The Mother* in *Brecht Plays: One* (London: Methuen).
2. Mills C. Wright. 1959. *The Sociological Imagination* (Oxford: Oxford University Press) (p. 77).
3. Birkett, B. 1991. *Social Selves: Theories of the Social Formation of Personality* (London: Sage).
4. Kureishi, H. 1986. *My Beautiful Launderette and The Rainbow Sign* (London: Faber and Faber). Walker, A. 1988. *Living By the Word: Selected Writings 1973–1987* (London: The Women's Press).
5. Hayes, P. 1993. 'Transracial Adoption: Politics and Ideology' *Child Welfare.* Vol. LXXII. No. 3. May/June, for example, traces the discourse against transracial adoption to Malcolm X and Stokely Carmichael and their advocacy of separatism. This philosophy was then adopted by the National Association of Black Social Workers and eventually became influential in Britain during the 1980s. That it became a cornerstone of professional practice in adoption and fostering alone shows how the poorer constituencies of Britain and America may be more vulnerable to state intervention in race mixing.
6. See Harris, C. 1988. 'Images of Blacks in Britain: 1930–1960' in Allen, S. and Macey, M. *Race and Social Policy* (Surrey: Economic and Social Research Council).
7. Braidwood, S.J. 1994. *Black Poor and White Philanthropists: London's Blacks and the Foundation of the Sierra Leone Settlement 1785–91* (Liverpool: Liverpool University Press).

8. Stoler, A. 1995. 'Mixed Bloods and the Cultural Politics of European Identity in Colonial Southeast Asia' in Pieterse, J.N. and Parekh, B. (eds) *The Decolonisation of the Imagination: Culture, Knowledge and Power* (London: Zed Books).
9. Morgan, S. 1988. *My Place* (London: Virago).
10. Walker, A. 1988. *Living by the Word: Selected Writings 1973–1987* (London: The Women's Press).

Index

Compiled by Auriol Griffith-Jones

205

giving voice to, 188–9
ideological construction of, 40,
    70, 152, 178–9
and ideology, 15–16, 180–7
importance of study, 2–3
and loyalties, 183
rights to self-identity, 63–4
social construction of, 40–3, 115,
    178
as undermining racial difference,
    157–9
see also métissage; race
mixed race condition, 3–5
ambiguous social location of,
    70–1, 155, 180–2
as conditional state, 184–6
and constituent cultures, 101
as contested site, 182–3
experience of, 4–5, 71
and genocide, 88–90
imagery of, 99
induced dependency, 183–4
positive aspects of, 9–10, 91, 94–8
strategies, 136–49
terminology of, 109–12
mixed race identity
assumption of mental problems,
    50–2, 74
pathologised, 8, 115–17, 118,
    157, 171
mixture
geographical areas of, 141–2
historical, 150, 152–3
social construction of, 6, 72
as unnatural, 155–6
modernity, race in, 25–6
Momoh, C.S., 21–2, 23
Morgan, Sally, autobiographical
    experience, 68, 69, 186–7
mothers of mixed race children,
    58–60, 105–8
and adoption criteria, 114–16,
    172–3, 197n
Mouffe, C., 15–16
multiracialism, 57

Nakashima, C.L., 10–11
National Association of Black Social
    Workers (US), 196n, 203n

need, racially defined, 59
networks, of support, 137–8
Nigeria, 33

'one drop rule', 11, 48, 191n
Other, the
defined by difference, 25
and 'one's own kind', 67, 159
Own-kind, 67, 159–60

Pakistan, class in, 66
parents
role in support of children,
    99–102
'wrong', 105–8, 134
Park, R.E., 48
passing
'passing as...', 10–11
as strategy, 142–4
use of term, 8–10
Pentecostal churches, 166
People in Harmony organisation,
    137, 176–7
pigeonholing, 130–1
Plato, *The Republic*, 21
Poliakov, L., 24
police, 167, 169
politicians, 169
Population Trends (1988), 61
Portugal, and India, 77
poverty, 7–8, 183
among mixed race populations,
    82, 83
and welfare work, 196n
prejudice, natural, 66–7
Provine, W., 40, 43, 44, 47, 60
psychological tests, on mixed race
    children, 56–8
psychology
and concept of 'marginal man',
    47–9
and culture, 150
and racial identity, 50–2, 157

race
and biological difference, 43–4,
    71
and class, 27–30, 174–5
to define community, 70